Instructor's Manual

INVESTMENTS:
A GLOBAL
PERSPECTIVE

Instructor's Manual

INVESTMENTS: A GLOBAL PERSPECTIVE

First Edition

Jack C. Francis

Robert Ibbotson

Marianne Plunkert

University of Colorado at Denver

Pearson Education

Upper Saddle River, New Jersey 07458

Executive editor: Mickey Cox
Assistant editor: Beth Romph
Production editor: Carol Zaino
Manufacturer: Bradford & Bigelow

ISBN 0-13-060403-8

10 9 8 7 6 5 4 3 2 1

PREFACE

The topical coverage of INVESTMENTS: AN INTERNATIONAL VIEW by Jack Clark Francis and Roger Ibbotson is readily adaptable to a number of different types of investments courses. Suggested course outlines for four alternative courses have been provided by Professor Jack Francis and immediately follow this introduction.

The rest of this Instructor's Manual is devoted to providing detailed solutions to the end-of-chapter questions and problems appearing in the textbook. The answers have been written to be easily understood by students. Every effort has been made to insure the accuracy of the solutions. I would particularly like to thank Alan Eastman at Indiana University of Pennsylvania, who served as the problem checker for this manual. His comments were very thorough and helpful.

A test bank, containing a minimum of 20 multiple-choice and 5 short answer questions for each chapter, is being published as a separate supplement to the textbook. Detailed solutions are provided for each test bank question, including rationales for every multiple choice question. I have often been frustrated when my answer to a multiple choice question differs from the indicated answer; I am then left to wonder if I have missed an important element or if the indicated answer is a typographical (or author) error. I hope to eliminate this frustration for others by providing my rationales. James Brown of Delta State University served as the accuracy checker for the test bank, and I am thankful to him for his very helpful input.

Acknowledgments
As anyone who has ever worked on a book knows, there are many people along the way who make valuable contributions to the final product. I would be remiss if I did not thank Professors Jack Clark Francis and Roger Ibbotson for the opportunity to be a part of this production. I feel especially honored to have been selected for this task by these two, who have made such notable contributions to the field of investments. I would also like to thank Cheryl Clayton, a former assistant editor for finance at Prentice-Hall, who worked closely with me through much of the production process. Her patience and her professionalism in responding to my many questions was greatly appreciated.

My deepest gratitude, however, goes to my husband Jack, who was understanding when I was preoccupied with this project to the exclusion of all else, peeled me off the ceiling when I had climbed the walls of frustration, provided me with an anchor of perspective for the duration, and, most of all, was always able to make me laugh in spite of it all.

Marianne Plunkert

FOUR COURSE OUTLINES FOR INVESTMENTS: AN INTERNATIONAL VIEW

I.   A first semester Introductory Course
II.   Semester #2 in a sequence of Introductory and Advanced Courses
III. One semester Advanced Course in Portfolio Theory
IV.   One semester Advanced Course in Security Analysis

Course Outline I: A first-semester Introductory Course

SECTION 1 - INTRODUCTION

Ch. 1 – Investment Setting, Week 1
Ch. 2 – Rates Of Return, Week 1
Ch. 3 – Investment Values, Week 2
Ch. 4 - Financial Analysis Of The Issuers, Week 3
Ch. 5 - Primary Securities, Week 4
Ch.6 – The Global Stock Markets, Week 5
Ch.7 - Statistical Analysis Of Investments, Week 6
Ch.8 - Efficient Capital Markets And Anomalies, Week 7
Ch.9 - Futures And Options, Week 8

SECTION 2 - - INVESTMENT INDEXES

Ch.10 – Creating Price Indexes, Week 9
Ch.12 – Using Indexes, Week 10

SECTION 3 - - PORTFOLIO THEORY

Ch.13 – Asset Allocation, Week 11
Ch.14 - Portfolio Analysis, Week 12

SECTION 4 - - INTERNATIONAL INVESTING

Ch. 18 - Global Investing, Week 13

SECTION 5 - - FIXED INCOME INVESTMENTS

Ch. 19 - Global Bond Markets, Week 14
Ch. 22 - Credit Risk, Week 15

Course Outline II: *Semester two of a two-course sequence of Introductory and Advanced Courses*

SECTION 2 - - INVESTMENT INDEXES

Ch.11 – Selected Market Indexes, Week 1

SECTION 3 - - PORTFOLIO THEORY

Ch.15   The CAPM And APT, Week 2 and 3
Ch. 16 Portfolio Performance Evaluation, Week 4

SECTION 4 - - INTERNATIONAL INVESTING

Ch. 17 – Foreign Exchange, Week 5

SECTION 5 - - FIXED INCOME INVESTMENTS

Ch. 20 - Market Interest Rates, Week 6
Ch.20 Appendix - Yield Curves Based On Spot & Forward Rates
Ch. 21 - Interest Rate Risk And Horizon Risk, Week 7

SECTION 6 - - EQUITY SHARES

Ch. 23 - Stock Valuation - A Microview, Week 8
Ch. 24 – Measuring Earning Power, Week 9
Ch. 25 - Stock Valuation Issues, Week 10
Ch. 26 - Technical Analysis, Week 11

SECTION 7 - - DERIVATIVES AND ALTERNATIVE INVESTMENTS

Ch.27 - Futures, Week 12 and 13
Ch.27 Appendix - Options On Futures
Ch. 28 - Options, Week 14
Ch. 29 - Alternative Investments, Week 15

Course Outline III: *A one-semester advanced course on Portfolio Theory*

SECTION 1 - INTRODUCTION

Ch. 1 – Investment Setting, Week 1
Ch. 2 – Rates Of Return, Week 1
Ch. 3 – Investment Values, Week 2
Ch.7 - Statistical Analysis Of Investments, Week 3
Ch.8 - Efficient Capital Markets And Anomalies, Week 4
Ch.9 - Futures And Options, Week 5

SECTION 2 - - INVESTMENT INDEXES

Ch.10 – Creating Price Indexes, Week 6
Ch.11 – Selected Market Indexes, Week 7
Ch.12 – Using Indexes, Week 8

SECTION 3 - - PORTFOLIO THEORY

Ch.13 – Asset Allocation, Week 9
Ch.14 - Portfolio Analysis, Week 10
Ch.14 Appendix A – Statistical Foundations Of Portfolio Theory
Ch.14 Appendix B – Mathematical Portfolio Analysis
Ch.15   The CAPM And APT, Week 11
Ch. 16 Portfolio Performance Evaluation, Week 12

SECTION 4 - - INTERNATIONAL INVESTING

Ch. 17 – Foreign Exchange, Week 13
Ch. 18 - Global Investing, Week 14

SECTION 7 - - DERIVATIVES AND ALTERNATIVE INVESTMENTS

Ch. 29 - Alternative Investments, Week 15

Course Outline IV: A one-semester advanced course on Security Analysis

SECTION 1 - INTRODUCTION

Ch. 1 – Investment Setting, Week 1
Ch. 2 – Rates Of Return, Week 1
Ch. 3 – Investment Values, Week 2
Ch. 4 - Financial Analysis Of The Issuers, Week 3
Ch.7 - Statistical Analysis Of Investments, Week 4
Ch.8 - Efficient Capital Markets And Anomalies, Week 5
Ch.9 - Futures And Options, Week 6
Ch. 9 Appendix – Warrants, Embedded Options, And Convertibles

SECTION 2 - - INVESTMENT INDEXES

Ch.10 – Creating Price Indexes, Week 7

SECTION 5 - - FIXED INCOME INVESTMENTS

Ch. 19 - Global Bond Markets, Week 8
Ch. 20 - Market Interest Rates, Week 9
Ch.20 Appendix - Yield Curves Based On Spot & Forward Rates
Ch. 21 - Interest Rate Risk And Horizon Risk, Week 10
Ch. 22 - Credit Risk, Week 11

SECTION 6 - - EQUITY SHARES

CHAPTER 2: RATES OF RETURN

SOLUTIONS

Questions

QA2-1   The formula for a bond's one-period rate of return before income taxes and other transactions costs are deducted is:

$$\text{Bond's before - tax rate of return} = \frac{\left[\begin{array}{l}\text{price change during}\\\text{holding period}\end{array}\right] + \left[\begin{array}{l}\text{coupon}\\\text{interest}\end{array}\right]}{\text{beginning of period purchase price}}$$

QA2-2   An "opportunity cost" of an economic resource is determined by what it could earn in its highest paying alternative use. The opportunity cost of holding cash rather than investing in long-term government bonds is the 5.5% arithmetic average annual rate of return that was forgone.

QA2-3   Since Lynette's stock is a small cap trading on the NASDAQ, both an equity risk premium and a size premium must be added to the risk-free rate to determine a required rate of return. As Table 2-3 indicates, the required rate of return should be 14.5%. If Lynette expects a return of 18%, this is a good investment for her since the expected return exceeds the required rate of return, which will result in an increase in wealth for Lynette if her expected return is realized.

QA2-4   False. Society as a whole actually benefits from the wealth maximization goal. Investors supply funds that allow firms to do research and development to develop new products that society wants and to improve on existing products. These funds also may create new jobs or make jobs easier. Firms, in order to maximize the wealth of their shareholders, compete with other firms to try to produce the highest quality, lowest cost products for society as a whole. Society also benefits because firms provide convenient locations and times for consumers to purchase their products. Friendly, courteous service is encouraged in order to attract (and keep) customers. The residents of countries that have government-controlled businesses do not enjoy these advantages.

QA2-5   A day trader is a speculator. While day traders have very short investment horizons, usually making the purchase and sale within a 24-hour period, they do so in expectation of a positive risk-return tradeoff, unlike gamblers who have negative expected returns. The extremely short holding period of day traders, however, makes it impossible to classify them as investors. Furthermore, day traders often know nothing of the stock in which they decide to take a position. Many times trades are made based only on the price movements they observe.

QA2-6   The probability of receiving 3 percent interest is 1.0 (or, 100 percent), as indicated in the probability distribution below.

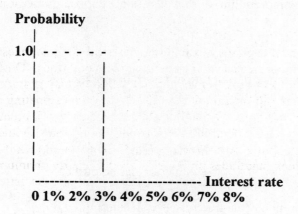

Probability

1.0

------------------------------------- Interest rate

0 1% 2% 3% 4% 5% 6% 7% 8%

Since there is zero probability of earning any interest rate other than 3 percent, the variability of possible returns is zero. An asset with zero variability of return is defined to be a riskless asset.

QA2-7   The table below compares and contrasts the investment characteristics of two different investment vehicles: a Treasury bill and a share of stock in a small corporation.

Investment characteristic	Common stock in a small firm	Treasury bill
Default risk	high	zero
Maturity	infinite	less than one year
Expected rate of return	high	low
Voice in management decision-making	some	zero
Guaranteed claim to income Payments	uncertain claim on residual	contractually scheduled
Purchasing power risk	significant	large
Interest rate risk	modest	large

The Treasury bill and the common stock in a small corporation are at opposite ends of the spectrum of risk-return possibilities. Some of the characteristics that a highly risk-averse investor would value in the T-bill would be disdained by an aggressive investor who would select a risky common stock investment, and vice-versa. Thus, it is impossible to say that one of these investments is better or worse than the other. Each of the investments would be considered best by investors who had certain investment goals, and investors in each would shun the other type of investment.

QA2-8   A historical return is the return an investment actually earned over a particular period in the past. A required return is what an investor needs to induce him to invest in the security rather than invest in another security or use his money for some other purpose.

QA2-9   Both Treasury bonds and corporate bonds must earn at least what Treasury bills return. Additionally, because Treasury bonds are longer-term investments and involve more risk, investors must earn a horizon premium to induce them to purchase Treasury bonds instead of the shorter-term Treasury bill. Corporate bonds are also longer-term and must offer investors this horizon premium, but corporate bonds have default risk as well, which Treasury bonds do not. Therefore, investors must also be given a default premium in addition to the horizon premium, or they would not choose to invest in corporate bonds.

QA2-10 When estimating a cost of capital by examining historical data, an investor must be sure that the sample data is representative of current market conditions. Outdated data from periods in time that had very different economic conditions may provide valuable information to investors, but should not be considered when estimating a cost of capital under current market conditions. Secondly, when considering risk premiums, an appropriate benchmark should be used. For example, an investor should not use the historical equity risk premium earned on the NYSE Composite Index if his stock is a small capitalization stock that trades on NASDAQ. The equity premium earned by the NASDAQ Composite Index or by a Small Cap Index would be the better choice. Once an estimate has been made for a cost of capital, it should not be considered static. New estimates should be made periodically as market conditions change.

Problems

PA2-1 The one-year holding period return is calculated as follows:

$$\text{One} - \text{year holding period return} = \frac{\left[\text{Price change}\right] + \left[\text{dividends}\right]}{\text{purchase price}}$$

$$= \frac{100(\$55 - \$48) + 100(\$0.60)}{100(\$48)}$$

$$= \frac{\$700 + \$60}{\$4,800} = 15.8\%$$

PA2-2 The one-year holding period return is calculated as follows:

$$\text{One} - \text{year holding period return} = \frac{\left[\text{Price change}\right] + \left[\text{dividends}\right]}{\text{purchase price}}$$

$$= \frac{200(\$12 - \$16) + 200(\$0.08)}{200(\$16)}$$

$$= \frac{-\$800 + \$16}{\$3,200} = -24.5\%$$

PA2-3 The terminal value of Leah's investment is calculated using the formula below:

Terminal value of investment = [present value of investment][1 + rate of return]
= $2,000(1.22) = $2,440

PA2-4 (a)   Justin's 3-month rate of return is calculated as follows:

$$3\text{ - month rate of return} = \frac{\text{terminal value - initial value}}{\text{initial value}}$$

$$= \frac{\$10,000 - \$9,900}{\$9,900} = 1.01\%$$

(b)   The annualized rate of return is calculated below:

Annualized rate of return $= (1.01)^4 - 1 = 4.06\%$

PA2-5 (a)   Derrick's 6-month rate of return is calculated as follows:

$$6\text{ - month rate of return} = \frac{\text{terminal value - initial value}}{\text{initial value}}$$

$$= \frac{\$10,000 - \$9,750}{\$9,750} = 2.56\%$$

(b)   The annualized rate of return is calculated below:

Annualized rate of return $= (1.0256)^2 - 1 = 5.19\%$.

PA2-6   The rate of return for each one-year holding period is calculated using the following formula:

$$r_{year} = \frac{\text{close price at year - end + dividend - price at beginning of year}}{\text{price at beginning of year}}$$

$$r_{1994-1995} = \frac{\$18.625 + \$0.10 - \$23.75}{\$23.75} = -21.2\%$$

$$r_{1995-1996} = \frac{\$23.50 + \$0.11 - \$18.625}{\$18.625} = 26.8\%$$

$$r_{1996-1997} = \frac{\$31.25 + \$0.13 - \$23.50}{\$23.50} = 33.5\%$$

$$r_{1997-1998} = \frac{\$28.50 + \$0.13 - \$31.25}{\$31.25} = -8.4\%$$

$$r_{1998-1999} = \frac{\$33.375 + \$0.13 - \$28.50}{\$28.50} = 17.6\%$$

The geometric mean return is

$$\sqrt[5]{[(1 + (-0.212)][(1 + 0.268)][(1 + 0.335)][(1 + (-0.084)][(1 + 0.176)]} - 1 = 7.5\%.$$

PA2-7 The arithmetic average rate of return is:

$$\frac{-21.2\% + 26.8\% + 33.5\% - 8.4\% + 17.6\%}{5} = 9.7\%.$$

The variance of the returns is calculated as follows:

$$\sigma^2 = VAR(r) = \frac{1}{T}\sum_{t=1}^{T}(r_t - \bar{r})^2$$

$$= \frac{(-21.2 - 9.7)^2 + (26.8 - 9.7)^2 + (33.5 - 9.7)^2 + (-8.4 - 9.7)^2 + (17.6 - 9.7)^2}{5}$$

$$= \frac{954.81 + 292.41 + 566.44 + 327.61 + 62.41}{5} = 440.736,$$

so the standard deviation is

$$\sigma = \sqrt{440.736} = 20.99\%.$$

PA2-8 No. For large company stocks, the required rate of return is 13.0%. The arithmetic mean calculated in Problem 2-7 can proxy for an expected return on GAP stock. Since the expected rate of return of 9.7% is less than the required rate of return, an investor would experience a decrease in his wealth from this investment.

PA2-9 (a) The arithmetic mean return on Smith-Tinker's stock is
$$\frac{10 + (-1) + 15 + 12}{4} = 9\%.$$

(b) The variance of the returns on the STC stock is calculated as follows:
$$\sigma^2 = VAR(r) = \frac{(10 - 9)^2 + (-1 - 9)^2 + (15 - 9)^2 + (12 - 9)^2}{4} = 36.5.$$

(c) The standard deviation of the returns on the STC stock is
$$\sigma = \sqrt{36.5} = 6.04\%.$$

PA2-10 The real returns are calculated by subtracting the arithmetic mean rate of inflation from the arithmetic mean return for each asset class.

Asset class	Real returns
Large Company Stocks:	13.3% - 3.2%=10.1%
Small Company Stocks:	17.6% - 3.2% = 14.4%
Long-term Corporate Bonds:	5.9% - 3.2% = 2.7%
Long-term Government Bonds:	5.5% - 3.2% = 2.3%
Intermediate-term Government Bonds:	5.4% - 3.2% = 2.2%
U.S. Treasury bills	3.8% - 3.2% = 0.6%

It can be seen that small company stocks provided the highest real returns.

CFA Exam Solutions*

The following are the guideline answers provided by the AIMR for the CFA Exam questions:

1.   B
   Solution: The formula for the arithmetic mean is

   $$\text{Arithmetic mean} = \frac{\sum r_i}{n}$$

   $$= \frac{14\% + 19\% - 10\% + 14\%}{4} = \frac{37\%}{4} = 9.25\%$$

2.   A
   Solution: Geometric mean (GM) $= \pi^{1/n} - 1$, where π = the product of the annual holding period returns.

   GM $= (1.14 \times 1.19 \times 0.90 \times 1.14)^{1/4} - 1$
           $= (1.392)^{1/4} - 1$
           $= 1.0862 - 1$
           $= 0.0862$ or 8.62%.

3.   A
   Solution:
   Geometric mean (GM) $= \pi^{1/n} - 1$
                       $= [(1.10) \times (0.90)]^{1/2} - 1$
                       $= (0.99)^{1/2} - 1$
                       $= 0.995 - 1$
                       $= -0.005$, or -0.500%

CHAPTER 3: INTRODUCTION TO VALUATION

SOLUTIONS

Questions

QA3-1   The present value equation (3.3) is as follows:

$$PV = \frac{\text{Cash flow}_1}{(1+k)^1} + \frac{\text{Cash flow}_2}{(1+k)^2} + ... + \frac{\text{Cash flow}_T}{(1+k)^T}$$

This is the equation used to determine the economic value of a security. The "k" represents a risk-adjusted discount rate and is based on the relative risk of the security. Table 2-3 in Chapter 2 depicts how the risk premia are combined to calculate required rates of return for the various asset classes. The cash flows represent what the analyst is expecting the security to return. Both are necessary to estimate the value of a security.

QA3-2   No. To be in equilibrium, a security's price must equal its value. When new information enters the market, the value of a security can change. So long as the price of the security adjusts to reflect the new value, equilibrium continues to exist. Because new information enters the market continuously, these changes can also occur continuously.

QA3-3   An efficient price is one that reflects the true economic value of a security. If all the securities' analysts estimate the same value (or very similar values) for a security, then the price will fluctuate in a narrow range around its changing equilibrium economic value, and the price is said to be efficient.

QA3-4   No learning lags or gradual reactions will be observable in GM's stock price movements. The stock market is open around the world and around the clock, and it is, therefore, possible to trade large blocks of GM stock 24 hours a day. When the announcement regarding GM's oil wells is made on the 11 P.M. news in New York City (when the NYSE is closed), the huge, sudden price appreciation will probably happen within a few minutes through the Tokyo office of Goldman Sachs and/or Merrill Lynch and/or J.P. Morgan and/or some other large international banks. Although 99% of the world's investors may experience learning lags, there are always a few professional investors awake and at work somewhere in the world who are managing multi-billion dollar stock portfolios. The immediate actions of these highly paid professional investors will probably cause the price of GM stock to complete most of its price appreciation before the NYSE begins trading on the morning after the announcement of the oil wells.

QA3-5   Short sellers may be either speculators *or* risk-averse hedgers. A short seller who takes the short position without having an offsetting long position is simply betting that the price of a stock will decrease and is a risk-taking speculator. If the price of the security decreases as he expects, he will make money. If instead, the price increases, he will lose money. However, an investor who has a long position in a security and wants to maintain that position, but is concerned about a temporary price decrease, can hedge his position by taking a short position in the same security. If, in fact, the price *does* decrease, his gains from his short position will offset the losses from his long position. On the other hand, if the price increases rather than decrease, his gains from his long position will be offset by his losses from his short position.

QA3-6   Although the number of professional investors is far less than that of nonprofessional investors, professional investors trade in large blocks—i.e., 10,000 or more shares at a time. The market value of a single one of their trades, therefore, exceeds the market value of a single trade made by a nonprofessional investor, and, due to this, the professional investors dominate the market. In fact, even if a million investors who each have $10,000 apiece all purchased the same stock at the same time, this $10 billion aggregate transaction might have a smaller dollar value than one large transaction by a multi-billion dollar portfolio. (For example, Fidelity had a total of $625 billion under management in 1997.) In financial markets it is the "dollar votes" that are important; the number of investors involved is irrelevant. Therefore, the manager of one large institutional portfolio can have a larger impact on market prices than millions of independent investors.

QA3-7   No. When a security's price differs *significantly* from its intrinsic, or economic, value, information traders find it profitable to correct the disequilibrium and respond by bidding up the low prices and/or selling overpriced securities. In effect, information traders erect **reflecting barriers** around the intrinsic value. Prices will fluctuate freely within these reflecting barriers. In this case, the price of the stock is close to its economic value, and when commissions are considered, such a small deviation is not profitable to correct.

QA3-8   If the pension fund was underfunded, it would be safer to pursue the passive investment policy. Over the long-run, the costs associated with the aggressive investment management program could reduce the average annual return below the 12% return earned on the portfolio, and the manager of an underfunded fund cannot afford to take big risks. A pension fund manager who believes in efficient markets would probably always choose this option. However, if the pension fund was overfunded, a manager who believed that the markets were less efficient might choose the more aggressive strategy in hopes of earning the higher rate of return. When the pension fund is overfunded, the manager can afford to take more risks.

QA3-9   Because Mr. Malone and others who have sold ATT stock short are responsible for dividend payments made while their short position is open, the dividend announcement will reduce their returns on the short sales. Remember that Mr. Malone must take money out of his own pocket to pay the cash dividends owed the party who lent him the shares he sold short.

QA3-10   The "law of one price" is an economic principle that states that goods that are perfect substitutes for one another should sell for the same price. Otherwise, arbitrage profits are available. Therefore, the price of Microsoft stock should be the same in Japan as it is in the U.S., after factoring in such frictions as exchange rate fees and differing brokerage commissions. If it is not, then arbitragers will buy Microsoft in the market that offers the lower price and sell it in the market that offers the higher price, thereby earning a profit.

8

Problems

PA3-1 (a) $r = \dfrac{(42-40)+2}{40} = 10\%$

(b) $r = \dfrac{(40-42)-2}{40} = -10\%$

PA3-2 $\text{Price} = PV = \$8.000 \sum\limits_{t=1}^{20} \dfrac{1}{(1.10)^t} = \$68,109$

PA3-3 (a) $\text{Price} = PV = \dfrac{\$2}{(1.14)^1} + \dfrac{\$3}{(1.14)^2} + \dfrac{\$4}{(1.14)^3} + \dfrac{\$4}{(1.14)^4} + \dfrac{\$75}{(1.14)^5} = \$48.08$

(b) If Quonset is currently selling for $2, Mr. Clay should not buy the stock. Based on his estimates, its economic value is $48.08, so at $52, the stock is overpriced.
If he pays $52 for the stock, he will not earn a 14% return on his investment.

PA3-4 $\$30 = \$2 \sum\limits_{t=1}^{5} \dfrac{1}{(1.12)^t} + \$3 \left[\sum\limits_{t=1}^{5} \dfrac{1}{(1.12)^t} \right]\left[\dfrac{1}{(1.12)^5} \right] + \text{Price}_{10} \left[\dfrac{1}{(1.12)^{10}} \right]$

$\$30 = \$7.210 + \$6.136 + \text{Price}_{10} \left[\dfrac{1}{(1.12)^{10}} \right]$

$\$16.654 = \text{Price}_{10} \dfrac{1}{(1.12)^{10}}$

$\text{Price}_{10} = \$51.72$

PA3-5 $PV = \dfrac{\$100}{(1.14)^1} + \dfrac{-\$50}{(1.14)^2} + \dfrac{\$200}{(1.14)^3} + \dfrac{\$400}{(1.14)^4} + \dfrac{-\$300}{(1.14)^5} = \$265.26$

PA3-6 $\$50,000 = \$100,000 \left[\dfrac{1}{(1+k)^5} \right]$

$\$50,000(1+k)^5 = \$100,000$

$k = \sqrt[5]{\dfrac{\$100,000}{\$50,000}} - 1 = 14.9\%$

PA3-7 (a) $PV = \$100 \sum\limits_{t=1}^{10} \dfrac{1}{(1.12)^t} + \$1,000 \left[\dfrac{1}{(1.12)^{10}} \right] = \$887$

(b) $PV = \dfrac{\$100}{0.12} = \$833$

9

PA3-8 $$PV = \frac{DIV_0(1+g)}{k-g} = \frac{\$0.75(1.08)}{0.12-0.08} = \$20.25$$

Yes. Based on Jim's estimates, the value of the stock is $20.25. If it is currently selling for $13.75, it is underpriced.

PA3-9 $$PV = \$50,000 \sum_{t=1}^{5} \frac{1}{(1.18)^t} + \$350,000 \left[\frac{1}{(1.18)^5} \right] = \$309,347$$

Te Cheih should pay no more than $309,347 for the condo.

PA3-10 (a)

Sell 100 shares at $65	$6,500
Cover short position	($5,000)
Pay dividends	($ 45)
Net profit	$1,455

(b) $$r = \frac{(\$6,500 - \$5,000) - \$45}{\$6,500} = \frac{\$1,455}{\$6,500} = 22.4\%.$$

CFA Exam Solutions*

The following are the guideline answers provided by the AIMR for the CFA Exam questions:

1. C

2. B

3. A
   Solution:
   $1,000 x 0.312
   = $312;
   n = 20 periods
   i = 6% per period

CHAPTER 4: ANALYSIS OF FINANCIAL STATEMENTS

SOLUTIONS

Questions

QA4-1   Not necessarily. Since assets are carried at the lower of cost or market and fixed assets are depreciated, firms that have been in the industry for a longer period of time likely have lower book values for their total assets. Even given the same sales levels, older firms would have a higher total asset turnover ratio because of this.

QA4-2   Coverage ratios are designed to measure the ability of a company's annual earnings to pay (or cover) the firm's fixed financing costs (such as interest payments, sinking fund payments, and lease payments). Coverage ratios are supposed to convey information about the ability of the firm to meet its debt servicing costs to bond analysts and other parties who might consider investing long-term funds in the firm. Most debt servicing costs are contractual fixed periodic payments; if they cannot be paid on time the firm that issued the defaulting bonds will quickly find itself in front of a bankruptcy judge. The times-interest-earned ratio is one of the more popular coverage ratios. Financial analysis services such as Standard & Poors, Moodys, and Fitchs are very interested in the coverage ratios for the bonds that they are paid to analyze and to assign quality ratings. Long-term lenders, such as life insurance companies and banks also consider a firm's coverage ratios when deciding whether or not to lend money.

QA4-3   Airline companies face <u>highly</u> <u>cyclical</u> <u>sales</u> <u>fluctuations</u> that vary directly with the level of general business activity. Not only does the number of passengers fluctuate cyclically, but, during recessions, the number of passengers flying in economy-class instead of in the more profitable first-class accommodations also increases. This cyclically fluctuating sales revenue is matched with a <u>fixed</u> <u>cost</u> <u>structure</u>. The passenger airlines must make all scheduled flights whether the plane is one-fourth, one-half, or 100 percent full. The airline company's cost of maintaining its flight schedule under these widely varying load conditions is practically invariant. The "bottom line" is that the airlines typically experience soaring profits during economic booms when many of their flights are near full capacity and many of their first-class seats are sold at premium prices. During recessions, when many flights must be carried out with less-than-50-percent-full plane loads, the airline can lose money on every flight. Federal airline regulations will not let the airlines cancel scheduled flights simply because the flight may be unprofitable. The combined effect of all these factors is that the annual profits of the passenger airline companies typically alternate between "very high" during booms and "very low" during recessionary conditions. One or two airlines usually go bankrupt during every recession, and the common stock prices of almost all airlines react directly to the business cycle.

        In contrast to the cyclical airline industry, most public utilities (and, in particular, ATT) enjoy stable demand that does not rise and fall as the economy alternates from its recession to boom phases. After all, someone who has the misfortune to become unemployed during a recession does not typically have the telephone disconnected -- this would make it more difficult to find another job. Conversely, periods of economic boom do not usually motivate people to have more telephones installed. This non-cyclical demand pattern facilitates the ability of public utility companies like ATT to report stable profits from year to year. Furthermore, public utility rate-setting commissions typically allow public utilities to raise their customer service charges to cover any cost increases the company might experience; this no-harsh-competition environment also helps the public utilities to report positive, and increasing, dollar profits year after year. All the factors described above may be readily discerned by perusing the financial statements of airline companies and public utilities over a complete business cycle.

QA4-4   No, KO's growth rate is not as large as its rate of return on equity (ROE). The equation below shows the relationship between a corporation's ROE and its growth rate.

$$\text{Growth rate} = [\text{Retention rate, RR}] \times [\text{ROE}]$$

Assuming the corporation obtains zero external financing, the equation above shows that any corporate growth that occurs will have to be financed through retained earnings. Let us assume KO retains about half of its after-tax earnings as retained earnings to finance its growth internally since this is about average for NYSE listed corporations. Since 50 percent of earnings is retained inside of the Coca Cola Corporation, the corporation cannot grow at a rate faster than 50% of its ROE. Only external financing can allow the corporation to finance growth and/or expansion in excess of its ROE.

QA4-5   IBM's change in the unit of account increases the number of shares outstanding, but does not alter the corporation's aggregate sales, assets, earnings, or cash dividend payments. As a result, after the appropriate adjustments for the change in the unit of account have been made on a per share basis, the common stockholders are economically unaffected in any way. Many investors erroneously think that their welfare has somehow been magically changed by the paper shuffling and bookkeeping entries that are associated with a stock split or stock dividend, but this is popular folklore. The actual dollar amounts for the IBM 4:1 stock split that occurred in May 31, 1979 are shown below.

Year/Qtr.	Data unadjusted for the split			Data adjusted for the split		
	Price per share	Earnings per share	Dividends per share	Price per share	Earnings per share	Dividends per share
1979-Q1	$315.50	$4.56	$3.44	$78.875	$1.14	$0.86
1979-Q2	$73.375	$4.60	$3.44	$73.375	$1.15	$0.86
1979-Q3	$74.125	$1.14	$0.86	$74.125	$1.14	$0.86
1979-Q4	$64.375	$1.73	$0.86	$64.375	$1.73	$0.86

If IBM's adjusted earnings and cash dividends per share after the stock split are multiplied by four to reflect the fact that every shareholder has four times as many shares, then every shareholders' total cash dividends and earnings per share are the same whether or not the stock split occurred.

    It is interesting to note that IBM's adjusted market price per share declined from $78.875 to $64.375 in the months after the stock split. According to the folklore, which suggests that stock dividends and splits increase the investors' wealth, this is the opposite of what should have occurred. (Stock dividends and stock splits are discussed in detail in Chapter 8.)

QA4-6   If a firm has a current ratio that is significantly higher than the industry average, it may mean that it has too much of its funds tied up in current assets, which typically do not produce as high a return as longer term investments. For example, a firm may have a lot of money tied up in cash, a non-earning asset.

QA4-7   Each type of financial analyst has different focal points and interests.

(a) Potential investors are interested in discerning those factors that can be expected to affect the market price of the company's securities in the future. Since the company's future earning power is the principal determinant of the value of the firm's marketable securities, the firm's profitability is the quantity on which potential investors tend to focus. Potential investors typically focus on ratios that indicate whether the firm is growing profitably.

(b) The hired executives who run a company may (unfortunately) be more interested in the size of their salaries, the executive perquisites (such as the company car and country club membership) that their positions provide, and their job security than they are in the company's earnings. (This is what agency theory tells us.) However, the managers' salaries and their job security are indirectly dependent on the earnings of the firm that employs them. So, hired executives are interested in the firm's earnings to the extent they think it impacts on their own personal welfare. Hired executives' interest in the company's earnings differs from the shareholders' interest, however. Most shareholders want their firm to maximize its earnings while, in contrast, the hired executives probably prefer for the earnings to grow slowly but steadily. Steady earnings growth makes management look like it is doing a good job year after year. As a result of their own selfish interests, hired business managers may be endeavoring to increase earnings without taking any risks that might cause the company's earnings to diminish (and perhaps get them fired). Stated differently, hired executives may maximize profits within some risk constraints that they secretly impose on the firm for their own welfare.

(c) Raw material suppliers that extend credit to the firm are interested in the earnings of the firms to the extent that they want the firm to earn enough to pay its bills. But, credit suppliers are usually not concerned with whether their credit customers are maximizing profits or merely earning profits that are modest but grow steadily. Credit suppliers are more interested in the solvency ratios of their customer than in the firm's profitability, because solvency ratios measure bill-paying power.

QA4-8   The classifications are as follows:

a.	The firm buys a new piece of equipment	**Cash flow from investing activities**
b.	The firm pays cash for additional inventory	**Cash flow from operations**
c.	The firm buys back shares of its common stock	**Cash flow from financing activities**
d.	The firm sells inventory at a loss	**Cash flow from operations**
e.	The firm pays dividends on its common stock	**Cash flow from financing activities**
f.	The firm pays off its accounts payable	**Cash flow from operations**
g.	The firm sells some equipment it no longer needs	**Cash flow from investing activities**

QA4-9   About Similarities Within An Industry. The classic industrial organization theories are presented by E. H. Chamberlin, **THE THEORY OF MONOPOLISTIC COMPETITION**, seventh edition, 1956, Harvard University Press, and also, Joan Robinson, **THE ECONOMICS OF IMPERFECT COMPETITION**, Macmillan Press, London, 1933. The portion of economic theory dealing with the organization of

industries suggests that firms that manufacture similar products should maximize their profits by adopting similar policies with respect to the following factors.

(1) The labor-capital ratio within each firm.

(2) Markups, profit margins, and selling prices.

(3) Advertising and promotional programs.

(4) Research and development expenditures.

(5) Reliance on legislated competitive aids (such as tariffs in the import-export business or monopoly franchises by public utilities).

Since each different industry usually uses some unique technological process and a similar set of operating policies to produce its product, economic theory also suggests that the competitive firms in each industry should experience similar levels of risk and similar rates of return. In fact, empirical research has shown that the firms in the same industry do experience similar average rates of return that are typical of their industry. Furthermore, the industry average rates of return differ significantly from industry to industry. [1]

About Differences Between Firms Within An Industry. Benjamin King used a mathematical statistical analysis tool called multivariate factor analysis to analyze the price movements of 63 stocks over a period of 33 years and found the results summarized in the table below:

TABLE QA4-9: PROPORTION OF STOCK PRICE VARIATION DUE TO VARIOUS FACTORS

Industry	Firm	Market	Industry	Industry subgroups
Tobacco	.25	.09	.17	.49
Oil	.15	.37	.20	.28
Metals	.15	.46	.08	.31
Railroad	.19	.47	.08	.26
Utilities	.22	.23	.14	.41
Retail	.27	.23	.08	.42
Overall	.20	.31	.12	.37

Source: B.J. King, "Market and Industry Factors in Stock Price Behavior," **JOURNAL OF BUSINESS**, January 1966, pp. 139-190.

King statistically decomposed the causes of price movements in the stocks he studied. For all the stocks in all the industries he studied King found that, on average, 20 percent of the stock price movements were the result of factors unique to each firm; 31 percent were due to general market factors; 12 percent were the result of industry factors; and 37 percent were the result of factors tied to industry subgroups. King's findings document the importance of the industry factor in explaining stock price movements. But, the fact that 20 percent, on average, of the variance in the stocks' prices were due to firm effects is evidence that industry factors alone cannot explain all of the price movements of a common stock. The high proportion of each firm's stock price movements which are

---

[1] See Marc Nerlove, "Factors Affecting Differences Among Rates Of Return On Investments In Individual Common Stocks", **THE REVIEW OF ECONOMICS AND STATISTICS**, August 1968, Volume 50, pages 312-331. See also Frank J. Fabozzi and J. C. Francis, "Industry Effects And The Determinants Of Risk", **THE QUARTERLY REVIEW OF ECONOMICS AND BUSINESS**, Autumn 1979, Volume 19, No. 3, pages 61-74. Also see Barr Rosenberg and James Guy, "Prediction Of Beta From Investment Fundamentals", **FINANCIAL ANALYSTS JOURNAL**, July-August 1976, Volume 32, pages 62-70.

determined by factors that are unique to that firm attest to the need for financial ratio analysis of the individual firms to explain non-industry and non-market factors that are idiosyncratic to each individual firm.

QA4-10   A firm's return on equity is the product of its ROA and its financial leverage ratio:

$$ROE = ROA \times \frac{assets}{equity}$$

Therefore, if both firms have identical ROAs, the firm with the higher ROE must be more highly leveraged—i.e., use more debt.

Problems

PA4-1   It would be easier to analyze Ultima if some industry average ratios or Ultima's own historical ratios were made available. However, it is possible to reach some conclusions even without these standards of comparison.

(a)

(i)   The current ratio of 2.31 times seems too high.

$$\frac{Current\ assets}{Current\ liabilities} = \frac{\$162,000}{\$70,000} = 2.31\ times$$

(ii)   Ultima`s quick ratio of 1.17 times current liabilities also seems a little too high.

$$\frac{(Current\ assets) - (Inventory)}{Current\ liabilties} = \frac{(\$162,000) - (\$80,000)}{\$70,000} = 1.17\ times$$

However, even without any standards of comparison it is clear that Ultima's $70,000 investment in accounts receivable is too large. If most of Ultima`s sales are made COD, as explained in the problem, the firm should have accounts receivable near zero.

(iii)   Ultima's inventory turnover of 4 times per year seems too slow.

$$Inventory\ turnover = \frac{Cost\ of\ goods\ sold}{Inventory\ (at\ cost)} = \frac{\$320,000}{\$80,000} = 4.0\ times$$

An inventory turnover of 4 times per year implies that the average age of the inventory is about 91 days old.

$$\frac{365\ days\ per\ year}{Inventory\ turnover} = \frac{365}{4\ times} = 91.25\ days\ old$$

It seems unlikely that an order filling firm needs an inventory of three months of raw materials to operate profitably. Excess inventory can be stolen, can rot, is subject to property taxes and insurance, and must be stored in a costly warehouse.

(b) Even if \$60,000 (that is, ten percent) of Ultima's annual sales are made on credit, the firm's accounts receivable turnover would be only 0.83 times per year -- too slow for a company that carries zero inventory of finished goods.

$$\frac{\text{Annual credit sales}}{\text{Accounts receivable}} = \frac{\$60,000}{\$72,000} = 0.83 \text{ times per year}$$

Ultima is granting some of its customers such lenient credit terms they are inviting bad debt losses. Ultima's accounts receivable turnover of only 0.83 times per year is too slow. An accounts receivable turnover of 0.83 times per year implies that the average age of Ultima's accounts receivable would be 439.8 days old.

$$\frac{365 \text{ days}}{\text{Accounts receivable turnover}} = \frac{365 \text{ days}}{0.83 \text{ times}} = 439.8 \text{ days}$$

Customers should not be given credit in excess of one year in a COD business. Mr. Davis appears to be <u>too</u> <u>nice</u> and has accumulated some bad debts as a result.

(c) In conclusion, it appears that Ultima has too much inventory and far too much accounts receivable. The owner\manager needs to get better control over his firm's inventory and accounts receivable. The firm appears to be so highly profitable that the owner/manager is ignoring his inventory and accounts receivable. It is impossible to reach further conclusions without additional facts.

PA4-2 (a) Mohawk's common-sized income statements:

	1999$	1999%	2000$	2000%
Sales	$870,000	100%	$960,000	100%
Less: Cost of goods sold	-500,000	-57%	-600,000	-63%
Equals: Gross profit	$370,000	43%	$360,000	37%
Less: Operating expenses	300,000	35%	320,000	33%
Equals: EBIT*	$ 70,000	8%	$ 40,000	4%

(b) Mohawk's percentage changes:

	1999$	2000$	Percentage change
Sales	$870,000	$960,000	10%
Less: Cost of goods sold	-500,000	-600,000	20%
Equals: Gross profit	$370,000	$360,000	(3%)
Less: Operating expenses	300,000	320,000	7%
Equals: EBIT*	$70,000	$40,000	(43%)

*EBIT stands for earnings before interest and taxes, or, identically, operating income.

(c)   The percentage change calculations in section (b) indicate that Mohawk has suffered a 43 percent decline in its earnings before interest and taxes even though its sales are up 10 percent. This profit erosion is totally attributable to a 20 percent increase in Mohawk's cost of goods sold. From the common-sized calculations in section (a) we see that, stated as a percent of its sales, Mohawk's cost of goods sold rose from 57 percent to 63 percent of its sales. This substantial increase could be the result of either (i) higher quality goods being produced from more expensive raw materials and more labor, or (ii) production inefficiencies and wasteful production procedures, or (iii) some combination of (i) and (ii). The decrease in profits would have been even worse if Mohawk's operating expenses had not shrunk from 35 percent of sales to 33 percent to absorb some of the increase in the cost of goods sold. If Mohawk has intentionally increased the quality of the goods it manufactures, the firm must raise its selling price in order to operate as profitably as it did before the quality increase.

PA4-3   No comparative ratios are furnished to complicate this problem. The objective of this problem is to get students to calculate several ratios and think about how they inter-relate.

(a)   Mohawk Manufacturing Corporation's common-sized balance sheet for 2000 with total assets of $700,000 as 100%.

CURRENT ASSETS $200,000 28.6%	CURRENT LIABILITIES $100,000 14.2%
FIXED ASSETS $500,000 71.4%	LONG-TERM LIABILITIES $300,000 (at 9% interest) 42.9%
	NET WORTH $300,000 42.9%

(b)   Mohawk's total asset turnover in 2000 was $960k/$700k = 1.37 times.

Mohawk's after-tax income (or profit) is calculated as follows:

EBIT	$40,000
less: Interest expense	- 27,000 = 9% x $300,000
Taxable income	$13,000
less: 30% taxes	- 3,900 = 30% of $13,000
After-tax income	$9,100

Mohawk's after-tax profit margin on sales is $9,100/$960,000 = 0.0095 = 95/100 of one percent.

Mohawk's financial leverage is measured by the ratio below:

$$\frac{\text{Total assets of } \$700,000}{\text{Equity of } \$300,000} = 2.333 \text{ times}$$

Mohawk's rate of return on equity is calculated component by component below.

$$\frac{\text{Net income}}{\text{Equity}} = \frac{\text{Sales}}{\text{Total assets}} \times \frac{\text{Total assets}}{\text{Equity}} \times \frac{\text{Net income}}{\text{Sales}}$$

$$\frac{\$9,100}{\$300,000} = \frac{\$960,000}{\$700,000} \times \frac{\$700,000}{\$300,000} \times \frac{\$9,100}{\$960,000} = 0.030 = 3.0\%$$

(c)   Mohawk's growth rate can be decomposed as follows:

(Growth rate)=(percent of net income retained) x (return on equity)
1.8% = (100% - 40% = payout rate = 60%) x (3.0%)

Or, in a more elaborate form Mohawk's growth rate can be decomposed as shown below:

$$\text{Growth rate} = \frac{\text{Retained earnings}}{\text{Net income}} \times \frac{\text{Net income}}{\text{Sales}} \times \frac{\text{Sales}}{\text{Total assets}} \times \frac{\text{Total assets}}{\text{Equity}} = \frac{\text{Retained earnings}}{\text{Equity}}$$

1.8% = 0.018 = (0.6) x (0.0095) x (1.37 times) x (2.33 times)

Mohawk's low growth rate of 1.8% could be doubled if Mohawk could cut its cost of goods sold enough to regain the rate of profits it had in the preceding year. Reduced income is hindering the firm's growth.

PA4-4 (a)   Dopler's dividend payout ratio was $0.30/$2.40 = 12.5%
(b)   Dopler's P/E was $24/$2.40 = 10 times
(c)   For every dollar of earnings, investors are paying ten times that amount for the stock of the firm. Whether this is good or bad depends on current industry averages. Historically, the average P/E for all firms in a bull market was 19. However, in the bull market of the mid-1990s, the average P/E ratio was closer to 22-24. A low P/E relative to the industry may mean that investors are not looking favorably on the firm for whatever reason.

PA4-5 (a)   The International Telecommunications Corporation's sales = asset turnover ratio x total assets = 0.29 x $7,130,000 = $2,067,700.
(b)   ROA = asset turnover ratio x net profit margin = 0.29 x 17% = 4.93%.
(c)   ROE = net profit margin x asset turnover ratio x financial leverage ratio

$$\text{financial leverage ratio} = \frac{1}{1 - \dfrac{\text{debt}}{\text{assets}}} = \frac{1}{(1 - 0.45)} = 1.82$$

ROE = 0.29 x 17% x 1.82 = 8.97%

PA4-6 (a)   Seenew's return on equity has been decreasing steadily each year, as shown below:

	1 year ago	2 years ago	3 years ago
ROE	$\dfrac{\$15K}{\$250K} = 6\%$	$\dfrac{\$13K}{\$200K} = 6.5\%$	$\dfrac{\$12K}{\$175K} = 6.9\%$

(b)   The factors contributing to this decline can be determined by using the DuPont system:

Years ago   ROE = net profit margin x asset turnover x financial leverage ratio

1     $6\% = [\dfrac{\$15K}{\$1,000K} = 1.5\%] \times [\dfrac{\$1,000K}{\$500K} = 2.0] \times [\dfrac{\$500K}{\$250K} = 2.0]$

2     $6.5\% = [\dfrac{\$13K}{\$900K} = 1.4\%] \times [\dfrac{\$900K}{\$300K} = 3.0] \times [\dfrac{\$300K}{\$200K} = 1.50]$

3     $6.9\% = [\dfrac{\$12K}{\$800K} = 1.5\%] \times [\dfrac{\$800K}{\$200K} = 4.0] \times [\dfrac{\$200K}{\$175K} = 1.14]$

The net profit margin has remained fairly steady, and even increased one year ago from the prior year's level. The use of debt has also increased, and, all else equal, this would increase the return on equity. However, the asset turnover ratio has been falling steadily, which has caused the decline in the ROE. The firm needs to focus its attention on which assets may be being mismanaged.

PA4-7   The following relationship can be used to determine Mystery's sales level:

$$\text{Gross profit margin} = \dfrac{\text{Sales - Cost of goods sold}}{\text{Sales}}$$

(Sales - $3,650)/Sales = 0.40, so sales = $6,083

Mystery's inventory balance can be determined by using the inventory turnover ratio:

$$\text{Inventory turnover} = \dfrac{\text{Cost of goods sold}}{\text{Inventory}}$$

Inventory = $3,650/5 = $730

PA4-8 (a)   Telform's <u>solvency ratios</u>

$$\text{Current ratio} = \dfrac{\$1,750K}{\$685K} = 2.55$$

$$\text{Quick ratio} = \dfrac{\$1,750K - \$950K}{\$685K} = 1.17$$

Telform has a better current ratio (2.55 compared to 2.35), but a lower quick ratio (1.17 compared to 1.40) than the industry average, indicating it may be holding excessive inventory that may, in fact, not be very liquid, due to damage, obsolescence, or a number of other factors.

(b)   The <u>turnover ratios</u> measure Telform's asset management.

$$\text{Inventory turnover ratio} = \frac{\$3,800K}{\$950K} = 4.0$$

$$\text{Accounts receivable turnover} = \frac{\$6,500K}{\$700K} = 9.29$$

$$\text{Fixed asset turnover} = \frac{\$6,500K}{\$2,500K} = 2.60$$

$$\text{Total asset turnover} = \frac{\$6,500K}{\$4,250K} = 1.53$$

Telform appears to be doing slightly better than the industry in accounts receivable management. They are turning over their accounts receivable 9.29 times a year, compared to the industry average of 9.0 times a year, and they seem to be doing a better job utilizing their fixed assets (2.60 compared to 2.55). However, as was surmised when looking at the liquidity of the firm, their inventory turnover is slower than that of the industry (4.0 compared to 5.5). This is causing the total asset turnover to be below the industry average as well (1.53 compared to 1.60).

(c)   The <u>leverage ratios</u> and <u>coverage ratios</u> measure the debt management of Telform. Industry averages are given only for the total debt-to-assets ratio and the times-interest-earned ratio.

$$\text{Times-interest-earned} = \frac{\$1,500K}{\$800K} = 1.88$$

$$\text{Total debt-to-assets} = \frac{\$1,985K}{\$4,250K} = 0.47$$

Telform uses 47% debt in financing its assets while the industry average is only 38%. The firm has more interest expense and less ability to cover that expense from its earnings as indicated by a times-interest-earned ratio of 1.88, compared to the industry average of 2.10.

(d)   The <u>profitability ratios</u> measure the productivity of money invested in Telform.

$$\text{Net profit margin} = \frac{\$420K}{\$6,500K} = 6.5\%$$

$$\text{Return on assets} = \frac{\$420K}{\$4,250K} = 9.9\%$$

$$\text{Return on equity} = \frac{\$420K}{\$2,265K} = 18.5\%$$

Telform has a lower net profit margin than the industry (6.5% compared with 7.2%), possibly due to their higher use of debt, and, therefore, greater interest expense. This, coupled with their inventory problem, causes their ROA to be lower than the industry average (9.9% compared to 11.5%). In spite of this, their ROE is slightly better than the industry average (18.5% compared to 18.3%) because of Telform's greater financial leverage. Of course, this greater use of debt also means a greater risk to the shareholders of the firm.

PA4-9   The sustainable growth rate of a firm, assuming no additional external financing can be determined by the following formula:

g = net profit margin x asset turnover x financial leverage x retention rate

Breaking each firm's potential growth into these components yields the following results:

Firm	Growth =	Profit margin	Asset turnover	Financial leverage	Retention rate
A	11.2%	4%	2.50	1.60	0.70
B	9.6%	5.15%	2.04	1.32	0.69

From this, it can be seen that Firm A can be expected to have a higher growth rate under the present conditions, even though Firm B has the higher profit margin. This is due to the fact that Firm B does not appear to be utilizing its assets as well as Firm A. Firm B also uses less debt and reinvests slightly less of its earnings into the firm.

PA4-10 (a-g)   The ratio calculations yield the following results:

Ratio	BigCorp	SmallComp
Total debt-to-assets*	$250M/$885M = 28.2%	$6M/$41M = 14.6%
Total debt-to-equity	$250M/$635M = 39.4%	$6M/$35M = 17.1%
Long-term debt-to-equity	$175M/$635M = 27.6%	$2M/$35M = 5.7%
Long-term debt-to-capitalization	$175M/$810M = 21.6%	$2M/$37M = 5.4%
Times-interest-earned	$600M/$140M = 4.29	$22M/$6M = 3.67

*Total assets = total debt + preferred stock + common equity

Based on the above ratios, it is apparent that BigCorp utilizes more debt than SmallComp. All of their financial leverage ratios are considerably greater. Even so, BigCorp has a better ability to meet its interest expense than does SmallComp, as indicated by the times-interest-earned ratios, and one might conclude that it has less financial risk.

CFA Exam Solutions*

The following are the guideline answers provided by the AIMR for the CFA Exam questions:

1.   A

2.   D

3.   C
     Solution:
     ROE = Equity turnover x Net profit margin
     = 4.2 x 5.5%
     = 23.1%

4. **Part A**

The equation for the implied or sustainable growth is [ROE][Retention rate], but where the retention rate is (1 - Dividend payment ratio), there are several alternative ways to compute the growth rate:

If 1993 net income used. Using 1993 ending equity:

$$\text{Aspen} \qquad\qquad\qquad\qquad \text{PSI}$$

$$\frac{2{,}800}{4{,}000}\left(1-\frac{1.10}{2.80}\right)=42.5\%; \qquad \frac{150}{600}\left(1-\frac{0}{1.50}\right)=25.0\%.$$

Using estimated 1993 beginning equity: ($4,000 - $1,700 increase in retained earnings) for Aspen; ($600 - $150 increase in retained earnings) for PSI:

$$\frac{2{,}800}{2{,}300}\left(1-\frac{1.10}{2.80}\right)=73.9\%; \qquad \frac{150}{450}\left(1-\frac{0}{1.50}\right)=33.3\%.$$

Using average equity: ($4,000 + $2,300)/2 = $3,150 for Aspen; ($600 + $450)/2 = $525 for PSI:

$$\frac{2{,}800}{3{,}150}\left(1-\frac{1.10}{2.80}\right)=54.0\%; \qquad \frac{150}{525}\left(1-\frac{0}{1.50}\right)=28.6\%.$$

If 1994 estimated net income is used. Using estimated 1994 ending equity: ($4,000 + $1,660 increase in retained earnings) for Aspen; ($600 + $200 increase in retained earnings for PSI:

$$\text{Aspen} \qquad\qquad\qquad\qquad \text{PSI}$$

$$\frac{2{,}800}{5{,}660}\left(1-\frac{1.14}{2.80}\right)=29.3\%; \qquad \frac{200}{800}\left(1-\frac{0}{2.00}\right)=25.0\%.$$

Using estimated 1994 beginning equity:

$$\frac{2{,}800}{4{,}000}\left(1-\frac{1.14}{2.80}\right)=41.5\%; \qquad \frac{200}{600}\left(1-\frac{0}{2.00}\right)=33.3\%.$$

Using average equity: ($4,000 + $5,660)/2 = $4,830 for Aspen; ($800 + $600)/2 = $700 for PSI:

$$\frac{2{,}800}{4{,}830}\left(1-\frac{1.14}{2.80}\right)=34.4\%; \qquad \frac{200}{700}\left(1-\frac{0}{2.00}\right)=28.6\%.$$

Part B

Internal growth rates can be helpful in providing clues for forecasting future growth rates of companies but should only be used with a proper understanding of certain limitations.

First, the return on equity and payout ratios must be at sustainable (i.e., normalized) levels. If either ratio is trending upward or downward, a calculation made at a single point in time will produce a misleading result. Similarly, a calculation made at a cyclical peak or trough can be highly misleading.

Second, this calculation assumes that only retained earnings affect the amount of equity. However, repurchases or sales of shares, acquisitions for stock, accounting changes, and write-offs can also have a material impact.

Third, over the long term, few companies can sustain well-above-average growth rates. As businesses mature and become a larger portion of the total economy, growth will necessarily slow. Also, above-average growth (if profitable) will attract competition.

NOTES FOR RESEARCH QUESTION

There is no unique solution to this question; however, the instructor may wish to assign the class a specific stock to research. The purpose of this problem is to introduce the student to a web site that contains a wealth of information. The students can find comparison ratios for an actual firm and practice their financial analysis skills. Students are also asked which comparison figures should be used. Obviously, the industry comparisons are more relevant than those for the sector or the S&P 500. Alternatively, the instructor may ask the students to research financial ratios of two firms in the same industry to conduct a comparative analysis--say, Hasbro and Mattel.

CHAPTER 5: PRIMARY SECURITIES

SOLUTIONS

Questions

QA5-1   All money market securities are (a) high quality, (b) highly liquid, (c) short-term securities with less than one year to maturity. They are sold at a discount so their interest income is paid via price appreciation income instead of via coupon interest payments, and they are not subject to SEC registration requirements. Most such instruments only come in large denominations.

QA5-2   A discount instrument is a security that is selling for less than its face value. The return that investors will receive is the difference between the price they pay for the security and the face value they will receive at maturity. This is referred to as "implicit interest."

QA5-3   A bond issue that is callable is likely to be called in by the issuer only when it is to the issuer's benefit to do so. It will be beneficial for the issuer to call in a bond issue at times when market interest rates are low. At such a time the issuer can call in an outstanding issue and issue new bonds with lower interest rates to get the funds to pay off the old debt. Refinancing debt in this manner reduces the issuer's interest expense. But, it is disadvantageous to the bondholder because the investor unexpectedly gets his or her bond investment returned at a time when interest rates are low, and it will probably be possible to reinvest the money only at a disadvantageously low rate of return.

QA5-4   A municipal bond's coupon interest is exempt from federal income taxes in the United States. As a result, an investor in the 50% income tax bracket, for instance, would have to earn twice the coupon rate from a taxable bond (such as a U. S. Treasury bond) as from a tax-exempt municipal bond in order to earn an equivalent after-tax return. Because of this tax advantage, investors in high income tax brackets prefer municipal bonds.

   The following equation can be used to relate the interest rates on taxable and non-taxable municipal bonds that are equally risky and have equivalent protective provisions.

$$\frac{\text{Municipal bond yield}}{1 - \text{tax rate}} = \text{yield on a fully taxable bond of equivalent risk}$$

The capital gains income on municipal bonds is taxable; only the coupon interest is tax-exempt. And, most states charge state income taxes on the interest income on bonds issued by out-of-state municipalities. The basis for the municipal bond interest tax-exemption is in the Constitution of the United. States. The Constitution states that the federal government should not interfere with the operations of the state governments. However, some legal experts are dubious about this interpretation as it applies to the tax exemption of municipal bond interest.

QA5-5   False. Although the material in this chapter does not present the student with a method to calculate the actual price, this Treasury bill would sell for $9,747.22 if the quoted discount is 5%. Students should be cognizant of the fact that the price will be greater than $9,500, however. The difference is due to the fact that it is the convention to assume a 360-day year, rather than a 365-day year, for money market transactions.

QA5-6   STRIPS is an acronym that stands for Separate Trading of Registered Interest and Principal of Securities. STRIPS emulates the successful TIGRs and CATS that were invented by Merrill Lynch and Salomon Brothers. Under the U. S. Treasury's 1985 STRIPS program, the coupons and the corpus (or underlying principal) of U. S. Treasury bonds are separated and registered separately in a book-entry system at the Federal Reserve to facilitate trading in the zero-coupon component bonds that result from stripping. For reasons that are unknown, the Treasury decided to authorize the creation of STRIPS instead of simply issuing its own zero-coupon bonds. More generally, zero-coupon bonds of all kinds were invented to eliminate the set of coupon investment problems that are summarized under the phrase "reinvestment risks."

QA5-7   Agencies of the U.S. government are institutions that were created by the federal government to serve some specific purpose. These governmental agencies are allowed to issue bonds to raise the funds they need to operate. The government makes no written promise that the interest and principal of most agency bonds will be paid. As a result, agency bonds must pay slightly higher yields than non-callable U.S. Treasury bonds of the same maturity in order to induce investors to buy the slightly riskier agency bonds. As a practical matter, however, the U.S. government would probably never allow any of its agencies bonds to default. Therefore, agency bonds do not yield much more than similar Treasury securities.

QA5-8   In some ways, preferred stock is similar to a debt security. From both the investors' and the issuer's points of view, one big difference between preferred and common is that common stockholders always get to **vote** at the stockholders' meetings. Preferred stockholders usually get to vote only if the issuer is in arrears in the fixed annual payments, and in this way are more like bondholders, who do not have voting rights. Another big difference between preferred and common is that preferred stockholders are supposed to get a **fixed cash payment** every year (with the exception of those who hold adjustable rate preferred.) Preferred stock's invariant rate of cash dividends is the reason why preferred stock, like a bond, is called a fixed income security. In contrast, the issuer is encouraged to change (more specifically, increase) the cash dividend payments to the common stockholders. Unlike the preferred investors, the common stockholders expect to get a stream of annual incomes that fluctuate significantly.

    In other ways, however, preferred stock is more like an equity security. From the issuer's points of view, one big difference between preferred and common is that the cash dividends paid to both common and preferred stock investors are not **tax-deductible** while the interest paid on debt securities is a tax-deductible expense. Another big difference between preferred and common is that the board of directors can decide to omit the cash dividend payments on common and preferred stock, and those two categories of stockholders can only protest, they cannot sue. But, management **cannot omit a single interest payment**, or they will quickly be in bankruptcy court. (An exception to this is interest paid on an income bond.) It is much easier for management to miss payments on common and preferred stock than it is to miss payments on debt instruments.

QA5-9   True. Contrary to the popular folklore, changes in the unit of account (such as stock dividends and splits) are merely paper shuffling and bookkeeping exercises, which do not change any of the economic facts that determine the value of an equity share. If a corporation pays a 10% stock dividend, or equivalently, an 11-for-10 stock split, there are 10% more shares of stock outstanding -- either way. But, each share is worth 10% less than it would have been if there had been no change in the unit of account. The aggregate value of the corporation or its securities is not changed by such devices. The classic research on this topic is the study by E. Fama, L. Fisher, M. Jensen and R. Roll, "The Adjustment Of Stock Prices To New Information", **INTERNATIONAL ECONOMIC REVIEW**, February 1979, pages 1-21.

QA5-10   False. Corporations cannot be sued for missing cash dividend payments to either their preferred or common stockholders (even if the preferred stock is cumulative) because common and preferred stockholders get cash dividends only if the board of directors wishes to pay them. In contrast, a bond issuer can be sued in bankruptcy court by a bond investor for missing a single penny of coupon interest payment because bonds are debt securities.

Problems

PA5-1   The price of the bond is equal to the present value of its expected future cash flows. We can, therefore, determine the average annual rate of return that the Burton-Heally bond is offering by solving the following equation:

$$\$360 = \frac{\$1,000}{(1+r)^{12}}$$

$$\$360(1+r)^{12} = \$1,000$$

$$r = \sqrt[12]{\frac{\$1,000}{\$360}} - 1 = 8.89\%$$

PA5-2 (a)   If non-cumulative voting is used, an investor would need to control one more than 50% of the shares to insure the election of a person of her choice to the Board: Since 0.50 x 79,115,000 = 39,557,500, she would need to control 39,557,501 shares.

(b)   If cumulative voting is used, the number of shares required can be calculated using the following formula:

$$REQ\text{-}SHS = \frac{(NUM\text{-}DIR) \times (TOT\text{-}OUT)}{(NEW\text{-}DIR)+1} + 1$$

$$= \frac{(1\,director) \times (79,115,000\,shares)}{(3\,directors)+1} + 1$$

$$= 19,778,751$$

PA5-3   Since the stock price was the same at the end of the year, the entire return on Archstone's preferred stock issue is from dividend income and is equal to $2.07/$30.875 = 6.7%.

(a)   Trudy must pay taxes on the total amount of the return at her marginal tax rate of 28%. Her after-tax return is, therefore, 6.7%(1 - 0.28) = 4.8%.

(b)   Federal tax law in the U. S. says that only 30% of inter-corporate cash dividend income is taxable by the receiving corporation. This law applies to both preferred and common stock cash dividend payments. The purpose of this law is to reduce double taxation of income. As a result, only 30% of the 6.7% from the preferred stock will be taxable at the assumed 39% corporate income tax rate. Stated differently, only [(6.7% pretax return) x (30% taxable proportion) x (39% tax rate) =] 0.7839% of the 6.7% rate of return must be paid to Uncle Sam for taxes. Thus, NationsBest's rate of return from the preferred stock investment is [(6.7%) - (0.7839% income taxes) =] 5.9% after taxes.

PA5-4   Sally has two alternatives:

Alternative A: The after-tax yield on the corporate bond would be 1.0 - tax rate of 0.25 or 75% of the 10% yield to maturity. This yield equals 7.5% per year after taxes.

Alternative B: The IRS says that cash dividend income received from another corporation is 70% tax free, to prevent triple taxation of inter-corporate cash dividend income. So, (1.0 - 0.70 = 0.30 =) 30% of the cash dividend from the preferred stock is taxable income. Thus, the 25% marginal corporate income tax rate applies to only 30% of the cash dividend income from the preferred stock investment. Stated differently, (0.30 x 0.25 = 0.075 =) 7.5% of the 8% yield must be given up to pay taxes. This leaves [1.0 - (0.075)(0.08) = 1.0 - 0.006 = 0.994 =] 99.4% of the 8% yield or .07952 = 7.952%, for the life insurance company.

Sally's Choice: The after-tax yield from the preferred stock is higher (7.952% > 7.5%) than the after-tax yield from the corporate bond, even though the bond's yield to maturity before taxes is higher (10% > 8%). So, select the preferred stock.

PA5-5   John has two alternatives. Alternative A: The 7.0% before-tax rate of return is also the after-tax rate of return for the tax-exempt municipal bond. Alternative B: For the taxable corporate bond we have: [12% x (1 - tax rate)] = [12% x (1 - 0.33) =] 8.04% is the after-tax corporate return. Therefore, the corporate bond is the better choice.

PA5-6   Alice's United Motors Corporation (UMC) bond will provide a single period rate of return of r = 8.76% before taxes and commissions.

$$r_t = \frac{\text{Price change} + \text{Cashflow}}{\text{Price at beginning of the period}} = \frac{(P_t - P_{t-1}) + CF_t}{P_{t-1}} = 0.0876$$

where r_t = one period rate of return during the holding period = 8.76%

P_t = market price at end of period t = $1,032

P_{t-1} = price at end of period $t - 1$ = $1,050

CF_t = cashflow from coupon interest received during holding period = $110

PA5-7 (a)   The one period rate of return on the Zall bond is r = 15.38%, computed as follows: r =[($980 - $910) + $70]/$910 = $140/$910 = 15.38%.

(b)   The negative 4.4% rate of return on the Zall bond is computed as follows: r = [($800 - $910) + $70]/$910 = -$40/$910 = -4.4%

PA5-8 (a)   In order to be able to elect at least one member to the Gulton board a shareholder must have at least 501 shares if the Gulton stock has non-cumulative (or straight one-share-one-vote) voting. In this case, an investor who owed 501 shares would own a majority of the outstanding shares and could elect the entire board of directors one-at-a-time.

(b) Let us adopt the following conventions:
TOT-OUT = 1,000 shares outstanding
NUM-DIR = 1, the number of directors that we want to elect is one in this problem.
NEW-DIR = 6 new members to be elected to the board
REQ-SHS = Number of shares required to elect new directors that equal the value of NUM-DIR.

$$REQ\text{-}SHS = \frac{(NUM\text{-}DIR) \times (TOT\text{-}OUT)}{(NEW\text{-}DIR) + 1} + 1$$

$$= \frac{(1\,director) \times (1,000\,shares\,outstanding)}{(6\,directors) + 1} + 1$$

$$= \frac{1,000}{7} + 1 = 143.86\,shares$$

If Gulton has cumulative voting a minority stockholder would need to own at least 144 shares to elect one director. Let us consider the facts intuitively. Under cumulative voting there will be 6,000 aggregate cumulative votes cast for the 6 new directors, as computed below:

(NEW-DIR) x (TOT-OUT) = (6 directors) x (1,000 shares outstanding) = (6,000 cumulative votes in aggregate). If our minority shareholder owns 144 shares, that ownership will bestow 864 cumulative votes on the investor. (REQ-SHS = 144 shares) x (NEW-DIR = 6 directors) = 864 cumulative votes.
Since all other shareholders could possibly act in concert against our minority shareholder, let us assume that one rich shareholder owns the (6,000 - 864 =) 5,136 adversarial aggregate cumulative votes. If the adversarial shareholder casts her 5,136 aggregate cumulative votes evenly for 5 of the 6 new directors, that will elect all 5 with (5,136/5=) 1027.2 votes each. Then, you can cast your 864 votes and elect the sixth new director. But, if the rich shareholder acts stupidly and tries to elect all 6 new directors, she will cast her 5,136 adversarial aggregate cumulative votes evenly over all 6 of the new directors that will be (5,136/6=) 856 votes each. In this case you get to cast your 864 votes for a single individual, guaranteeing his or her election.
        Let us consider the sophistry in the problem. It may or may not be true that Gulton has a total of 12 members on its board. In any event, the number 12 is irrelevant because it is not needed to solve the math problem. Sophistry makes solving a case (and real life) more difficult and/or confusing. For that reason some case users oppose the use of sophistry in educational cases.

PA5-9 (a) The Biddle Corporation investors' one period rate of return for year two is calculated as follows:

r = [($30 - $50) + $1]/$50 = -$19/$50 = -0.38 = -38%
        The Biddle investor's rate of return for the third year is:
r = [$45 - $30) + $1.50]/$30 = $16.50/$30 = 0.55 = 55.0%.

(b)   If a two-for-one stock split occurred, all the per share values must be halved before the split to produce consistent calculations, as shown below:

Year	Ending Price	Cash Dividend
t+1	$25.00	$1.00
t+2	$15.00	$0.50
t+3	$22.50	$0.75

For year t+2: $r = [(\$15 - \$25) + 0.50]/\$25 = -\$9.50/\$25 = -0.38 = -38\%$.
For year t+3: $r = [(\$22.50 - \$15) + 0.75]/\$15 = \$8.25/\$15 = 55.0\%$
Conclusion: The rates of return are the same whether or not a change in the unit of account occurs.

PA5-10 (a)   Mr. Dowd's pre-tax rate of return is 23.3% on his one-year Baltic stock investment, as calculated below:

$$r = [(P_t - P_{t-1} + DIV_t)/P_{t-1}] = [(\$35 - \$30 + \$2)/\$30] = \$7/\$30 = 0.2333 = 23.3\%$$

(b)   Mr. Dowd's after-tax rate of return is 16.3%:
$r = [(P_t - P_{t-1} + DIV_t)(1 - \text{Tax Rate})]/P_{t-1} = [(\$35 - \$30 + \$2)(1.0 - 30\%)]/\$30 = \$7(0.7)/\$30$
$= \$4.90/\$30 = 0.1633 = 16.3\%$, after paying taxes at the rate of 30%.
The fact that Mr. Dowd traded 200 shares is sophistical.

PA5-11   Federal tax law in the U. S. says that only 30% of inter-corporate cash dividend income is taxable by the receiving corporation. This law applies to both preferred and common stock cash dividend payments. The purpose of this law is to reduce double taxation of income. As a result, only 30% of the 10% rate of cash dividends from the preferred stock will be taxable at the assumed 34% corporate income tax rate. Stated differently, only [(10% pretax return) x (30% taxable proportion) x (34% tax rate) = 0.0102=] 1.02% of the 10% rate of return must be paid to Uncle Sam for taxes. Thus, Albacore's rate of return from the preferred stock investment is [(10.0% dividend yield) - (1.02% income taxes)=] 8.98% after taxes. An additional point is that if a parent corporation owns more than 80% of a subsidiary corporation, the parent may file a consolidated income tax return.

CFA Exam Solutions*

The following are the guideline answers provided by the AIMR for the CFA Exam questions:

1.   C

2.   D

3.	B
	Solution:
	102 and 5/32 of 1,000 = 1,021.56.

CHAPTER 6: THE GLOBAL STOCK MARKET

SOLUTIONS

Questions

QA6-1   Supply and demand interact to determine an equilibrium price. Beyond these major price-level determinants, the type of market mechanism is a less powerful but, nevertheless, significant price determinant. Consider the effects of the two major market-making systems.

      (a)   Over-the-counter (OTC) securities have a spread between the bid and ask prices posted by the OTC brokers and dealers. These bid and ask prices are determined by competition among dealers who own an inventory and compete with each other to make a market in a given security. No single person controls the bid and ask prices of any security in the OTC market.

      (b)   People called specialists make the market in the stocks traded on an organized exchange. The exchange assigns every listed stock to some specialist and instructs the specialist to make an orderly and continuous market in that assigned stock. The specialists keep a secret book of stop, GTC, and limit orders for their assigned stocks. The specialists' limit order books gives them valuable monopolistic information that allows them to see the outlines of the stock's supply and demand curves. Then, they buy and sell for their own inventory in such a way as to equate supply and demand at a market price that changes little from trade to trade. The specialists also have different bid and ask prices, like the OTC. But, in an organized exchange the specialist sets these bid and ask prices at his or her sole discretion. This allows one person to manipulate the prices within the limits imposed by supply and demand conditions.

QA6-2   A broker is a matchmaker and matches buyers with sellers for securities. A broker earns a commission for his services. As a broker, he does not own the securities and, therefore, does not have his own money at risk. A dealer buys and sells securities out of his own inventory. Because the dealer owns the securities, he is exposed to risk. A dealer has several potential sources of income: capital gain income on the securities in which he has invested, dividend and interest income on the securities he holds in inventory, and the difference between the ask price and the bid price (the bid-ask spread). Sometimes a broker may be acting as a dealer in a transaction--i.e., buying and selling out of his own inventory. When this is the case, the other party in the transaction must be informed of it.

QA6-3   The conflict is clear, yet most inexperienced investors overlook it.

      (a)   Since most stockbrokers are more interested in earning commission income for themselves than they are in seeing their customers earn trading profits, many brokers churn (that is, turn over fruitlessly) a client's account as much as they think they can safely do without getting caught. This churning is accomplished by giving the customer "hot tips" to buy and sell more frequently than is profitable. Although churning is illegal, it is difficult to prove that broker churned a client if the broker only churned the account modestly and obtained the client's permission for every transaction before completing it.

      (b)   Contrary to popular belief, security brokers are some of the worst people from whom to take investment advice. Many security brokers have never studied economics or finance. Furthermore, the "broker schools" that the large brokerage houses provide for their new brokers stress telephoning techniques, how to fill out the necessary paperwork, and selling skills. These schools teach surprisingly little about economics, accounting, or finance to the security brokers. As a result, security brokers are salespeople with very little financial analysis skill.

QA6-4   A market order is an order from a client to a broker instructing the broker to buy or sell a specific security as soon as possible at whatever the current market price may be when the order reaches the trading arena. Market orders are the easiest and most sure-to-be-executed type of order that a client can give a broker.

QA6-5   **Impact costs** are those incurred when the market price of a security moves disadvantageously in response to the presentation of the order to the market. These costs occur between the time an order is presented to the broker and the time the order is executed and ranges in value from zero to as much as a few dollars a share. **Commission costs** are simply the administrative costs of executing a trade through the normal market channels. Commissions can be close to zero for block traders or as much as a dollar a share. **Opportunity cost** refers to the cost of not executing a trade. An investor might decide not to place an order if he observes the price of the security he was considering move up. In doing so, he may lose out if that security's price continues to increase steadily. Opportunity costs are difficult to quantify because this steady price increase may be a trend that ends up lasting several years.

QA6-6   Ed stands to lose money if the price of AT&T rises, forcing Ed to buy back the shorted shares at a higher price than what he received for them when he executed the short sale. Therefore, Ed should use a stop loss buy order to limit his losses, specifying a price somewhere above the $35 price at which he did the short sale. If, for example, Ed specifies a price of $38 a share, he will limit his losses to *somewhere around* $3 a share. If AT&T's price hits $38, the stop loss order becomes a market order and will be executed at the next available price. (This assumes that Ed does not use a stop loss limit order since a stop loss limit order may never get executed, leaving Ed to face extreme losses if the price of AT&T shoots up.)

QA6-7   A **call market** is one in which the buy and sell orders for a particular stock are batched for simultaneous execution at a single price when an auction for that stock is called. For this reason, call markets are also referred to as periodic auctions or single price auctions. Call markets may be operated by small stock exchanges that experience a small flow of buy and sell orders. This allows them to consolidate their order flow temporally.

QA6-8   An **order crossing network** is an electronic communication network (ENC) that matches buy and sell orders off the floor of a securities exchange. Some networks execute trades at the last reported price that the security traded on an organized exchange. Others execute trades at a price that is midway between the bid price and the ask price existing on an organized exchange at the time the trade is consummated. Others use still different techniques. Regardless, an advantage is the minimization of impact costs when publicly unidentified buyers and sellers who are compatible turn up in the crossing network at the same time. This results in good execution prices. Too, variable trading costs may be reduced to zero if a fixed annual fee is charged for the use of the network. Block traders, tax evaders, and corporations investing in a competitor's stock also find the anonymity that these networks offer advantageous. On the disadvantage side, these networks are not continuous 24-hours-per-day auction markets, so the network may not be available when it is needed. It may also be the case that a transaction falls through because no active market-makers are present to provide continuous liquidity. This is a major drawback of order crossing networks.

QA6-9   The answer to this question goes back to the concept of risk/return trade-offs. While margin transactions expose investors to more risk, they also hold the promise of higher returns. A very risk-adverse investor would not buy on margin because the higher expected return would not be enough to induce her to take on the additional risk. However, an investor who is less risk-adverse and desires higher expected returns on her investment would be willing to do so.

QA6-10   The four functions of the investment banker are consultation, administration, underwriting, and distribution. The investment banker that initially reaches an underwriting agreement with the issuing firm is called the **originator** and help the firm decide on the best way to obtain the needed financing. (That is, what type of security would be best to issue, given the economic environment and the financial situation of the issuing firm.) Next, the originator handles the **administrative duties** involved in bringing the issue to market, such as obtaining the necessary information and filing a registration statement with the SEC if one is required. The originator will form an **underwriting syndicate**, comprised of other investment banking firms, to help purchase the issue from the issuing firm for immediate resale to the public. The issuing firm is thus guaranteed to receive a set amount from the issue of the security. The underwriting syndicate shoulders the risk if the issue is not well received in the market. A selling group, consisting of investment bankers, brokers, and dealers may be formed to help **distribute** the issue to the public, or, in the case of a private placement, the originator may simply act as an intermediary and sell the issue to a few large investors.

Problems

PA6-1   The minimum initial margin that is required for this transaction is:
(500 shares) x $40 x 0.6 = $12,000.

PA6-2   The minimum initial margin that is required for this transaction is:
(500 shares) x $40 x 0.75 = $15,000.

PA6-3   The minimum initial margin that is required for this transaction is:
(100 shares) x $50 x 0.65 = $3,250.

PA6-4   The equation presented below can be used to solve for the investor's rate of return. The interest rate, i, the investor's brokerage firm charged him for the $45 per share loan is given in the problem as 10%. No cash dividends were received while the investor held the stock, so DIV = 0. The initial margin requirement, m, is 55%.

$$r_t = \frac{P_{t+1} - P_t + DIV_t - i(1-m)P_t}{m(P_t)}$$

$$= \frac{\$200 - \$100 + 0 - [(0.1)(1.0 - 0.55)(\$100)]}{(0.55)(\$100)} = \frac{\$95.50}{\$55.00} = 1.736$$

The equation above shows that the investor made a 173.6% return when the price of the stock he bought doubled. Stated differently, margin transformed a 100% price rise into a 173.6% net gain for the lucky investor.

PA6-5   Mr. Jones purchased 300 shares x $50 = $15,000 for his initial position. His minimum initial margin of 65% was $9,750, which means he had to borrow $5,250 from his broker. The maintenance margin on 300 shares is 300 x $50 x 0.35 = $5,250. Solving for the value of P yields a price of $26.92 per share as shown below:

$$0.35 x (Px300) = [(Px300) - \$5,250]$$
$$195P = \$5,250$$
$$P = \$26.92 = \text{price at which a margin call will occur.}$$

The price of the stock must decline by ($50 - $26.92 =) $23.08 before Mr. Jones will receive a margin call.

PA6-6   Mr. Jones minimum initial margin is $9,750:
300 shares purchased on margin x $50 purchase price per share = $15,000 total purchase price. $15,000 x 0.65 = $9,750. In addition, we can see that Mr. Jones has to borrow [$15,000 - $9,750 =] $5,250. By coincidence, his minimum maintenance margin requirement is the same amount. [90.35)($15,000)=]$5,250. The algebra below indicates that if the price per share falls to $15, Mr. Jones must deposit at least $2,325 additional cash in his account to meet the minimum maintenance margin call of 35%.

$$(0.35)(\$15 \times 300 \text{ shares}) = (\text{Cash needed}) - (\$5,250 \text{ debt}) + (\$15 \times 300 \text{ shares})$$
$$(0.35) \times \$4,500 = (\text{Cash needed}) - \$5,250 + \$4,500$$
$$\text{Cash needed} = \$2,325$$

PA6-7 $r_t = [(\$75 - \$50) + \$0 - 0.12(1 - 0.65)(\$50)]/0.65(\$50)$
        $= (\$25 - \$2.10)/\$32.50 = \$22.90/\$32.50 = 70.46\% \text{ return}$

PA6-8 $r_t = [(\$75 - \$50) + \ 0]/\$50 = \$25/\$50 = 50\% \text{ return}$

PA6-9 $r_t = [(\$75 - \$50) + \$4 - 0.12(1 - 0.65)\$50]/0.65(\$50)$
        $= \$26.90/\$32.50 = 82.77\% \text{ return}$

PA6-10(a)   Regardless of what the stock sells for when it reaches the market place, GNU will have received the agreed upon price, which is 90% of the initial offer price:
0.9($18)(1,000,000) = $16,200,000.

(b)   The investment banker, however, bears the risk, and if the issue sells for only $12 a share, the investment banker will experience a loss as shown below:

Proceeds from sale	$12,000,000
-Purchase of shares (from GNU)	16,200,000
-Administrative expenses	500,000
Loss	$ 4,700,000

CFA Exam Solutions*

The following are the guideline answers provided by the AIMR for the CFA Exam questions:

1.   B

2.   A

3.   A.   Wagner defines the three elements of indirect trading costs as *impact* (the cost of buying liquidity), *timing* (the cost of not executing the entire order at once), and *opportunity* (the cost of not executing the trade at all).

            Impact Cost. This cost is measured as the change in price between the time an order is presented to a broker and the actual execution. A simple example is stepping across the bid-ask spread to complete a small trade immediately. Impact Cost is the price change during the time the order is exposed to the market by the broker and represents the cost of getting the order executed quickly.

            The difference or spread between the bid and ask prices can be a significant expense, even on small trades, and purchasing liquidity for large institutional trades can be very costly. If a large trade is presented to the market and there is not enough immediate liquidity to meet the demand, the stock price will be driven up or down significantly by the trade. This price change is the Impact Cost.

            Timing Cost. This cost is measured by what happens to the stock price while an order is held on the buy-side trading desk. It is the difference between the stock price at the time that the original order was presented to the trader and the prices that exist when the trader presents the order to the market. As the order is parceled out to the market over time, the price may rise or fall. This movement in price is the Timing Cost.

            Many institutional trades are larger than can be presented to the marketplace at once. Therefore, it may take several days for the trader to execute the trade; in the interim, the stock price could move substantially, creating a significant cost. In addition, timing costs have the potential to increase as the time period increases.

            Opportunity Cost. An Opportunity Cost occurs because the price moves away from the implicit value of the information on which the trade was based. For example, if the order is too large, it can result in execution that is too slow to capture the short-term gain potential of the underlying investment idea. If the order cannot be executed at an acceptable price, it creates an opportunity cost. Opportunity Cost can be measured as the difference in price at the time the order was placed from the price at the time the order was canceled.

            Opportunity Cost is significant because it represents the entire value of the investment idea. To the extent the trade can not be executed, the portfolio manager's alpha is lost.

        B.   The conflict: Impact Costs and Timing Costs can be interrelated (i.e., trying to reduce the cost of one means risking an increase in the cost of the other). For example, buying liquidity on the floor of the exchange is one way to execute a trade. The costs should not be large if the order is small. However, as the trade size increases, Impact Cost can increase significantly. It may be wiser to parcel out the trade over time. Time can often be a tool for seeking lower-cost trades. The problem is that time can also move against the trade if the stock value begins to reflect the value of the underlying investment idea. Overemphasis on minimizing Impact Costs may increase Timing Costs so that total costs are actually increased. A trader needs to realize when to pay up. Paying the highest price of the day may, in fact, be the cheapest way of executing the trade. The trader has to manage this trade-off between Impact Cost and Trading Cost as he or she attempts to minimize total trading costs.

4.   **Part A**

Noncommission trading costs are difficult to identify but can be measured through study of trading records. "Best execution" includes not only the commission but also the impact costs associated with the size and urgency of the trade, the timing costs encountered in finding and negotiating liquidity and the opportunity costs of unexecuted trades. In the aggregate, these costs can be large. The following is a simple, but by no means a complete sample, of sources of noncommission trading costs.

Market Impact Cost is the cost of buying liquidity. It is the change in price between the time an order is given to a broker and the actual execution. It is the price change during the time the order is exposed to the market by the broker. This is the intraday costs. It is a measure of the effect that the order had on the market. If it is a large order relative to the normal trading volume of the security, the impact on the price of the security can be significant.

Timing Cost is the cost of not executing an entire order at one time. Sometimes a trade is too big to be immediately executed without significantly affecting the current market price. As an alternative, the trade can be parceled out into the market over time, but the price of the security may rise or fall adversely before the entire order is filled. This is the cost of seeking liquidity. It can be thought of as the interday cost.

Opportunity Cost is the cost of not executing the trade. The price moves away and the manager pulls the order, the liquidity is not there at the desired price. This is the cost of liquidity failure.

Bid-Ask Spread is also a noncommission cost of trading. Securities are purchased at the ask price (the higher price) and sold at the bid (the lower price). This spread represents compensation to the market maker for providing liquidity.

Execution-Related Charges and Taxes (administrative charges) like stamp taxes, withholding taxes, and transaction-related custodian charges are also sources of noncommission trading costs.

Administrative Delays applies to costs associated with the delay because an investment decision had to go through an approval process. By the time a recommendation passes through committee, goes through data entry, and goes back for verification, the price of a security can change adversely and significantly.

Part B
1.   Exploit the multiple execution channels available, including crossing networks, electronic systems, various nonbroker "markets,", etc.
2.   Aggregate orders to larger sizes to use the skills of your most competent traders.
3.   Limit orders may be useful (to keep the transaction costs below the alpha expected to be added by the analyst/manager).
4.   Be patient in your pursuit of trades, unless you expect a significant reward from execution speed per se.
5.   When possible, use derivatives instead of the cash markets in transactions, including international transactions.
6.   Match trade size to market volume to avoid dominating the order flow.
7.   Use the "transaction trading" technique to implement global strategies simultaneously in multiple markets (global program trading).

8.   Know where trading costs are being incurred (analyze the data critically; get professional help).

Please note that if the foregoing (and the many other possibilities not listed) were to be distilled into methods for lowering and controlling noncommission transaction costs, four principal ideas would be: (1) Analyze your trading costs/measure your market impact. (2) Broaden the range of channels used for order execution to include at least one nonbroker electronic system or crossing network. (3) Adopt transition trading or some variant thereof when you have a number of transactions to execute in several markets and would like simultaneous executions of all trades in all markets/consider the use of derivatives. (4) Liquidity costs money; patience pays. Accordingly, organize and carry out your trading activities, insofar as possible, around the idea of being a "liquidity supplier," not a "liquidity demander."

NOTES FOR RESEARCH QUESTIONS

1.   The bid-ask spread equals the difference between the lowest ask (or offer) price and the highest bid price. The bid-ask spread is like a commission on each share traded that a dealer earns for making a market in a security. The market is said to lack depth when the bid-ask spread is wide. Bid-ask spreads measure the price of transacting. Bid-ask spreads are inverse measures of an asset's liquidity.

Bid-ask spreads are simultaneously determined by the following economic forces: (i) the volume of shares traded, (ii) the continuity with which a security trades, (iii) the riskiness of the security, (iv) the number of institutional investors holding the stock, (v) the average price level of the stock, (vi) the concentration of trading, which equals the reciprocal of the number of markets (such as NYSE, AMEX, OTC, etc.), in which the stock is traded, and (vii) the number of different stocks handled by the specialist.

2.   The theory of financial markets suggests that the development of more unique securities and more markets will tend to raise the general level of social welfare. The development of more different securities and more security markets is expected to improve the welfare of the general population by providing investors with (i) more opportunities to reduce their risks by hedging, (ii) more ways to correct mispriced assets via arbitrage, (iii) more different securities mover which to diversify away risk, (iv) more instruments with which to create profitable investment positions tailored to different situations, (v) more pathways on which to move closer to an optimal allocation of resources, and/or (vi) more complete markets in which to develop unambiguous security prices. Essentially, having more securities and more markets should move the society closer to Pareto optimality.

CHAPTER 7: STATISTICAL ANALYSIS AND THE SML

SOLUTIONS

Questions

QA7-1   It is true that the rate of return is the most important outcome from an investment. Glamour, prestige, power, excitement, and other things that might possibly be obtained from investing should all be secondary to maximizing the return within an acceptable risk class. If the investor earns enough high returns, the other goods that are desired can be purchased. Utility (or happiness) can be derived from many sources; but, do not forget that money can buy most of the things that yield utility (or contribute to happiness). The investment risk level, however, must be considered.

QA7-2   The ex-post rate of return is a historical return. In contrast, the ex-ante rate of return is an anticipated return that has not yet occurred. Investors base their decisions on their expectations about the future; that is, investment decisions are based on ex-ante rates of return. But, these ex-ante rates of return cannot be observed. So, investors must find some way to estimate the future rates of return before they can make their decisions. Since there is some tendency for history to repeat itself, the ex-post rates of return can provide estimates of the ex-ante rates of return. In fact, a good way to obtain estimates of a security's ex-ante rates of return is to analyze the relative frequency distribution that can be obtained from the historical returns. If the stochastic process that generates the returns has remained stable through time, the historical probability distribution and the future probability distribution should be identical. However, the stochastic processes often change with the passage of time as new competition emerges, laws are changed, and other factors alter the environment. When this occurs, subjective adjustments can be made in the objective historical data to derive ex-ante returns. Ex-post returns are helpful in estimating ex ante returns.

QA7-3   False. The expected rate of return on a margined investment will be higher since the investor has less of his own money invested. However, the risk is also greater since an investor must pay back the borrowed funds with interest, regardless of whether the asset generates a positive return. The expected return on a margined investment is $E(r^m) =$

$E(r^u)/m$, where m is the initial margin requirement, and the risk is $\sigma_m = \dfrac{\sigma_u}{m}$. Since m <

1.0, both the expected return and the risk of the investment will be greater.

QA7-4   The E(r) measures the average rate of return that the investor expects to earn over the holding period planned for that investment. Statistically speaking, if the probability distribution of returns is symmetric, then the E(r) also equals the median and mode rate of return. The E(r) is a measure of central tendency that is a location parameter for the asset's probability distribution of returns. More subjectively, the E(r) is a gauge of desirability that is useful in investment decision making.

QA7-5   Skewness refers to the lopsidedness in a probability distribution. If a probability distribution of returns is lopsided to the left (that is, there is a chance of large losses), that probability distribution is said to be negatively skewed. If a probability distribution is symmetric, it has zero skewness. If an investment offers a chance of a very high return, that probability distribution is said to be positively skewed, or skewed to the right. Positive skewness is desirable and negative skewness is undesirable (unless the investor is holding a short position or some other position in which they profit from large downward price moves).

QA7-6 Common stocks are more risky than bonds that are issued by the same corporation because bankruptcy law in the U. S. gives the bondholders a prior claim over the assets of the corporation in case of bankruptcy. However, the common stock of a high quality AAA-grade rated corporation (like Exxon, for instance) is usually safer than junk bonds. But, as a general category of investments, common stocks are riskier than bonds.

QA7-7 The range enjoys the advantage of simplicity. But, the range is based on only the highest and lowest observations within the sample. The range ignores all observations other than the highest and the lowest and, in so doing, wastes valuable information. In contrast, the variance, denoted VAR(r), considers every observation in the sample and wastes no information. The variance is also more desirable because there is a valuable sampling theory that is based on the variance that does not exist for the range. The variance is also convenient because many hand-held calculators are pre-programmed to calculate the variance (and/or the standard deviation). Unfortunately, neither the range nor the variance is a perfect quantitative risk surrogate. They are both too sensitive to outliers; that is, both risk statistics explode when either an unusually large or unusually small number is sampled.

QA7-8 Careful examination will reveal that there is definitely a risk-return relationship between the probability distributions of returns illustrated in Figure 7-3. Essentially, the common stocks pay the highest average returns of the categories of investments in that figure because the common stocks, on average, are the riskiest and investors require the highest E(r)s to induce them to assume the highest levels of risk.

Most economic theories presume that (i) a positive-risk-return tradeoff exists, and, (ii) rational people are risk-averse. This economic focus on risk grows out of the fact that there are many risk-return relationships in life. For example, the choice of lifetime careers can be formulated as a risk-return choice, as illustrated on the next page.

Average
annual
income
in dollars
|
| Bill Gates of Microsoft
|
| Plastic surgeon
| Medical doctor
| Cabinet level position in Washington, D.C.
|
|
| Tenured business professor
| GS-13 in U. S. federal government's civil service
| High school teacher with MS degree
| GS-7 in the U.S. civil service
| Janitor
|
-----------------|-------|------|----------------- Riskiness of income

Various kinds of risk also play an important role in investments theories and practice, as illustrated below.

Average
annual
yield
|
| Junk bonds
|
| C-grade corporate bonds
| CC-grade corporate bonds
| KO-grade corporate bonds
| B-grade corporate bonds
| BB-grade corporate bonds
| BBB-grade corporate bonds
| A-grade corporate bonds
| AA-grade corporate bonds
| AAA-grade corporate bonds
| U. S. Treasury bonds
|
-- Default risk

Risk-return relationships are at the core of many theories, and there are many interesting examples that can be cited.

QA7-9   It is true that the rate of return measure *implicitly* assumes the investment is purchased at the start of each holding period and then sold at the end of that holding period in order to compute the price gain or loss over the holding period. However, this does not mean that the investor must *actually* buy and sell the asset every period. For example, consider a hypothetical investor who reconsiders and remakes his or her retirement investment decisions every year with a one-year planning horizon while expecting to stay invested for 30 consecutive years (say, until reaching retirement age). This investor can actually hold onto the same investments year after year for decades if the investment remains desirable at each year's annual investment re-evaluation. Nevertheless, this investor should consider each potential new investment's probability distributions of returns and each old existing investment's probability distributions of returns, computed _as if_ every investment were purchased at the start of each holding period and then sold at the end of that holding period for the purpose of computing the returns. Furthermore, all potential and existing investments should have their rates of return computed over the same *identical holding period* because it would be like comparing apples and oranges to compare one asset's bull market rate of return with another asset's bear market rate of return (that is, rates of return from different holding periods).

QA7-10   Basing investment decisions on only the risk and return statistics, namely, the VAR(r) and E(r) statistics, does not waste any information about the underlying investment opportunities. The VAR(r) and E(r) statistics are summary statistics that should be formulated to represent all information the investor has about each investment candidate. Stated differently, all information that the investor has about an investment candidate should be summarized in the probability distributions of returns from which the investment's VAR(r) and E(r) statistics are calculated. Unless the probability distributions of returns is significantly skewed, the VAR(r) and E(r) statistics should convey enough information to make optimal investment decisions. And, the powerful central limit theorem suggests that portfolio returns will be symmetrically distributed (according to a normal probability distribution that is completely defined by its mean and variance).

Problems

PA7-1   Equation (7-1) indicates that Sharon's stock earned a rate of return of ten percent during the year she owned it.

$$r = \frac{(P_t - P_{t-1}) + CF_t}{P_{t-1}} = \frac{(\$42 - \$40) + \$2}{\$40} = \frac{\$4}{\$40} = 0.10 = 10.0\%$$

where P_t denotes the market price at the end of time period t and CF represents the cash flow (from cash dividends in this case).

PA7-2 (a)   Shelly's 6-month rate of return is the same as in the preceding one-year problem. Shelly's stock earned a ten percent rate of return during the six-month investment period. This question was designed to introduce the concept of annualizing a rate of return.

(b)   There are 2 ways to annualize the 6-month rate of return. Since there are two consecutive six-month periods in one year, we can simply multiply the 6-month rate of return by 2 to annualize it. Thus, we get: (10%)(2 periods) = 20%. This is the annualized rate of return with no compounding. The more precise way to solve this problem is to compound the 6-month rate of return for two time periods. After adding one to the 6-month rate of return it is compounded twice as follows: $(1.0 + r)^2 = (1 + 10\%)^2 = (1.1)^2 = 1.21 = (1.0 + 21\%)$ The calculation indicates the stock yielded a 21% annualized rate of return with compounding considered. The compound rate of return includes interest-on-the-interest.

PA7-3   The stock price and cash dividend data for the Consolidated Business Corporation (CBC) from Table P7-3 are below, and the annual rates of return are shown, too.

Year	End-of year close price	Annual cash dividends	Annual return, Eqn. (7-1)
1995	$ 60.00	$3.00	Insufficient data to calculate.
1996	69.00	3.00	($9.00+$3.00)/$60 = 20%
1997	100.50	3.00	(31.50+3.00)/69 = 50%
1998	47.25	3.00	(-53.25+3.00)/100.50 = -50%
1999	39.53	3.00	(-7.72+3.00)/47.25 = -10%
2000	72.10	3.00	(32.57+3.00)/39.53 = 90%
2001	82.52	4.00	(10.42+4.00)/72.10 = 20%

PA7-4   Using the CBC data in Table P7-3 to compute the annual rates of return required in the preceding problem results in a five point finite probability distribution that has four points that equal $1/6 = 0.16666$ and one point that equals $1/3 = 0.333333$, as shown below:

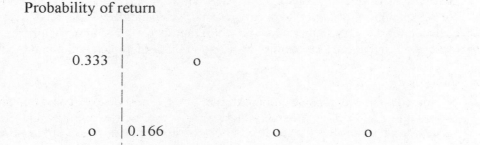
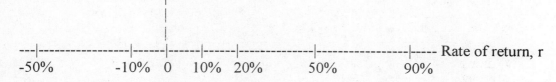

PA7-5   The Consolidated Business Corporation (CBC) expected return and risk statistic computations are below.

Year	Return	Probability	Probability x Return	Deviations from E(r) [Return - E(r)]	Probability times squared deviations
1996	20%	0.166	(.166)(.2) = .03333	(.2-.2) = 0	$(.166)(0)^2 =$ 0
1997	50%	0.166	(.166)(.5) = .08333	(.5-.2) = .3	$(.166)(.3)^2=$ .015
1998	-50%	0.166	(.166)(-.5) = -.08333	(-.5-.2) = -.7	$(.166)(-.7)^2 =$ .08166
1999	-10%	0.166	(.166)(-.1) = -.01666	(-.1-.2) = -.3	$(.166)(-.3)^2 =$ .015
2000	90%	0.166	(.166)(.9) = .14999	(.9-.2) = .7	$(.166)(.7)^2 =$ .08166
2001	20%	0.166	(.166)(.2) = .03333	(.2-.2) = 0	$(.166)(0)^2 =$ 0
Totals		1.000	E(r) = 0.20 = 20%		VAR(r) = .19333

The standard deviation is $\sigma = \sqrt{VAR(r)} = \sqrt{0.19333} = 0.439696$.

PA7-6　　　　　　Susan could use the dominance principle to narrow down her choices, as shown below:

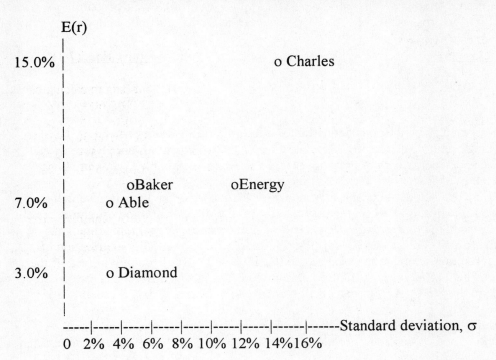

E(r)
|
15.0% | o Charles
|
|
|
|
|
| oBaker   oEnergy
7.0% | o Able
|
|
|
3.0% | o Diamond
|
|
-----|-----|-----|-----|-----|-----|-----|------|------Standard deviation, σ
0   2% 4% 6% 8% 10% 12% 14%16%

Perusal of the graph above reveals that Baker dominates Energy and that Able dominates Diamond. This dominance eliminates two of the five choices. The dominant assets are Able, Baker and Charles. Susan should choose between Able, Baker and Charles based on her own risk-return preferences. For instance, if Susan is an aggressive investor she should select the Charles investment. But, if Susan is a highly risk-averse investor, she should pick Able.

Some bright student might suggest the possibility of portfolios made up of various combinations of the assets. A solid straight line of portfolio possibilities can be drawn between Able and Charles, for instance -- if we either (i) ignore the risk reducing effects of diversification, or (ii) assume that all the assets are perfectly positively correlated. The instructor may want to plunge ahead into a discussion of the risk-reducing effects of diversification in Chapter One or postpone such discussions until the appropriate chapter later in the book.

PA7-7　　　　　　The variance of returns is defined mathematically below.

$$VAR(r) = \sum_{t=1}^{T} p_t [r_t - E(r)]^2$$
$$= p_1 [r_1 - E(r)]^2 + p_2 [r_2 - E(r)]^2 + \cdots + p_T [r_T - E(r)]^2$$

The semi-variance of the returns, denoted SVR, is like the variance in the sense that they both measure deviations away from the expected value (or mean) of the probability distribution of returns. However, the SVR differs from the formula above in one important respect.

$$SVR = \sum_{t=1}^{T} p_t \left[BAR_t - E(r) \right]^2$$

Unlike the variance, which considers all rates of return, the SVR only considers the below average returns, denoted BARs. Comparing the two equations above reveals that the variance considers the rates of return that are above the mean, $r > E(r)$, while the semi-variance (SVR) ignores these pleasing rates of return.

If the probability distribution of returns is symmetric, then the variance will be double the value of the SVR. In the case that the probability distribution of returns are all symmetric, ranking N different VAR(r)s will yield the same identical risk ranking as ranking the same N assets' SVR statistics. However, if the probability distribution of returns is asymmetric, then the variance and the SVR will differ in value. In fact, as the skewness of the probability distribution of returns increases, the difference between the variance and the SVR risk surrogates will increase, too. You may ask, do such differences exist?

In fact, the probability distribution of returns for many stocks, bonds, and, especially, put and call options, are not symmetric. At first, this may seem to suggest that we should make investments decisions using the three statistics {E(r), VAR(r), SKEW} instead of only the two statistics {E(r), VAR(r)}. Secondly, asymmetry might seem to suggest that we should use the E(r) and the SVR for our dominance criteria instead of the E(r) and VAR(r) statistics. Or, thirdly, you might wonder if the probability distribution of returns of the stocks and bonds are skewed, are we not ignoring valuable information if we ignore skewness in our investment decisions? All three of these problems are premature and over-simplified. The solution to this dilemma lies in a venerable mathematics theorem. A robust theorem from mathematical statistics called the Central Limit Theorem says that, essentially, totals will always be symmetrically distributed (according to a two parameter normal probability distribution) even if the underlying component probability distribution of returns that are added up to obtain the totals are all skewed. Since portfolios' returns are totals of returns from individual assets, the Central Limit Theorem becomes relevant in investment decision-making. The Central Limit Theorem implies that the probability distribution of returns of diversified portfolios should be symmetrically (normally) distributed even if all the component probability distribution of returns are highly asymmetric. Later in this book you will learn that diversified portfolios (and not individual stocks and bonds) are the objects of choice that an investor should analyze. As a result, there is no reason to consider skewness or the semi-variance because the portfolios' probability distribution of returns will (in the limit, as N approaches infinity) always be (asymptotically) symmetric (and normally distributed).

PA7-8   The formula for the third statistical moment, denoted SKEW, is below. The probability distribution of returns has $E(r) = 0.1 = 10\%$; this statistic is used in the SKEW computations.

$$SKEW(r) = \sum_{t=1}^{T} p_t [r_t - E(r)]^3$$

$$= p_1 [r_1 - E(r)]^3 + p_2 [r_2 - E(r)]^3 + p_3 [r_3 - E(r)]^3$$

$$= (.3)[.3 - .1]^3 + (.4)[.1 - .1]^3 + (.3)[-0.1 - .1]^3$$

$$= (.3)[.2]^3 + 0 + (.3)[-0.2]^3 = 0 = \text{Zero skewness}$$

This probability distribution of returns is symmetric.

PA7-9 (a)   All three securities have the same expected return, $E(r) = 10.1\%$; however, Security A is the least risky, having the lowest variance of returns.

$E(r_A) = 0.3(10\%) + 0.6(12\%) + 0.1(-1\%) = 10.1\%$
$VAR(r_A) = 0.3(10\% - 10.1\%)^2 + 0.6(12\% - 10.1\%)^2 + 0.1(-1\% - 10.1\%)^2 = 14.49$

$E(r_B) = 0.4(20\%) + 0.4(8\%) + 0.2(-5.5\%) = 10.1\%$
$VAR(r_B) = 0.4(20\% - 10.1\%)^2 + 0.4(8\% - 10.1\%)^2 + 0.2(-5.5\% - 10.1\%)^2 = 89.64$

$E(r_C) = 0.3(9\%) + 0.5(6\%) + 0.2(22\%) = 10.1\%$
$VAR(r_C) = 0.3(9\% - 10.1\%)^2 + 0.5(6\% - 10.1\%)^2 + 0.2(22\% - 10.1\%)^2 = 37.09$

(b)   In light of these statistics, Security A is the most desirable since it has the same return as Securities B and C, but offers a lower risk.

PA7-10   To calculate a beta value, we need first to calculate the covariance of the returns of Juxta-Med Prosthetics (JMP) with the S&P 500 and the variance of the returns of the S&P 500. First, the expected returns of each must be calculated:

$E(r_{S\&P}) = 0.2(22\%) + 0.3(18\%) + 0.5(13\%) = 16.3\%$
$E(r_{JMP}) = 0.2(25\%) + 0.3(22\%) + 0.5(15\%) = 19.1\%$

The variance of the returns on the S&P 500 is 12.81, calculated as follows:

$VAR(r_{S\&P}) = 0.2(22 - 16.3)^2 + 0.3(18 - 16.3)^2 + 0.5(13 - 16.3)^2 = 12.81$

The covariance of the returns for JMP and the S&P 500 is 14.97:

$COV(r_{JMP}, r_{S\&P}) = 0.2(22-16.3)(25 - 19.1) + 0.3(18 - 16.3)(22 - 19.1) +$
      $0.5(13 - 16.3)(15 - 19.1) = 14.97$

The beta for Juxta-Med Prosthetics $= \dfrac{14.97}{12.81} = 1.17$.

CFA Exam Solutions*

The following are the guideline answers provided by the AIMR for the CFA Exam questions:

1.   **D**
   Solution:
   $r = \text{Cov}(R_A, R_B)/\sigma_A \sigma_B$
   $= (0.0096)/(0.20 \times 0.12)$
   $= 0.40$.

2.   **C**
   Solution:
   The S&P 500 Stock Index is a market index, has a beta equal to 1.0, and consists only of systematic risk. If the correlation coefficient between the Baker Fund and the S&P 500 Stock Index is 0.70, the coefficient of determination is 0.49, or 49 percent (i.e., 0.70^2). Because 49 percent of the Baker Fund's total risk is systematic risk, the remaining 51 percent of the total risk is specific or unsystematic risk.

   Total risk = systematic risk and unsystematic risk;
   100% = 49% - unsystematic risk;

   Unsystematic risk = 100% - 49%
   = 51%.

3.   **C**

CHAPTER 8: EFFICIENT CAPITAL MARKETS AND ANOMALIES

SOLUTIONS

Questions

QA8-1   The statement made by Keynes in 1936 undoubtedly still has a large element of relevance in the 2000s. The persistent anomalies in the efficient markets hypotheses leave little doubt that the kind of short-term price change speculating that Keynes described in 1936 correctly describes a significant number of successful traders who are operating today.

QA8-2   If a technical analysis stock price pattern that repeated itself occasionally could be delineated, that pattern would have valuable predictive power and would violate the weakly efficient markets hypothesis. More specifically, Hermann Rorschach's activities would violate the weakly efficient markets hypothesis because historical price information is used to earn trading profits. Since some respectable evidence that is anomalous to all the efficient markets hypotheses has been published, we should give some consideration to assertions like the ones made by Mr. Rorschach. However, his claims are so strong that objective observers could reasonably be a little dubious. It would be appropriate to ask Mr. Rorschach to write a computer program to recognize the repetitive pattern and execute trades based on it. Then, if Mr. Rorschach's computer program yielded risk-adjusted rates of return after deducting trading commissions that were better than some market index (like the S&P 500), that would comprise solid evidence that could be examined by outside researchers in order to verify Hermann Rorschach's claims. NOTE: A world famous Swiss psychiatrist named Hermann Rorschach invented the Rorschach Ink Blot Test during the early 1900s. The Rorschach Ink Blot Test requires the psychiatric patient to observe meaningless ink blots and tell the psychiatrist what they represent. This technique is supposed to draw out patients who are shy and timid about discussing their psychological problems. It has been suggested by those who are dubious of technical analysis that there is some resemblance between the Rorschach Ink Blot Test and pattern recognition by technical analysts.

QA8-3   Mr. Fohx will have to earn a consistent rate of return that is very high to earn a comfortable living from $200,000 of investments if he does not want to consume his $200,000 principal.   Even under the best of circumstances, the return regularities do not offer the high abnormal rates of return Wiley needs to pay his trading costs and live comfortably. Furthermore, if a bear market pulls the S&P500 and Dow Jones Averages down 20, 30, or more percentage points, Mr. Fohx could find himself in dire circumstances.

    Mr. Fohx seems to have given little consideration to what he will do when the buy and sell signals issued by the January effect, the day-of-the-week effect, the time-of-the-day effect, and the within-the-month effect conflict with each other. For instance, what should Wiley Fohx do on the Monday mornings that occur during the early part of January? Also, if he buys and sells too frequently his commission costs could exceed his trading gains.

    Wiley Fohx is also probably naively adding up the abnormal independent returns he has read that each return regularity will yield.   Instead, he should be trying to estimate the net return that could be expected after the counter-productive interactions and double-counting of the simultaneous positive effects are deducted from the gross abnormal returns.

Finally, Wiley Fohx's portfolio is so small that he will be highly subject to sampling errors. Stated differently, a few unlucky trades could bankrupt an investor who has a portfolio as small as Mr. Fohx's.

Wiley Fohx would be well advised to give up his trading scheme. He should consider his liquidity needs, his ability to tolerate risk, his needs for income from the invested funds, and select an appropriate buy-and-hold strategy. In addition, he should look for a job to support himself until his investment portfolio increases substantially.

QA8-4   Eqn.(7-7) is the characteristic line that was introduced in Chapter 7 of this textbook.

$$r_{i,t} = a_i + b_i r_{M,t} + e_{i,t}$$
Eqn. (7-7)

where

$r_{i,t}$ =   the one-period rate of return from the ith stock in time period t = the dependent variable in the regression,

$r_{m,t}$ =   the one-period rate of return from the market portfolio in time period t = the independent variable in the regression,

a_i =   alpha = the characteristic regression line's intercept term,

b_i =   beta = the characteristic regression line's slope coefficient = an index of undiversifiable risk,

$e_{i,t}$ =   epsilon = the residual return that is unexplained by the regression

t =   a subscript that is the time period counter over t = 1, 2, 3,...T time periods.

A review of an empirical study of stock dividends and splits that was conducted by Fama, Fisher, Jensen and Roll (FFJR) was provided in this chapter. FFJR focused on the unexplained residual error term from the characteristic line, e_{it}, to study the effects of stock dividends and splits. This unexplained residual return has had the bull and bear market effects filtered out by the characteristic line regression. The residual terms that remain unexplained by the regression for asset i are:

$$e_{i1}, e_{i2}, e_{i3}, \ldots e_{iT}$$

These idiosyncratic terms contain many of the return regularities that comprise flaws in the efficient markets theory. Careful statistical analysis of these idiosyncratic residual terms from a cross-section of different stocks is a form of security analysis that can yield valuable insights. This is how many of the return regularities introduced in Chapter 7 were discovered.

QA8-5   The statement is uncertain. Compared to the overall average results reported by Dr. Jaffe, the statement espouses exaggerated claims of the profitability of insider trading. A study of trading on insider information that was conducted by Jaffe was reviewed in this chapter. Jaffe used the CAPM to purge bull and bear market effects from a sample of stocks that were traded by insiders. Then he studied the unexplained residuals from the CAPM, denoted u_{it}, and found only the small abnormal returns displayed in the textbook when he averaged over all inside trades. While these additional returns are positive, they are not large. Further research by Seyhun, which was also reviewed in the chapter, suggested that the modest abnormal returns enjoyed by insiders that Jaffe reported were upward biased. These scientific studies leave us with the conclusion that most insiders are not able to get rich quick by trading on the information to which they have access.

QA8-6   The study by Fama, Fisher, Jensen, and Roll indicated that no abnormal returns could be earned, on average, by purchasing stocks once the split was announced although shareholders did earn abnormal returns prior to the split announcement. This is probably the result of positive new information about the firm. Therefore, it is neither a good time nor a bad time for Jake to buy the IBM stock. He can expect to earn a return that compensates him for his risk--no more and no less.

QA8-7   There is no single correct answer to this question. Your approach to investment management should be guided by your beliefs about market efficiency. If you believe that the stock market is perfectly efficient, you should argue for some passive investment system--such as indexing the portfolio to the S&P 500 index, for instance. A passive investment system would be best if markets were perfectly efficient because (i) it could be executed at less cost than an active investment strategy, and (ii) if the market were perfectly efficient, it would be impossible to earn any abnormal returns from any active investment system. At the other extreme, if you believed that the stock market was highly inefficient and that substantial divergences between price and value were common, then you should argue in favor of an active investment system in order to profit from buying under-priced and selling over-priced securities. Between these two extremes, if you believe the stock market is moderately efficient, but not perfectly efficient, then you would favor some mix of passive and active investment management.

QA8-8   Empirical efficient markets tests that employ explicit models (such as the characteristic line, CAPM, or x percent filter rules) from financial theories are actually simultaneous tests of both theories. This is true regardless of whether or not the researcher realizes it or is willing to acknowledge it.

It would certainly be more desirable if empirical tests of the efficient markets theory were based on one independent test; this would allow the efficient markets theory to be tested in isolation. For example, if the efficient markets theory is rejected by employing some other theoretical apparatus, it is not clear whether the results of the test should be interpreted as a rejection of the efficient markets theory, a rejection of the other theoretical apparatus, or a rejection of both models. Using one model to test another model involves an inherent logical flaw that clouds the results.

QA8-9   One of the two events is an example of a flow in the efficient markets theory; the second is supportive of the theory.
(a) The October 1987 international stock market crash did not occur in response to any significant new information. Even a decade after the crash no compelling reason for the plunge had become evident. Furthermore, 18 months after the crash, the stock market had regained most of its losses. This is an example of panic selling and market illiquidity for which no rational explanation exists --it is a large and obvious flaw in the efficient markets theory.
(b) The risk and return from the S&P 500 index is an example of what picking stocks with an unaimed dart should accomplish. The fact that very few mutual funds are able to consistently earn higher risk-adjusted rates of return than S&P 500 is strong evidence that it is not easy to "beat the market." This piece of evidence supports all three hypotheses about efficient markets; it is evidence that all information is already impacted into the market prices.

QA8-10   No. The mutual fund may be investing in stocks that have greater risks than the S&P 500; that is, the beta of the mutual fund portfolio may be greater than 1.0. In this case, the fund *should* be earning a higher return than the S&P 500. An abnormal return is when a stock, or a portfolio of stocks, earns a return higher (or lower) than what is expected on a *risk-adjusted* basis.

Problems

PA8-1   After the Jaring Corporation's 200% stock dividend (a) the number of shares of stock that could be purchased for $150, and (b) the stockholders' one-period rates of return are shown below:

Quarters of one year	Q = 1	Q = 2	Q = 3	Q = 4
Beginning market price/share	$150	$150	$50	$50
Cash dividend per share	$7.50	$7.50	$2.50	$2.50
Earnings per share	$15	$15	$5	$5
Number of shares for $150 of investment	1	1	3	3
One-period rate of return	5%	5%	5%	5%

Summarizing, the change in the unit of account was a meaningless administrative change that had no economic effects or implications.

PA8-2   (a)   [($55 - $50)/$50] = 0.1 = 10.0% = r
         (b)   ln($55/$50) = ln(1.10) = 0.09531 = 9.53% = r
         (c)   The difference of (10% - 9.53% = 0.47 =) 47 basis points results from the fact that a dollar growing at 9.53% that is compounded continuously will grow to the same value as another dollar that is compounded once per time period at the higher 10% noncompounded rate. Mathematically, the two rates are related as shown below:

r = ln(1 + r)

PA8-3 (a)   IBM's characteristic line predicted returns, the actual IBM returns, and unexplained residual returns for 1979 are:

Year/Quarter	IBM's qrtrly. rate of return	IBM's predicted rate of return	Unexplained rate of return residual
1979/1	6.6600%	8.2636%	-1.56036%
1979/2	-5.883%	3.65274%	-9.53574%
June 11, 1979: a 4-for-1 stock split			
1979/3	-6.494%	8.6873%	-15.1813%
1979/4	-3.712%	0.9277%	- 4.6397%

     (b)   The third quarter of 1979 followed IBM's 4-for-1 stock split. The negative residual of -15.1813% for 1979-IIIQ indicates that IBM's stock price declined 15.1738% in the quarter following the stock split. Stated differently, if the stock split did anything (which it did not), it appears to have diminished the shareholders' wealth. What actually happened is that, purely by coincidence, IBM's price was declining at the time it happened to declare a stock split; the two events are coincidental and economically unrelated.

PA8-4 (a)   Buy when the price increases 5% to $44.10: $42 x 1.05 = $44.10
       (b)   Sell when the price drops to $57: $60 x (1 - 0.05) = $57

PA8-5 (a)   Dividend income = 500 x $1.00 = $500. If you are in the 28% tax bracket, the dividends
              will be taxed at this rate, and you will net $500(1 - 0.28) = $360 after taxes.
       (b)   Your capital gain income is $500. If this is taxed at 20%, you will net, after taxes,
              $500(1 - 0.20) = $400.

PA8-6 (a)   John will purchase Sun Microsystems when the price increases by 1% from its low price
              of $73. $73(1.01) = $73.73.
       (b)   John will sell his Sun Microsystems shares when the price falls by 1% from its high of
              $98.50. $98.50(1 - 0.01) = $97.515.
       (c)   Even though there is evidence that small filters may produce some abnormal returns,
              John would have to be very alert and very lucky to be able to buy and sell the shares
              when the price moved by exactly 1%, especially when the price of a stock is so volatile.
              In addition, these exact prices may never occur during an actual trading day.

PA8-7   The runs in the price data for Hiprotech are depicted by alternating italics:

Day	Price	Day	Price	Day	Price	Day	Price
1	*$86*	6	$83 1/2	11	$92	16	$105
2	*$83 1/16*	7	*$82*	12	$93 9/16	17	*$103 3/4*
3	$78	8	*$81 1/4*	13	$97	18	*$103*
4	$81 1/4	9	$85	14	$98 11/16	19	$110
5	$82 3/4	10	$87 1/2	15	$100 1/16	20	$111 1/2

              From this, it can be seen that there are 6 runs.

PA8-8 (a)   Growth investors invest in stocks with relatively low current yields, high price-earnings
              multiples, and high growth rates.

	Current yield	P/E	Growth rate
Stock A	$0.50/$12 = 4.2%	$12/$2.20 = 5.45	5%
Stock B	$0.25/$30 = 0.83%	$30/$1.25 = 24	10%

              Growth investors would, therefore, prefer to invest in Stock B.

       (b)   According to empirical research, value style managers earn higher risk-adjusted returns
              than growth managers, possibly due to overestimates of growth rates by growth
              managers.

PA8-9   William Sharpe suggests that one can differentiate between growth stocks and value
              stocks by examining their market value/book value multiples.

	Price per share	Shares outstanding	Market value	Book value	Market-to-Book
Peach	$30	10 million	$300 million	$75 million	4X
Pear	$25	12 million	$300 million	$50 million	6X
Plum	$18	18 million	$324 million	$300 million	1.08X

Plum Corporation, which has the lowest market-to-book ratio, would be classified as a value stock.

PA8-10   Prior to the split, the investor owned 1,000 shares of the stock with a market value of $1,400,000,000/20,000,000 = $70 a share. Total dividends were 1,000 x ($10,500,000/20,000,000) = $525.

$$r = \frac{((1,000x\$70) + \$525) - (1,000x\$60)}{(1,000x\$60)} = 17.5\%$$

After the split, the investor owns 2,000 shares of stock with a market value of $1,400,000,000/40,000,000 = $35 a share. (The market value of the firm's assets is unaffected by the split. Its shares outstanding, however, double.) His total dividend income would be 2,000 x ($10,500,000/40,000,000) = $525.

$$r = \frac{((2,000x\$35) + \$525) - (1,000x\$60)}{1,000x\$60} = 17.5\%$$

Nothing but an accounting change has occurred, and the investor's wealth is the same regardless of whether he sells his stock before or after the split takes place.

CFA Exam Solutions*

The following are the guideline answers provided by the AIMR for the CFA Exam questions.

1.   A

2.   B

3 (A)   Technical analysts search for recurrent and predictable patterns in the movements of individual securities, groups of securities, and securities markets. Trading rules are developed on the observations of patterns (such as "head and shoulders" and "catapult" patterns for individual stocks and "support and resistance" areas for markets) that they believe convey buy or sell signals. Technicians see no reason to study fundamental information about companies, industries, and the economy; indeed, they do not even need to know the name of the company whose securities price data is being studied. Although technical analysts believe that stock prices do react to fundamental data, they also believe that price and volume data will reveal future price moves to them before fundamental data reveals it to fundamental analysts. This belief is the key premise of technical analysis and is in conflict with even the weak form of the efficient market hypothesis (EMH).

Fundamental analysts make extensive use of company, industry and economic data, industry statistics, and accounting information to make estimates of future states of the economy and the markets and the values of individual securities. Such estimates ordinarily incorporate judgmental assessments of the attractiveness of issues for purchase or sale, assessments usually based on the insights the individual analyst believes he or she has gained ahead of other market participants. The key premise of fundamental analysis is that each security (and market) has an intrinsic value and appropriate study of the appropriate data and information will reveal to the astute investor whether the security is fairly valued, overvalued, or undervalued.

(B)   The weak form of the EMH states that all past data regarding given securities, groups of securities, or markets, are already reflected in current prices. Hence, such information is of no value and cannot be used to predict future prices or price changes. This form of the EMH directly challenges technical analysis.

The semistrong form of the EMH states that all publicly available information has been efficiently (i.e., quickly and accurately) incorporated into present prices so that possession of such information is of no value in predicting future prices or changes in prices.

The strong form of the EMH asserts that even nonpublic information (i.e., "inside" or "privileged" information) is not sufficient consistently to permit what economists would call supernormal profits from its possession over time. The strong form of the EMH is an extreme view that is totally inconsistent with theory and practice in U.S. securities markets, securities laws, and the rules of the SEC.

It is the semistrong form of the EMH that directly challenges fundamental analysis. This form maintains that there can be no incremental value to fundamental analysis because all of an analyst's public information has already been processed by the consensus and accurately embedded in current security prices. Because new information arrives randomly, the next significant "news" that will change security prices is not knowable.

(C)   In 1992, Fama and French published an empirical study using U.S. stocks that also could be interpreted as challenging the EMH. At about the same time Capaul, Rowley, and Sharpe published a similar study using international stocks. In both studies, stock indexes (or, in Fama and French, a large sample) were divided into groups based on stock price-to-book ratios (in Fama and French's study, book-to-price ratios). Those stocks with high price/book (low book/price) represented "expensive" stocks, which are commonly the stocks of companies with high growth prospects; investors are willing to pay high prices relative to book value for companies expected to have strong earnings and dividend growth. Stocks with low price/book (high book/price) represented "cheap" stocks with low growth prospects. Hence, stocks can be divided into "growth" stocks and "value" stocks based on relative price/book.

Fama and French evaluated the joint roles of CAPM-derived betas, size, and stock ratios of book value to market value for a large sample of U.S. stocks for the 1963-90 period. They found a weak relationship between beta and average return and a robust relationship between size and return, and between book/market values and return. In particular, small companies and companies with high stock book/market value had higher returns. If these findings are interpreted as suggesting that size and book/market are proxies for risk, then they may not conflict with the EMH. Alternatively, if these findings are interpreted as implying that book-to-market ratios predict stock returns, then they directly challenge the EMH.

Capaul, Rowley, and Sharpe analyzed the returns for value and growth stocks in six countries--France, Germany, the United Kingdom, Japan, and the United States--from 1981 to 1992. Value stocks outperformed growth stocks in each country both in terms of absolute and risk-adjusted return. Furthermore, the pattern of the positive spread between value returns and growth returns operated at different times and different ways in each of the six countries. This finding suggests that investors "tilting" toward value stocks should diversify their portfolios on a global basis.

If the semistrong form of the EMH were valid, one might expect that a passive indexing strategy that includes all stocks (value and growth), weighted according to market value, would prove superior to strategies that involve a tilt toward value stocks. In both the Fama and French and the Capaul, Rowley, and Sharpe studies, however, value stocks outperformed all stocks even on a risk-adjusted basis. Nevertheless, one must be careful in interpreting these results. For example, the dividend component is typically a larger portion of the total return of value stocks than of growth stocks. Because dividend return is subject to higher taxes than capital appreciation, value stocks might be expected to offer a larger return on a before-tax basis than growth stocks.

4A.   i.   The semi-strong form of the EMH receives support from numerous event studies that show that new information is rapidly assimilated into market pricing. The market appears to correctly differentiate between events that have economic importance and those that do not. A partial list of examples includes the following:

- **Price impact of dividend changes.** Various studies have concluded that dividend changes, which have economic significance, are quickly reflected in stock price changes. After the public announcement of a dividend change, stock prices generally adjust quickly, without further drift in CAR (cumulative abnormal return). These results support the semi-strong EMH because they indicate that the market quickly and correctly reflects the economic significance of new information.

- **Price impact of takeover announcements.** Similar to dividend announcements, announcements of takeovers have economic significance and are quickly reflected in market pricing with little further drift in CAR (in the absence of further information).

- **Price impact of stock splits**. Stock splits are popularly viewed as having positive implications for future stock price performance, even though they represent no change in a firm's economic fundamentals. Multiple studies have concluded that splits do no result in higher rates of return for shareholders. These results support the semi-strong EMH because they indicate that the market is correctly reflecting the economic significance (or lack thereof) of new information.

- **Initial Public Offerings (IPOs).** Under the premise that underwriters generally price IPOs below their true economic value, various studies have examined how quickly the market adjusts for the underpricing. Results indicate that the price adjustment takes place quickly (one day or less), which is essentially consistent with the semi-strong EMH.

- **Unexpected world and economic events**. Studies have shown that the economic significance of world or economic news is quickly reflected in security market pricing, consistent with the semi-strong EMH.

- **Active manager underperformance.** Studies have shown that active managers often underperform the relevant benchmark, which is essentially consistent with the semi-strong EMH.

ii.   Apparent pricing and performance anomalies have been documented in a growing number of studies. The ability to consistently predict stock price performance on the basis of publicly available information regarding company attributes or calendar effects is inconsistent with the semi-strong form of EMH.

- **Calendar effects.** Numerous studies have documented a seasonality to stock price performance. The January effect (in which small cap stocks outperform large stocks in January) and various other calendar effects appear to refute the semi-strong EMH, under which known seasonalities would be already reflected in market pricing.

- **Superior returns to small and/or neglected firms.** Small firms, often "neglected" by analysts, have been found to provide superior risk-adjusted returns relative to large stocks. Under the semi-strong EMH, public information regarding company attributes would already be reflected in pricing.

- **Superior returns of "value" stocks.** Several studies (e.g., Haugen, Fama) have observed that, over long time periods, stocks of companies with low valuations (especially those with low price-book ratios) appear, when adjusted for risk, to outperform stocks of companies with high valuations. Such results are in conflict with the semi-strong EMH, inasmuch as they imply that publicly available data and ratios can be used to produce superior returns.

- **Exceptional track records** of certain firms and individuals appear attributable to superior fundamental analysis of public information (e.g., the Value Line enigma). These achievements seem to refute the semi-strong EMH.

- **Extreme market moves**, such as those of October 1987, appear to indicate that market pricing is sometimes driven by more than just the rational processing of new information. To the extent that "crowd psychology" or other noneconomic factors drive prices away from "fair values," exploitable mispricings exist, in conflict with the semi-strong EMH.

- **Price reversals** (reversion to the mean), in which poorly performing stocks in one period systematically experience reversals in the subsequent period, are inconsistent with the semi-strong EMH. They imply that the market is overreacting to public information and that securities are mispriced.

B.   There are *client-specific needs* that must be met for counsel and management to be effective. Actively managed portfolios can be constructed to meet client objectives and constraints not reflected in a (passively managed) market portfolio, adding a "nonperformance dimension" to the value of active management. These client-specific needs include the following:
- **Special objectives** (e.g., social investing, special portfolio attributes, and similar nonstandard preferences); and
- **Special constraints** (e.g., security exclusions, special tax circumstances, unusual regulatory limits, abnormal liquidity needs and similar non-standard constraints).

Active management is justified when its rewards equal or exceed its associated costs. Although consistently superior risk-adjusted performance may be unattainable in a semi-strong efficient market *on average*, it may be possible to identify managers who posses superior mosaic-assembling abilities to create valuable information from publicly available data.

CHAPTER 9: FUTURES AND OPTIONS

SOLUTIONS

Questions

QA9-1   The statement is false. Short selling is done by both risk-averters and speculators. Consider a farmer who plans to harvest a good corn crop in August, but wants to lock in a price for which he can sell the crop today in order to insure that he can cover his expenses and earn a tidy profit. He could do so by short selling a futures contract in corn for August delivery.

QA9-2   There are three parties involved in the sale of put and call options: the option seller (or writer), the option buyer, and the broker. The option seller receives the option premium and must perform (i.e., either sell stock to the option buyer if he has written a call or buy the stock from the option buyer if he has written a put). The option buyer pays the option premium to the seller of the option and can choose to exercise the option or not. The broker matches option buyers and sellers and acts as their agent to consummate transactions. They receive a commission for doing so.

QA9-3   The main factors that determine the premiums on puts and calls are: (a) The optioned asset's price. The higher the price, the greater the call premium and the smaller the put premium required by the option writer. (b) The time to expiration on the option--the longer the time to expiration is, the higher the premium, regardless of whether it is a call or a put, because there is a greater possibility that the option will be exercised in the time remaining on the option. (c) The volatility of the optioned asset's price--the greater the probability of price change, the greater the probability that it will become profitable to exercise the option, so the greater the option premium. (d) The exercise price on the option. If this price is below the market price of the stock, the put writer's risk that the put will be exercised is less, and a lower premium will result. The opposite is true if the exercise price on the put is above the market price of the stock. The reverse is true for call option premiums. (e) The risk-free interest rate. The higher the interest rate, the higher the call premium and the lower the put premium due to opportunity costs. The effect of interest rates on premiums is small, however. (f) Cash dividend payments. Dividend payments decrease call premiums and increase put premiums due to the price dropoff effect that they have on the price of the optioned stock.

QA9-4   A warrant is, in effect, a call option on a corporation's stock, but it differs from a regular call option in several ways. The writer of a call option is just another investor, whereas the writer of the warrant is the corporation issuing the warrant. When a call option is exercised, no new shares are issued, but when a warrant is exercised, the corporation must issue new shares, which dilutes the earnings per share of the corporation. This could potentially result in a decrease in the stock price of the corporation. The exercise of a call option would not affect the price of the optioned stock. Warrants have longer times to expiration than call options; some may even have infinite lives. The exercise price on a warrant may change with the passage of time, but the exercise price of a call is fixed for the life of the call.

QA9-5   The option writer receives a payment, the option premium, to stand ready to perform should the option buyer decide to exercise his or her option. In order to insure that the writer will perform as promised, the writer must put up a "good faith deposit," the initial margin payment. Option buyers are not required to do so because they can simply let their options expire. They are not contractually obligated to perform.

QA9-6   The initial investment of $1,000 is the same regardless of whether the 100 calls on SKBC are purchased or the 10 shares of SKBC stock are purchased. Therefore, the maximum possible loss is the same with either alternative. The key difference between the two strategies lies in the amount of financial leverage that each provides. Buying the 100 calls will provide much more upside profit potential than investing the same amount of money in the long position of 10 shares. Therefore, if you expect the price of SKBC to rise significantly before the calls expire, the call buying alternative is clearly the more desirable. However, if there is a very large probability that the price of SKBC stock might not rise before the calls expire and become worthless, then the long position in SKBC looks more appealing.

QA9-7   Long and short positions in futures contracts are called linear because their prices move in a linear one-to-one relationship with the market price of the underlying asset. This is not true of puts and calls. The option premiums are related to the prices of their underlying assets in a discontinuous manner. The intrinsic value of the call option, for example, remains at zero until the value of the underlying asset is equal to the exercise price, and the option buyer will not earn a profit until the value of the call (which will be higher than its intrinsic value if any time is left to expiration) exceeds the option premium. This affects the price that the option buyer is willing to pay. Similarly, the intrinsic value of a put option remains at zero until the value of the underlying asset is equal to the exercise price on the option, and the buyer of the put option will not begin to earn a profit until the price of the optioned asset drops below the exercise price on the put by the amount of the put premium.

QA9-8   Futures contracts sell on organized exchanges and are regulated by government agencies whereas forward contracts are over-the-counter instruments and are governed only by contract law. Every futures exchange has a clearing house that guarantees that deliveries will be complete and on time, thus eliminating the risk of default that exists with a forward contract. (This default risk is also referred to as counterparty risk.) The futures exchanges also provide for a continuous, auction market, so futures contracts are highly liquid and marketable. Forward contracts, on the other hand, are not marketable. To get out of a forward contract, the buyer or seller must hope that the counterparty to the contract will be open to negotiation. There are no daily cash settlements in forward contracts as there are in futures contracts. Settlement occurs only on the specified delivery date. Transactions costs, both explicit and implicit, are higher for forward contracts.

While forward contracts have greater counterparty risk and lack liquidity, they have the advantage that they can be tailored to the specific needs of the buyer or seller. The size of the contract and delivery date, for example, can be negotiated between the counterparties, whereas the sizes of futures contracts and their delivery dates are standardized.

QA9-9   Commodities futures require the physical delivery of the asset, and the shipping and transportation costs (and delays) involved make international transactions in commodity futures less attractive. Financial transactions involving millions of dollars can, however, be wired around the world in seconds at a minimal cost.

QA9-10   If the stock market falls, the price of the S&P 500 Index futures contract will also fall. There is a linear relationship between the value of the futures contract and the price of the underlying asset. If Doug takes a short position (sells) a futures contract in the S&P500 Index, the decrease in value of his stock portfolio will be offset (at least partially) by his gain in his futures position. His gain on the futures position will be the difference in the value of the futures contract on the day he sells it and the value of that same contract when he reverses his position (i.e., buys the S&P 500 futures contract at a now lower price.)

QA9-11   Open interest refers to the number of futures contracts that remain outstanding. The greater the open interest, the greater the public interest in that contract.

Problems

PA9-1 (a)   The TI option would be worth at least its intrinsic value of $108.75 - $90.00 = $18.75 per optioned share. (If there remained any time to expiration, it would actually be worth a little more than this.)

(b)   The percentage gain $= \dfrac{\$18.75 - \$1.375}{\$1.375} = 12.64 = 1,264\%$.

PA9-2   The recommendation is to buy the convertible bond and convert it to shares of common stock. The conversion value of this bond is 50 x $25 = $1,250, so by buying the convertible bond and converting, you make an immediate profit of $1,250 - $1,100 = $150 per bond. The non-convertible bond appears to be overpriced since it is selling for more than the convertible bond. Its price should be less than the price of the convertible security by the value of the call premium on the issuer's stock.

PA9-3   The intrinsic value of a call option = max[0, (stock price - exercise price)].
(a)   The intrinsic value = max[0, ($33 - $30)] = $3 per optioned share.
(b)   The intrinsic value = max[0, ($24 - $30)] = $0 per optioned share.
(c)   The maximum potential loss to the option buyer is the premium paid for the call, or in this case, $6 per optioned share.
(d)   Sam has limitless potential profit as the stock price increases beyond the exercise price.
(e)   Profit = max[0,(stock price - exercise price)] - call option premium =
        $3 - $6 = -$3 per optioned share.

PA9-4 (a)   (i) The intrinsic value = max[0, ($82 - $70)] = $12 per optioned share.
        (ii) The intrinsic value = max[0, ($51 - $70)] = $0 per optioned share.
(b)   Your maximum loss is the price you paid for the option--$7 per optioned share.
(c)   Joe's losses are limitless if he doesn't already own the stock. Even if he owns the stock, he will have an opportunity loss as the stock price increases and the stock is "called away" from him.
(d)   Profit = intrinsic value of call - call option premium = $12 - $7 = $5 per optioned share.

PA9-5   The intrinsic value of a put = max[0, (exercise price - stock price)].
   (a)   The intrinsic value = max[0, ($85 - $97)] = 0.
   (b)   The intrinsic value = max[0, ($85 - $79)] = $6 per optioned share.
   (c)   The maximum amount the option buyer can lose is the price of the option,
        or $3 per optioned share in this instance.
   (d)   The maximum gain will occur if the optioned stock price goes to zero, in
        which case the profit will equal the intrinsic value less the cost of the   option: $85
        -$3 = $82.
   (e)   Profit = intrinsic value - option premium = $6 - $3 = $3.

PA9-6   The put writer's intrinsic value = min[0, (stock price - exercise price)].
   (a)   Intrinsic value = min[0, ($51 - $50)] = 0.
   (b)   Intrinsic value = min[0, ($33 - $50)] = -$17.
   (c)   The maximum value the put writer can lose occurs if the price of the
        optioned asset goes to zero. At that point, the writer's loss is equal to the
        exercise price on the option less the premium he or she received for
        writing the option. In this case in would be $50 - $7 = $43.
   (d)   Profit = min[0, ($135 - $50)] + $7 = $7 per optioned share.
   (e)   Profit = min[0, ($33 - $50)] + $7 = -$17 + $7 = -$10.

PA9-7 (a)   European puts can only be exercised at expiration. If, at expiration, the intrinsic value of
        the put is greater than $7, the price Tanya paid for the option, Tanya will earn a profit,
        ignoring commissions and taxes.
   (b)   Tanya might choose to exercise the put if the price at expiration is anything less than $70
        in order to recoup at least part of her option premium.
   (c)

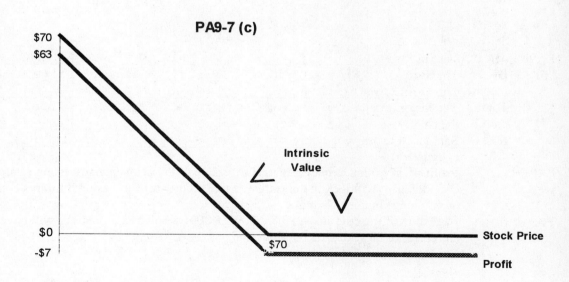

PA9-8 (a)   The conversion value = conversion ratio x market price of stock, so 20 x $40 = $800.
   (b)   The conversion premium = market price of the convertible - the conversion value of the
        convertible, so $955 - $800 = $155.

PA9-9 (a)   If Addison believed that the price of heating oil would go up, he would take a long
        position in a heating oil futures contract.

(b)　Value of contract = 42,000($0.4574) = $19,210.80, and Addison would have to deposit 10% of this or $1,921 (= 0.10 x $19,210.80).

(c)　Addison's purchase price in July:　　$0.4574 per gallon
　　 Addison's selling price in January:　$0.4225 per gallon
　　　　　　　　　　Loss　　　　　　　　$0.0349 per gallon

　　$0.0349 (42,000 gallons) = $1,465.80 loss

(d)　Addison's investment was $1,921, so his holding period return was (-$1,465.80/$1,921) = -76.3%.

PA9-10　This problem was designed to demonstrate a perfect hedge. The solutions to all parts are presented in tabular form below:

	(a)	(b)	(c)	(d)	(e)	(f)	(g)
Value of mutual fund	$1,350	$1,400	$1,450	$1,500	$1,550	$1,600	$1,650
Payoff from short position = current futures price - futures price at delivery date = $1,550 - delivery date price	$200	$150	$100	$50	0	-$50	-$100
Div. income	$12	$12	$12	$12	$12	$12	$12
Total gain (loss)	$1,562	$1,562	$1,562	$1,562	$1,562	$1,562	$1,562

PA9-11 (a)　Since HOW wants to hedge against the value of the deutschemark rising relative to the U.S. dollar, it will lock in an exchange rate today buy purchasing a futures contract (going long) in deutschemark.

(b)　The value of the contract = $0.5565($125,000) = $69,562.50. HOW will have to deposit, therefore, (0.08)($62,562.50) = $5,565.

CFA Exam Solutions*

The following are the guideline answers provided by the AIMR for the CFA Exam questions:

1. **A**
   Solution:
   The put buyer could theoretically earn $40 - 0 - $2 = $38, so $38 is also the put seller's maximum loss. The call writer could earn only the option premium of $3.50.

2. **A**

3. **D**

4A. **Futures vs. Options**
   Using futures differs from using options for hedging the portfolio's equity exposure in the following ways.

   i. *Initial cost.* Futures require an initial margin which is usually costless. The initial cost of a stock index options strategy is the option premium. Thus, the option strategy has a higher initial cost than the futures strategy.

   ii. *Effect of implied volatility in pricing.* Implied volatility is not a factor in futures pricing, whereas it is a key factor in determining the initial option premium.

   iii. *Sensitivity to movement in value of the underlying.* The futures must move with the spot price or an arbitrage is possible. Sensitivity to movement in value of the underlying asset for options can vary from 0.01 to 1.00.

   iv. *Risk exposure.* Using futures to hedge the portfolio is the optimal hedge strategy because the symmetrical feature of the futures hedge ensures that losses (profits) on the underlying portfolio are offset by profits (losses) on the corresponding futures positions. Because of the asymmetrical characteristics of options, producing a "perfect hedge" with options may be more difficult. Both instruments are subject to "tracking error," or a "mismatch" of the hedging instrument's ability to adequately offset movements of the underlying portfolio.

B. **Covered Calls versus Long Puts**

   i. *Effectiveness of the hedges.* Because a covered call strategy provides only partial downside protection, it is not an effective hedge if the market declines greatly. The strategy's protection is limited to the amount of premium collected by selling the call contracts. A long put plus the current portfolio strategy offers essentially complete downside protection for market levels that are at or below the put's strike (exercise) price.

   ii. *Performance of the hedges during a rising market.* A covered call strategy limits the return that a portfolio can achieve in a rising market. The upside potential of the portfolio is limited by the exercise price of the option. A long put strategy allows unlimited upside participation by the portfolio in return for the premium. The put will not be exercised and will expire worthless.

iii.   ***Cost of the strategies.***   A covered call strategy has no explicit cost because the strategy calls for selling call options from which premium income is received. The real cost is the limit placed on the upside potential of the portfolio. The cost of the long put strategy is the initial premium paid for the put contracts.

CHAPTER 10: CREATING PRICE INDEXES

SOLUTIONS

Questions

QA10-1   The five factors to be considered are sample size, representativeness, weighting, convenient units, and economy of maintenance. The sample should be a statistically significant fraction of the underlying population. It needs to be large enough to minimize sampling errors, but not too large. If it is too large and diverse it might be uneconomical to compile and uninteresting to specialized investors. The sample also needs to be representative of all sections of the population to be useful. The elements in the sample should be assigned weights based on some rational methodology. Weighting the securities by market value or assigning equal weights are two of the most sensible options. An index should be stated in convenient units that are easy to understand and that will facilitate answering relevant questions. Index numbers meet this criterion better than averages. The indicator needs also to be economical to maintain. When the data gathering is expensive and/or the population being measured is small, smaller samples are more sensible. They are also appropriate if the population being sampled is very homogeneous and the elements in the population are all highly positively correlated.

QA10-2   The DJIA uses a very small sample of only 30 stocks, which represents less than two percent of the stocks listed on the NYSE. Furthermore, it uses only stocks of large, blue-chip firms, and is not very representative of the population being sampled. The DJIA is an arithmetic average and uses only prices, rather than market values, in its computation. This creates a downward bias when a stock splits since that stock's price movements no longer affect the average by as much as it previously did. A one percent increase in a higher priced stock will cause a greater movement in the DJIA than will that same percentage increase in a smaller priced stock. The DJIA is quoted in a unit called a "point," which translates into no useful economic meaning. If the DJIA has increased (or decreased) by a certain percentage, an investor cannot use that percentage movement as a benchmark by which to judge his portfolio's performance. In contrast, an investor can use percentage movements in market value weighted indexes as benchmarks. The DJIA is fraught with maintenance problems because of the manner in which it is constructed. As mentioned above, stock splits cause movements that have no economic logic. The DJIA also has historically added and deleted stocks for what seems to be no real logical reason. In spite of these problems, however, the DJIA is highly positively correlated with other respected indexes, such as the S&P 500 Index, and because of this, it is about as good an indicator as those indexes that are scientifically superior to the DJIA in construction.

QA10-3   When the Case Corporation's $20 stock rose ten percent, it had a small impact on the average because the average is a price-weighted average and Case is a low-priced stock. In contrast, when the price of the $80 Ace stock rose ten percent, it had a larger effect on the average because Ace is a high-priced stock.

         The DJIA is a price-weighted average, and, therefore, it reacts to changes in the prices of its component stocks, such as the three-stock average in this example. Most price-weighted averages are not based on any rational economic model or logical reflection of investment opportunities. Price-weighting is arbitrary and inappropriate in most applications and can result in misleading values for an inappropriate price-weighted average.

QA10-4   Indexes are more statistically refined than averages. Averages are merely weighted or unweighted arithmetic mean prices for a group of stocks. Indexes are pure numbers that are void of dollar dimensions. Indexes are usually weighted in some meaningful fashion. Multiplying the price of each stock times the number of shares outstanding is a common weighting method; this is called "value weighting" since the weight assigned to each stock corresponds to its aggregate market value weight. Indexes may be constructed from larger and more diverse samples of stocks than averages. Indexes are also more likely to be from more representative samples and contain less bias than averages. Nevertheless, some well-publicized averages, like the Dow-Jones Averages, for instance, are more widely discussed than most indexes, even though the Dow Jones Averages are unrepresentative, biased, and statistically inferior indicators.

QA10-5   The equally-weighted index is constructed to represent a portfolio that is selected by picking securities by some random technique (such as throwing a dart without aiming). Thus, an equally weighted index represents how an investor might perform if he had no skill, no good luck, or no bad luck. This is a good standard of comparison against which to judge a professional portfolio manager's investment performance. If the professional manager cannot outperform an index constructed to represent the performance of an unskilled investor, the professional manager's services aren't worth the price. The University of Chicago's Center for Research on Security Prices (CRSP) Equally Weighted Index is a well-known equally-weighted index. In addition, there exists a CRSP value-weighted index.

The value-weighted index is constructed to correspond to the investment opportunities that are available in the market. To assign each stock a weight that is proportional to the total dollar weight it commands in the market where it is traded, the index is constructed by multiplying each stock's market price times the number of shares outstanding for that stock. After this is done for every stock in the market, each stock's percentage of the aggregate market value can be calculated. This weighting system does not assign an equal weight to every stock. The stocks of large companies (like General Motors) are given larger weights than the stocks of small corporations. This weighting system is used to represent the dollar weighted investment experience of all investors.

The market-value-weighted weighting system is calculated by multiplying the market price of every stock in the index times the number of shares it has outstanding in order to obtain that issue's total market value.

Issue's total market value = price per share x number of shares outstanding

Then the aggregate value of all shares outstanding in all of the issues in the index is calculated simply by summing up each separate issue's total outstanding value.

(Total market value of first issue) + (Total market value of second issue) + . . (Total market value of last issue) = Aggregate market value of all the issues in the index.

Finally, the total market value of each issue is divided into the aggregate value of all issues in the index to obtain the fraction of the index's total market value attributable to each different issue.

$$\text{Weight of issue } i = \frac{\text{Total market value of issue } i}{\text{Aggregate market value of all issues}}$$

The Standard & Poor's 500 Composite Stocks Index is a popular example of a value-weighted stock market index.

QA10-6   An over-the-counter (OTC) stock market index would contain more small stocks than an index of NYSE-listed stocks; however, not all OTC stocks are growth stocks. Standard & Poor's does have about 90 different indexes for different homogeneous industry-oriented categories of stocks. If the researcher was interested in a new industry, then one or more of the S&P indexes might be appropriate. Finally, the researcher could construct a custom-made index from whatever sample of stocks in which she was interested.

QA10-7   While Treasury bills are considered to be free of default risk, investors are exposed to a great deal of purchasing power risk. Because of this, they are not a wise investment vehicle for retirement. Treasury bills offered a very low real return over the 73-year period from 1926 to 1999, and in some of those periods, the real return on Treasury bills was actually negative, meaning that investors lost purchasing power. In contrast, common stocks provided the highest real returns to investors over the 73-year period.

QA10-8   The 30 stocks used in 1999 in constructing the DJIA are listed below:

AT&T	DuPont	McDonalds
Alcoa	Eastman Kodak	Merck
Allied Signal	Exxon	Minnesota Mining and Manufacturing
American Express	General Electric	JP Morgan
Boeing	General Motors	Philip Morris
Caterpillar	Goodyear	Proctor and Gamble
Chevron	Hewlett Packard	Sears
Citigroup	IBM	Union Carbide
Coca Cola	International Paper	United Technologies
Disney	Johnson and Johnson	WalMart

The list of 30 stocks changes periodically. Nevertheless, the most striking thing about the DJIA list is the fact that all of the stocks are *not industrial firms* as the title of the Average implies. Utility stocks like AT&T, financial stocks like American Express, drug companies like Merck Labs, and retailers like Sears and WalMart, are hardly what one would call industrial firms that should be included in an industrial average.

Secondly, the DJIA is composed solely of large, old, blue-chip corporations. Thus, it is representative of that segment of NYSE-listed stocks that conservative investors and institutions like to buy. A more appropriate name for this Average might be "The Dow Jones Average of the Bluest of Blue-Chip Stocks" rather than the Dow Jones *Industrial* Average.

QA10-9 (a)   The arithmetic average rate of return is simple, well-known, and easy to calculate. This arithmetic mean return of T different single time periods' rate of return, each denoted r_t, is defined below:

$$\text{Arithmetic mean} = \bar{r} = \left[\frac{1}{T}\right]\sum_{t=1}^{T} r_i = \left[\frac{1}{T}\right](r_1 + r_2 + r_3 + \ldots + r_T)$$

(b)   The geometric mean of T different time periods' rates of return, each denoted r_t, is defined below as GMR:

$$GMR = \sqrt[T]{(1+r_1)(1+r_2)(1+r_3)...(1+r_T)} - 1.0$$

The geometric mean return is sometimes called a time-weighted rate of return because each time period's return is given an equal rate.

(c)   The arithmetic mean and geometric mean will be identical if there is no variability in the one-period rates of return; i.e., $VAR(r_t) = 0$. However, if there is variability, $VAR(r_t) > 0$, then the arithmetic mean will be greater than the geometric mean. The arithmetic mean assumes that a 1% decrease is exactly offset by a 1% increase, which is not the case, while the geometric mean takes compounding into account.

QA10-10   No. The DJIA uses only prices in its calculation. The percentage change in the DJIA cannot be equated to a percentage change in market value, which is price x shares outstanding. An investor can, however, use a percentage change in a value-weighted index, such as the S&P 500 Index, as a benchmark with which to judge her portfolio's return.

Problems

PA10-1(a) $MYVAL = \dfrac{\$30 + \$80 + \$100 + \$50 + \$20}{5} = \dfrac{\$280}{5} = \$56.00$

(b)   Given a 2-for-1 stock split, the price of Stock C is now $50.

$$MYVAL = \frac{\$30 + \$80 + \$50 + \$50 + \$20}{divisor} = 56.00$$

$$MYVAL = \frac{230}{56} = 4.1071$$

PA10-2(a)   The value-weighted three-stock index is calculated below:

Stock	Total shares outstanding on both dates	More recent market price July 1,2000	Total value = number of shares x price/share	Weights (total value = $11,700,000)
Middie	50,000	$ 60	$ 3,000,000	0.2564
Mite	10,000	$ 70	700,000	0.0598
Maxum	100,000	$ 80	8,000,000	0.6838
Totals	160,000	$210	$11,700,000	1.0000

66

Stock	Total shares outstanding on both dates	Base period market price July 1, 1970	Total value = number of shares x price/share	Weights (total value = $8,200,000)
Middie	50,000	$ 40	$ 2,000,000	0.2439
Mite	10,000	$ 20	200,000	0.0244
Maxum	100,000	$ 60	6,000,000	0.7317
Totals	160,000	$120	$8,200,000	1.0000

The value-weighted index is 1.4268, as calculated below:

$$\frac{\text{July 1, 2000 market value}}{\text{July 1, 1970 market value}} = \frac{\$11,700,000}{\$8,200,000} = 1.4268$$

This index value implies that the three-stock value-weighted index increased 42.68% from its base date of July 1, 1970 to the current date of July 1, 2000. This is the way other value-weighted indexes, such as the S&P 500 is calculated. Note that stock splits and stock dividends in any of the stocks would neither affect the way the value-weighted index is calculated nor its value.

(b)   The price-weighted three-stock index is calculated below:

Stock	More recent market price July 1, 2000	Weights (Total value = $11,700,000)
Middie	$ 60	0.2857
Mite	$ 70	0.3333
Maxum	$ 80	0.3810
Totals	$210	1.0000

Stock	Base period market price July 1, 1970	Weights (Total value = $8,200,000)
Middie	$ 40	0.3333
Mite	$ 20	0.1667
Maxum	$ 60	0.5000
Totals	$120	1.0000

The price-weighted index is 1.75, as calculated below:

$$\frac{\text{Total value of the three shares in 2000}}{\text{Total value of the three shares in 1970}} = \frac{\$210}{\$120} = 1.75$$

The index value of 1.75 implies that the three-stock price-weighted index increased 75% from its base date of July 1, 1970 to the current date of July 1, 2000. While the DJIA is a price-weighted indicator, it is not calculated as an index. Instead, it is calculated as an arithmetic average. Using the DJIA method, the value of the three-stock indicator would simply be $210/3 = 70. The computational procedure for both the index calculation and the arithmetic average would have been much more complicated if any stock dividends or stock splits had occurred.

(c) The equally-weighted three-stock index is calculated below:

Stock	Percentage price change per share from 1970 to 2000	Equal weights	Products (percent change x equal weight)
Middie	+50%	0.33333	16.667
Mite	+250%	0.33333	83.333
Maxum	+33%	0.33333	11.000
Totals	+333%	1.00000	110.999%

The equally-weighted index value of 110.999% implies that the three-stock index increased 110.999% from its base date of July 1, 1970 to the current date of July 1, 2000.

(d) The values of the three different indexes are summarized below:

Stock	Percentage price change	Index	Increase in index value
Middie	+50%	value-weighted	42.68%
Mite	+250%	equally-weighted	110.999%
Maxum	+33%	price-weighted	75.0%

The value-weighted index had the lowest percentage increase because the value-weighting procedure assigns the greatest weight to the largest issuer, Maxum, which happened to have the smallest percentage gain. The equally-weighted index registered the largest percentage gain, 110.999%, because it assigns equal weights, and therefore, the 250% gain in Mite stock had a large influence. The price-weighted index yielded an intermediate increase of 75%.

PA10-3 Each quarter's holding period return for Texaco must first be calculated, using the following formula:

$$\text{One - period holding period return} = \frac{(P_1 - P_0) + DIV_1}{P_0}$$

Quarter	Beginning price	Close price	Dividends paid	Quarterly return
1	$54.375	$60.25	$0.45	11.6%
2		$59.6875	$0.45	- 0.2%
3		$62.5625	$0.45	5.6%
4		$53.00	$0.45	-14.6%

The geometric return for the year is then calculated:

$$\text{GMR} = \sqrt[4]{(1.116)(0.998)(1.056)(0.854)} - 1 = \sqrt[4]{1.0044} - 1 = 0.1\%$$

PA10-4 The individual annual returns for A&P must first be calculated, using the following formula:

$$\text{One - period holding period return} = \frac{(P_1 - P_0) + DIV_1}{P_0}$$

68

Year	Close price	Dividends paid	Annual return
1993	$24.8526	not applicable	not applicable
1994	$17.2451	$0.80	-27.4%
1995	$22.0773	$0.20	+29.2%
1996	$30.8194	$0.20	+40.5%
1997	$29.0670	$0.35	- 4.6%
1998	$29.4255	$0.40	+ 2.6%

The arithmetic average return for the five-year period is calculated below:

$$\frac{-27.4\% + 29.2\% + 40.5\% - 4.6\% + 2.6\%}{5} = \frac{40.3\%}{5} = 8.1\%$$

PA10-5 A&P's geometric mean return for the five-year period is:

$$GMR = \sqrt[5]{(0.726)(1.292)(1.405)(0.954)(1.026)} - 1 = \sqrt[5]{1.2899} - 1 = 52\%$$

If you want the estimate the expected return on A&P's stock for 1999, the arithmetic average should be used. It is the better estimate of an expected return for a single future holding period. The geometric mean compounds returns and is a better measure of the historical, long-term performance of the stock.

PA10-6 The arithmetic mean for Biotech's stock is calculated below:

$$\frac{20\% - 5\% + 35\% + 5\% + 10\% - 10\% + 25\% + 2\% + 15\% + 18\%}{10} = \frac{115\%}{10} = 11.5\%$$

The geometric mean return for the ten-year period is:

$$GMR = \sqrt[10]{(1.20)(0.95)(1.35)(1.05)(1.10)(0.90)(1.25)(1.02)(1.15)(1.18)} - 1$$
$$= \sqrt[10]{2.767928} - 1 = 10.72\%$$

PA10-7 The inflation-adjusted returns are calculated by using the following equation:

$$\text{Inflation - adjusted return} = \frac{1 + \text{return}}{1 + \text{inflation rate}} - 1.$$

$$\text{real return on large company stocks} = \frac{1.0999}{1.0275} - 1 = 7.05\%$$

$$\text{real return on long - term government bonds} = \frac{1.1824}{1.0275} - 1 = 15.08\%$$

$$\text{real return on Treasury bills} = \frac{1.029}{1.0275} - 1 = 0.15\%$$

PA10-8(a) $\text{Arithmetic mean return} = \dfrac{10 + 18 + (-2) + 15}{4} = 10.25\%$

(b)

$$\text{Geometric mean return} = \sqrt[4]{(1.10)(1.18)(0.98)(1.15)} - 1$$

$$= \sqrt[4]{1.462846} - 1 = 9.98\%$$

(c)   The geometric mean is the more appropriate measure of the investment's compound average rate of return over the four-year period. The arithmetic mean return does not compound the returns.

PA10-9   The quarterly price relative for the fund is equal to $\dfrac{P_3}{P_0} = \dfrac{22.92}{21.28} = 1.0771$. The quarterly return is the price relative - 1, or 1.0771 - 1 = 0.0771 = 7.71%.

PA10-10 (a)   Carolyn's after-tax return was 12%(1-0.28) = 8.64%.

(b)   Her after-tax, inflation-adjusted return was $\dfrac{1.0864}{1.04} - 1 = 4.46\%$.

CFA Exam Solutions*

The following are the guideline answers provided by the AIMR for the CFA Exam questions:

1.   **B**
Solution:
There are seven annual periods between January 1, 1992 and December 31, 1998.
Market value end of 1998
EMV   = BMV x $(1 + \text{GMR})^n$
        = $100,000 x $(1.05)^7$
        = $140,710

2.   A

3.   Several reasons might cause an investor to prefer to use a GDP-weighted index rather than a market capitalization-weighted index as a benchmark. One reason is that a market-cap-weighted index may overweight or underweight certain markets. Another is that market-cap-weighted indexes may exhibit greater instability than a GDP-weighted index.

The circumstances that may cause a market-cap-weighted index to systematically over- or underweight a market or exhibit instability are excessively high or low relative market valuations in certain markets--for example, the "*maoichi* effect" in Japan, where cross-holdings of shares artificially inflate reported market capitalizations, thin public stock markets, and significant market moves.

Japanese stocks provide an example of the problem of the first point, valuation differences. When publicly listed Japanese companies trade at P/E multiples that are much higher than the rest of the world, Japan's relative stock market capitalization is greater than its relative economic production. The result is a systematic overweighting of Japan in a cap-weighted global index.

Cross-holdings inflate reported market capitalizations because some stocks are counted twice. Several studies have estimated the magnitude of cross-holdings for the Japanese market to be on the order of 40 percent. That is, Japan's market capitalization is about 40 percent higher than its underlying economic value. Again, the result is a systematic overweighting of Japan in a cap-weighted global index.

Furthermore, some countries have relatively large economies but relatively thin public stock markets. For example, because most equities are privately held in Germany, its various exchanges add up to a relatively small public stock market. Thus, the relative stock market capitalization of Germany is much smaller than its relative economic production. A mismatch may also exist between GDP and market capitalization in emerging countries with undeveloped securities markets. The result is a systematic underweighting in market cap-weighted global indexes.

Finally, market capitalization weights result in greater instability than GDP weights because of market movements, the third point. For instance, Japan's weight in the market-cap-weighted EAFE (Europe/Australia/Far East) Index was less than 15 percent at the start of 1970, when the EAFE Index was first launched. Its weight had grown to almost 70 percent by 1989 and was just under 40 percent in mid-1997. These changes in weightings because of market movements create instability and require frequent rebalancing in a portfolio benchmarked to a cap-weighted index, which can prove to be quite expensive in the long run.

CHAPTER 11: SELECTED INVESTMENT INDEXES

SOLUTIONS

Questions

QA11-1   Homoscedasticity refers to a stable standard deviation while heteroscedasticity refers to unstable standard deviations. While homoscedasticity is a desirable quality from a statistical point of view, the stock market indexes and longer-term bond indexes do not have this trait. The standard deviations are not constant and may, therefore, yield statistical estimates that are erratic and vary from sample to sample in a disconcerting manner.

QA11-2   Serial correlations (also called autocorrelations) measure the extent to which a value in one series is related to a later value in that same series. The serial correlations for stocks in Table 11-7 are not significantly different from zero, which means that an investor would not be able to forecast a future price of a stock by studying its past price information. A serial correlation of zero indicates that there is no relationship between future and past prices.

QA11-3   Callability risk refers to the risk that a bond issuer will redeem the bond prior to its maturity. The issuer will do this if interest rates fall below the coupon rate on the bond since this allows the issuing firm to borrow money at a lower rate and use the proceeds to pay off the old, higher coupon, issue. If this happens, the bondholders will have to reinvest the funds received from the bond redemption at a lower interest rate, thereby lowering the total rate of return on their investments. The bond default premium inadvertently captures the effect of callability risk.

QA11-4   The greatest diversification potential occurs when the correlation coefficient of securities returns is the smallest (and preferably negative). The data provided in Table 11-15 indicate that the Italian market has the lowest correlation with the United States market; therefore, if an investor had held a well-diversified portfolio of U.S. stocks over the period 1995-2000, the addition of Italian stocks could have provided greater diversification potential. Note, that this is the historical correlation, however; asset allocation should be based on expected correlations.

QA11-5   No. Even though the compound annual return in U.S. currency is 21.3% for Hong Kong stocks and only 11.9% for U.S. stocks, the standard deviation of the Hong Kong returns is significantly higher--53.5%, compared to 17.2% for the U.S. stock returns. This suggests that while there is a potential for greater returns, there is also greater risk. Thus, the risk-return relationship is upheld.

QA11-6   Time diversification refers to the concept that as an investor's holding period increases, the probability that his portfolio will appreciate in value also increases. The proponents of time diversification observe that the maximum and minimum annualized returns over longer holding periods are closer together than those same values when the holding period is shorter. This tendency is the result of what is called the mean reversion of returns. If the returns are either extremely high or low during one period, they tend to revert back toward their arithmetic mean, i.e., expected return, in the following period.

Proponents argue, therefore, that time diversification tends to average over the extreme fluctuations, thus reducing the risk of long-term investing.

QA11-7   Indexes are used to impart vast knowledge to inexperienced investors who can use them to observe how various investment vehicles have performed over the years. Additionally, academicians use them to confront theories about investing and determine whether the observable data supports the theories. The indexes are also studied in the hopes of unearthing a tendency or trend that might be potentially profitable. Lastly, indexes are used to make asset allocation decisions. Investors can study the historical risk-return statistics and structure their portfolios to meet their specific risk aversion levels.

Indexes, rather than individual securities, are easier to analyze since they are not affected by the idiosyncratic events that affect individual stock prices, such as a labor strike, the unexpected popularity of a new product, or the expose of fraudulent activity by an executive of the firm. The bad news regarding one firm is offset by the good news on another when looking at indexes.

QA11-8   No. The yield-to-maturity will be different from the compound growth rate (geometric mean return) due to a difference in the reinvestment rate assumptions on which the two measures are based. The yield-to-maturity assumes that all cash flows are reinvested at that particular bond's yield-to-maturity until the next sequential bond is encountered. Then, the next bond's yield-to-maturity is used as the reinvestment rate for the length of time that that bond is included in the index. In contrast, the compound growth rate is based on the aggregate sample period's single rate of return, as if all the different short-term bonds were rolled up into one long-term bond and one reinvestment rate was used throughout the total sample period.

QA11-9   No. The total return includes a reinvestment return. Thus, it assumes that cash flows received are reinvested in the portfolio. Mike, instead, spent his cash flow.

QA11-10   False. The total return on a portfolio includes the income return, the capital appreciation return, and the reinvestment return. As can be seen by examining the data in Table 11-4 the reinvestment return component of the total return is sometimes negative. This can occur when reinvested cash flows are used to buy assets that depreciate in value, thus reducing the total return to the investors.

Problems

PA11-1 $$\text{Index} = \frac{\text{Current value}}{\text{Base period value}} \times \text{Index value}$$

$$\text{Index} = \frac{\$15(1,000) + \$18(4,000) + \$22(3,000) + \$41(2,000) + \$53(5,000)}{\$10(1,000) + \$20(2,000) + \$30(3,000) + \$40(2,000) + \$50(5,000)} \times 100$$

$$= \frac{500,000}{470,000} \times 100 = 106.3830$$

PA11-2   Since historical average risk premia, rather than expected risk premia, are being calculated, geometric average total returns are used in the calculations.

$$\text{Equity risk premium} = \frac{(1 + \text{large stock total return})}{(1 + \text{T - bill total return})} - 1$$

$$= \frac{1.113}{1.038} - 1 = 7.2\%$$

$$\text{Small stock risk premium} = \frac{(1 + \text{small stock total return})}{(1 + \text{large stock total return})} - 1$$

$$= \frac{1.126}{1.113} - 1 = 1.2\%$$

$$\text{Bond default premium} = \frac{(1 + \text{long - term corporate bond total return})}{(1 + \text{long - term government bond total return})} - 1$$

$$= \frac{1.056}{1.051} - 1 = 0.48\%$$

$$\text{Bond horizon premium} = \frac{1 + \text{long - term government bond total return})}{(1 + \text{T - bill total return})} - 1$$

$$= \frac{1.051}{1.038} - 1 = 1.3\%$$

PA11-3a. Bob's ending wealth, in nominal dollars, is $\$1,000(1.178)^{10} = \$5,145.80$.

b. Since inflation also increased at an average annual rate of 3.2%, Bob's *real* wealth is $\$5,145.80/(1.032)^{10} = \$3,755.51$.

PA11-4 The bond horizon premium is calculated using the following formula:

$$\text{Bond horizon premium} = \frac{(1 + \text{long - term government bond total return})}{(1 + \text{T - bill total return})} - 1$$

Year	Long-term government bond total return	Treasury bill total return	Horizon premium
1975	9.2%	5.8%	3.2%
1976	16.75%	5.08%	11.1%
1977	-0.69%	5.12%	-5.5%
1978	-1.18%	7.18%	-7.8%
1979	-1.23%	10.38%	-10.5%
1980	-3.95%	11.24%	-13.7%
1981	1.86%	14.71%	-11.2%
1982	40.36%	10.54%	27.0%
1983	0.65%	8.8%	-7.5%
1984	15.48%	9.85%	5.1%
1985	30.97%	7.72%	21.6%

With the exception of 1982, the horizon premia for 1977-1983 were negative. This suggests that investors as a whole preferred to invest in long-term bonds over the short-term Treasury bills and, thus, long-term Treasury bonds did not have to offer an

74

additional return in order to induce investors to invest in them. The high negative premiums in 1979 through 1981 may be partly explained by the high volatility of interest rates during that period. Investors may have wanted to lock in the higher coupon rates offered during that period of time on the Treasury bonds. (Note the income return for long-term government bonds during this period of time as illustrated in Table 11-4.) Bear in mind that the total returns presented are historical returns, and obviously not what investors were *expecting* to earn. Rising interest rates resulted in capital losses from the bond investment as can be noted by observing the return due to capital appreciation in Table 11-4 for those years.

PA11-5   The small stock risk premium is computed using the following formula:

$$\text{Small stock risk premium} = \frac{1 + \text{small stock total return}}{1 + \text{large stock total return}} - 1$$

Year	Small stock total return	Large stock total return	Small stock risk premium
1986	6.85%	18.47%	-9.8%
1987	-9.3%	5.23%	-13.8%
1988	22.87%	16.81%	5.2%
1989	10.18%	31.49%	-16.2%
1990	-21.56%	-3.17%	-19.0%
1991	44.63%	30.55%	10.8%
1992	23.35%	7.67%	14.6%
1993	20.98%	9.99%	10.0%
1994	3.11%	1.31%	1.8%
1995	34.46%	37.43%	-2.2%

In 1986 and 1987, the small stock risk premium was negative. However, in 1988, it was positive, perhaps due to the stock market crash in October of 1987, which may have made investors more concerned about investing in small stocks. The risk premium was a large negative number in both 1989 and 1990, however. Note that small stocks offered a large negative total return in 1990, which may have caused investors to require higher expected returns in the following four years on small stocks, accounting for the large positive risk premiums in the three following years, 1991, 1992, and 1993. Bear in mind, however, that the above table reflects historical risk premia, and not what investors actually *expected* to occur.

PA11-6   Elaine's education account will be worth only $29,200 in eight years, given a 4% annual inflation rate. $\frac{1}{(1.04)^8} = 73\%$; and $(0.73)(\$40,000) = \$29,200$. This probably will not be enough to finance four years of college for her daughter.

PA11-7   The arithmetic average of the large stock returns is 15.58%, with a standard deviation of 13.83%. The arithmetic average of the long-term government bond returns is 12.53%, with a standard deviation of 12.17%. Next, the covariance of the returns must be calculated.

$$COV(r_x, r_y) = \frac{1}{T-1}\sum_{t=1}^{T}(r_{x,t} - \bar{r}_x)(r_{y,t} - \bar{r}_y)$$

COV(r$_{stock}$, r$_{bond}$) =

$$(18.47-15.58)(24.53-12.53)+(5.23-15.58)(-2.71-12.53)+(16.81-15.58)(9.67-12.53)$$
$$+(31.49-15.58)(18.11-12.53)+(-3.17-15.58)(6.18-12.53)+(30.55-15.58)(19.30-12.53)$$
$$+(7.67-15.58)(8.05-12.53)+(9.99-15.58)(18.24-12.53)+(1.31-15.58)(-7.77-12.53)$$
$$\frac{+(37.43-15.58)(31.67-12.53)}{9}$$

$$=\frac{1209.4913}{9}=134.39$$

The correlation of the returns is equal to $\dfrac{COV(r_x,r_y)}{\sigma_x\sigma_y} = \dfrac{134.39}{(13.83)(12.17)} = 0.80.$ In comparing this to the cross correlation coefficient for long-term government bonds and large company stocks provided for the period from 1926-1999, we see it is much higher than the 0.19 reported in Table 11-7. This demonstrates that the time period over which statistical measures are made can cause very different results.

PA11-8   Total return = capital appreciation return + income return + reinvestment return. 23.07% = 20.26% + 2.54% + reinvestment return. Therefore, the reinvestment return = 0.27%.

PA11-9   Since we are estimating an expected return for one year, the short-horizon premium on large corporation stocks should be used. Small-cap return = T-bill return + large corporation short-horizon risk premium + small stock risk premium. Thus, the expected return on the small-cap stocks is 5.2% + 9.5% + 4.3% = 19.0%.

PA11-10   The inflation-adjusted returns are calculated using Eqn. 10-7 as follows:

$$real\ return = \frac{1 + nominal\ return}{1 + inflation\ rate} - 1.$$

Large company stocks: $\dfrac{1.133}{1.032} - 1 = 9.8\%$

Small company stocks: $\dfrac{1.176}{1.032} - 1 = 14.0\%$

Long-term government bonds: $\dfrac{1.055}{1.032} - 1 = 2.2\%$

Treasury bills: $\dfrac{1.038}{1.032} - 1 = 0.6\%$

CFA Exam Solutions*

The following are the guideline answers provided by the AIMR for the CFA exam questions:

1.   C
      Solution: The *risk premium* is the required rate of return above the nominal risk-free rate. Because the risk premium is 10 percent and the risk-free rate is 6%, the rate of return for the equity fund is 16 percent (10 percent + 6 percent). The rate of return on Treasury bills is 6 percent. The portfolio weights are 60 percent ($60,000/$100,000) in the equity fund and 40 percent in the Treasury-bill money market fund. Therefore, the expected return on Webb's portfolio is:

$$E(R_{port}) = 0.60(16\%) + 0.4(6\%)$$

$$= 9.6\% + 2.4\%$$

$$= 12\%.$$

2.   B
      Solution:
      $r_{xy} = Cov(R_x R_y)/s_x s_y$
      $= 0.005/(0.20)(0.06)$
      $= 0.005/0.012$
      $= 0.417$

3.   **Part A**
      Although venture-capital rates of return have sometimes been in the 35-45 percent range cited by the investment committee members, those figures are very specific to a particular, relatively short time horizon, actually the late 1970s and early 1980s. Studies covering the last three decades have shown venture-capital returns of about 15 percent on an annualized basis, versus about 9 percent for large-cap stocks and 11 percent for small-cap stocks. Thus, as a rough rule of thumb, a venture-capital premium over U.S. common stocks should be about 6 percentage points, and, over small-cap issues, 4 percentage points.

      Note, however, that straight trend extrapolation may be difficult because of a variety of factors, including the more than fivefold increase in venture-capital funding in recent years, the proliferation of venture-capital groups, and increased competition.

      During the past 30 years, risk has been noticeably higher for venture capital. Measured by standard deviation, venture-capital risk is about twice as high as large-cap and 50 percent higher than small-cap stocks.

      Because the current capital market projections for other equity assets are below their long-term historical figures, venture-capital returns can be estimated to be a little less than 15 percent annualized. Risk levels will probably be consistent with the past, or perhaps somewhat higher in reflection of the fact that not all new venture-capital investors will be as skilled as older, more experienced investors. Thus, an annual standard deviation could be about 40 percentage points.

      Part B
      The correlation matrix shows that venture capital, as an asset class, is not highly correlated with bonds or Treasury bills (in fact, the correlation with T-bills is negative). Venture capital also has a relatively low correlation with large-cap stocks and with real estate. The highest correlation is with small-cap issues, although the relationship is not as strong as that between small-cap and large-cap equities.

Thus, the matrix data show that venture capital is an excellent diversifier for a pension portfolio. It offers the potential for a meaningful addition to expected return with little incremental risk.

CHAPTER 12: USING INDEXES

SOLUTIONS

Questions

QA12-1   A passive investor might choose to select some investments and then buy them and hold them for the duration of his or her investment horizon. Alternatively, a passive investor might choose to index his money. Using this method, the investor invests in a diversified portfolio that owns the same securities as whatever index he wants to emulate. One way to do this is to purchase shares of a mutual fund that is indexed to a well-known stock market index.

QA12-2   Mutual fund investors face four types of fees: entry fees, exit fees, management fees, and distribution fees. Some mutual funds are load funds and the load represents the entry fee. The maximum load allowed is 8 1/2%, but many funds have lower loads, and a lot of funds are no load. If a load exists of, say 8%, then an investor who buys into the fund with $1,000 actually only gets $920 invested in the fund. ($1,000 x (1- 0.08) = $920.) He pays an entry fee of $80.

        Both load and no load funds may charge a redemption fee, or a back-end load. This means that when an investor decides to sell his shares, he will receive something less than the net asset value at the time. If, for example, the redemption fee is 2% and the net asset value at the time of the sale is $40, then the investor will receive only $39.20 per share sold. ($40 x (1 - 0.02) = $39.20.) This fee is used to discourage investors from liquidating their investments, and many funds with back-end loads have a sliding schedule, so that the back-end load no longer exists once the shares have been held for a certain number of years.

        All funds charge management fees, although the amount of this fee varies in size from fund to fund. The average is about 1% a year, stated as a percentage of the managed assets. Studies have indicated that the performance of a fund varies inversely with the size of its management fee.

        Some funds also charge distribution fees, known as 12b-1 fees. The name of the fee refers to the Securities and Exchange Commission (SEC) Rule 12b-1 that allows funds to deduct up to 1% of their assets per year to pay distribution fees and promotional expenses.

QA12-3   Investors in mutual funds have three sources of income: they receive cash flow from dividend or interest distributions; they also receive their proportionate share of capital gains distributions, generated when the fund sells some of its assets at a gain; and they (hopefully) enjoy capital appreciation on the fund itself--i.e., increases in the net asset value of the fund.

QA12-4   Indexed funds tend to outperform actively managed funds for several reasons. First, indexed portfolios do not need a staff of highly paid securities analysts because whoever maintains the stock market index (e.g.,., Standard and Poors) tells the manager of the indexed portfolio which stocks to buy. Therefore, management fees associated with indexed funds are much smaller. Secondly, actively managed funds usually hold two to eight percent of their funds in cash in order to take advantage of good investment opportunities as they arise, but cash is a non-earning asset. In contrast, the indexed portfolios are 100% invested in the stocks of whatever index they mimic. Thirdly, the stocks that are included in a stock market index change infrequently, so the indexed portfolio's turnover rate is much lower than that of an actively managed fund. The lower turnover rate results in smaller brokerage commissions and, therefore, higher returns to investors. It also results in less realized capital gains on which investors would have to pay taxes.

On the disadvantage side, some indexed funds are not well-managed, resulting in tracking errors, i.e., the difference between the return on the targeted index and the return earned by the fund. Investors will be disappointed when the returns on these indexed funds are substantially less than the return reported on the actual index. Too, smaller indexed portfolios lack the economies of scale of larger portfolios--they have similar fixed costs and must pay larger brokerage commissions due to the smaller size of their trades--which erodes the return they can offer investors.

QA12-5   A tracking error is the difference between the return on the targeted index and the return earned by a fund mimicking the index. Tracking errors can result due to delayed reactions of the fund managers when the organizations that maintain the indexes add and/or delete stocks from the index, when an index is altered due to a merger or acquisition, or when it a corporation repurchases its shares, splits its stock, or pays a stock dividend. In these situations, the replicating portfolio will need to be rebalanced quickly. Some indexed fund managers also engage in what is called enhanced indexing, which means that these managers try to outsmart the market by tilting their portfolios in favor of some securities or sector of securities that they believe to be underpriced. If the managers are wrong, the portfolio's returns will be less than that of the targeted index. This can also occur when the index is replicated using derivative securities. Still other managers may not invest in all the stocks in the index in an effort to reduce transactions costs, but this, too, can result in large tracking errors.

QA12-6   The larger fund, if equally well-managed, might be the better choice since it enjoys economies of scale that the smaller fund does not. First of all, the smaller fund may have to pay higher brokerage fees because of smaller transactions. Secondly, there are certain fixed costs associated with portfolio management that do not vary with the size of the portfolio, so a larger percentage of the earnings of the smaller fund must go to pay these fixed costs. For both of these reasons, the management fees associated with the larger funds are typically smaller than those charged by the smaller funds.

QA12-7   SPDR stands for Standard and Poors Depository Receipt. This is a marketable security that is traded continuously on the AMEX. Like many indexed funds, SPDRs are indexed to the S&P 500 Index, using the same market-value weights that Standard & Poors uses in computing the S&P 500 Index. However, unlike a traditional indexed fund in which your order to buy or sell shares is transacted at the market close, an order to buy or sell SPDRs is executed on the floor of the AMEX within minutes.

The SPDRs represent ownership in the SPDR Trust, which is not a mutual fund; it is a unit investment trust (UIT). Under the Investment Company Act of 1940, UITs may only buy and sell securities in order to realign their holdings with the investment target they were organized to pursue; they may not engage in active trading. Unlike mutual funds, which may create as many new shares as there are buyers interested in the shares, UITs cannot sell more shares after their initial public offering, so the number of shares outstanding never changes.

QA12-8   iShares MSCI are shares in a no-load mutual fund that is indexed to a stock market index from one country. iShares is a creation of Morgan-Stanley, a large international investment bank. Morgan Stanley converts investors' U.S. dollars into the appropriate foreign currency, buys the securities in that foreign country, manages the mutual fund portfolio, and lists the iShares on the AMEX. Like any mutual fund, iShares can continue to sell new shares as long as there are investors interested in buying shares of the fund. They also have the advantages offered by other indexed mutual funds--i.e., lower management fees, fully invested monies, and low turnover rates. However, unlike traditional indexed funds, iShares are listed on an exchange. Therefore, they are continuously traded and continuously priced every day. An investor need not wait for market close for his trade to be executed. As they can for any exchange-listed security, investors can enter market orders, limit orders, stop orders, and stop limit orders for iShares. They can also issue fill or kill orders, good-til-cancelled orders, scale orders, or day orders. iShares can also be sold short--even on a downtick. This menu of orders is not available to investors in traditional indexed mutual funds.

QA12-9   True. Investors must pay taxes on their proportionate share of any capital gains distributions a mutual fund makes. These distributions result from gains earned when a fund sells securities it holds. Therefore, the more buying and selling a fund does, the greater the capital gains distributions, and the greater the tax liability of the fund investor. Indexed mutual funds have lower turnover rates than actively managed funds. That is, there is less buying and selling of securities and, therefore, less capital gain income that needs to be distributed to become taxable income of the investors.

QA12-10   The turnover rate measures the level of buying and selling of the investments held by a mutual fund. For example, if a fund held 100 different securities over the course of a year and traded 80 of them, the turnover rate would be 80%. The higher the turnover rate, the higher the fund expenses since trades trigger brokerage costs. This, then, reduces the return earned by investors in the fund. Higher turnover rates also result in greater capital gains distributions to the fund's investors, and the investors' must pay taxes on these distributions, so higher turnover rates mean higher tax bills.

Problems

PA12-1   The rate of return on a no-load mutual fund is calculated as follows:

$$r = \frac{CF_t + CGD_t + (NAVPS_{t+1} - NAVPS_t)}{NAVPS_t}$$

Sylvia's return is, therefore,

$$r = \frac{0.556 + 0.3122 + (23.04 - 18.18)}{18.18} = \frac{5.7282}{18.18} = 31.5\%.$$

PA12-2   Marcus' load was 4%, so only $960 ($1,000 x (1-0.04)) was invested in the fund. Marcus, therefore, purchased only $960/$36.04 = 26.6371 shares of the fund. Had the fund been a no-load fund, the entire $1,000 would have been invested, and he would have owned $1,000/$36.04 = 27.7469 shares.

PA12-3   The return on a no-load mutual fund is calculated as follows:

$$r = \frac{CF_t + CGD_t + (NAVPS_{t+1} - NAVPS_t)}{NAVPS_t}$$

Ji's return is, therefore,

$$r = \frac{0 + 3.222 + (26.88 - 32.03)}{32.03} = \frac{-1.928}{32.03} = -6.02\%.$$

PA12-4 The net asset value per share is calculated using the following equation:

$$NAVPS = \frac{\text{market value of assets - total liabilities}}{\text{total shares outstanding}}$$

$$NAVPS_A = \frac{\$25,000,000 - \$1,000,000}{1,100,000} = \$21.82$$

$$NAVPS_B = \frac{\$100,000,000 - \$6,000,000}{1,250,000} = \$75.20$$

$$NAVPS_C = \frac{\$50,000,000 - \$2,000,000}{1,420,000} = \$33.80$$

PA12-5 Because lower turnover rates translate into lower management fees and greater tax efficiencies, all else the same, an investor would prefer the fund with the lower turnover rate. The turnover rate is calculated using the formula below:

$$\text{Turnover rate} = \frac{\text{MIN(annual purchases, annual sales)}}{\text{average value of total assets}}$$

$$\text{Turnover rate}_A = \frac{\text{MIN}(80, 100)}{188} = \frac{80}{188} = 42.6\%$$

$$\text{Turnover rate}_B = \frac{\text{MIN}(600, 750)}{854.1} = \frac{600}{854.1} = 70.2\%$$

$$\text{Turnover rate}_C = \frac{\text{MIN}(550, 400)}{601.6} = \frac{400}{601.6} = 66.5\%$$

Therefore, Fund A provides the lower turnover rate and is the better investment, all else equal.

PA12-6 The tracking errors measure the difference between the return on the index being mimicked and the return on the indexed fund. The tracking errors for the three funds are as follows:

Fund	Tracking error
A	18.1% - 15.2% = 2.9%
B	18.1% - 17.3% = 0.8%
C	18.1% - 12.4% = 5.7%

Since the manager of Fund B produced a return closest to the return on the S&P 500 Index, which is the objective of the fund, his performance was better than that of the managers of Funds A and C.

PA12-7 Each investor's net return is the difference between the gross annual return earned by the fund and the annual management fee.

	Index20 Fund	Big20 Fund
Gross annual return	12.0%	12.00%
Annual management fee	0.5%	1.15%
Investor's net return	11.5%	10.85%

Barb, who invested in the Index20 Fund, will have $1,000(1.115)^5 = \$1,723.35$. Bob will have $1,000(1.1085)^5 = \$1,673.70$, so Barb's ending wealth will be $49.65 greater than Bob's.

PA12-8 Jack's money purchased only $980/$20 = 49 shares since only $980 was invested ($1,000(1-0.02) = $980). His purchase price for each share was $20/(1 - 0.02) = $20.41. His return was as follows:

$$r = \frac{\$1.25(49) + (\$24 - \$20.41)(49)}{\$1,000} = \frac{\$61.25 + \$196.00}{\$1,000} = 23.7\%$$

Judy's money purchased $1,000/$20 = 50 shares since the fund had no front-end load. However, when she sold the shares she received only $23.76 a share ($24(1-0.01) = $23.76). Her return was

$$r = \frac{\$1.25(50) + (\$23.76 - \$20)(50)}{\$1,000} = \frac{\$62.50 + \$188.00}{\$1,000} = 25.1\%$$

PA12-9 This problem illustrates the tax efficiencies offered by a passively managed fund. The total return on the ACTIVE FUND is 14%, 5% of which is taxed and 9% of which is unrealized gain on the appreciation of the net asset value of the fund. The after-tax return on the 5% portion that is taxed is 5%(1 - 0.28) = 3.6%, so the total after-tax return on the ACTIVE FUND is 9% + 3.6% = 12.6%.

The total return on the PASSIVE FUND is also 14%, but only 3% represents taxable return. The remaining 11% comes from the unrealized gain on the appreciation of the net asset value of the fund. The after-tax return on the 3% portion that is taxed is 3%(1 - 0.28) = 2.16%, so the total after-tax return earned on the PASSIVE FUND is 2.16% + 11% = 13.16%.

PA12-10 This problem demonstrates the advantage of the continuous pricing/continuous trading associated with SPDRs. Since dividends and transactions costs are ignored each investor's return is simply the price appreciation:

$$r_{Sally} = \frac{\$76 - \$64}{\$64} = 18.75\%$$

$$r_{Sam} = \frac{\$76 - \$70}{\$70} = 8.57\%$$

The fact that Sam's transaction was not executed until the close of the market, when the value of the S&P 500 Index had risen sharply, caused his return to be substantially less than Sally's return.

CFA Exam Solutions*

The following are the guideline answers provided by the AIMR for the CFA Exam questions:

1.   A

2.   C

3.   D

CHAPTER 13: ASSET ALLOCATION

SOLUTIONS

Questions

QA13-1   The first step in the investment allocation process is gaining understanding. The allocator must come to know his client intimately. He or she must know the age, education, work experience, and health of the client along with other details regarding the client's family and personal life. This allows the allocator to assess the client's financial situation, investment horizon, investment goals, tax situation, legal constraints, liquidity needs, and level of risk aversion better. The second step involves developing realistic expectations for your client. In this step, the allocator must educate the client regarding such things as real versus nominal returns, tax inefficiencies, and market volatility. A third, very important step, is the preparation of a written policy statement. The statement should contain information on the investment goals and the policies that will be used to meet these goals, including the asset allocation decision. A benchmark portfolio may be stipulated so that the client can better assess the allocator's performance. In step four, the allocator prepares a forecast after studying current conditions and analyzing alternatives. Most allocators use a risk-return analysis to prepare this forecast. Step five involves making the asset allocation decision, which the allocator does by considering the written policy statement along with the expected return and risk statistics that were developed for the various asset classes. In step six, the allocated funds are invested according to the asset allocation decision.   Finally, in the last step, step seven, performance reports are prepared which show the client the current market value of each asset and the aggregate value of the portfolio. This is typically done on a quarterly basis. During these performance reviews, the asset allocator should endeavor to detect significant changes in the client's position or views that may require an adjustment in the policy statement.

QA13-2   A defined benefit pension fund is one in which the benefits to be paid at retirement are stipulated at the outset. This means that the fund must earn a specific average annual return in order to meet the necessary payments as the employees retire. The extent to which the plan is underfunded or overfunded will dictate whether the asset allocator must pursue a more conservative or a more aggressive asset allocation. In a defined contribution pension fund, there is no prior stipulation of the benefits that will be paid when an employee retires. The asset allocator has much more leeway in the management of this type of fund for this reason and can pursue whatever type of asset allocation he chooses.

QA13-3   Municipal bonds are not a good investment vehicle for Mr. Crotchet. Mr. Crotchet pays little or no taxes, so the return on a municipal bond mutual fund will not offer as high a return as a corporate bond fund will, even after taxes are paid, and Mr. Crotchet is definitely going to need a good return in order to make his money last for the next 45 years. Additionally, although capital preservation is important to Mr. Crotchet since he will not be earning any money from employment in the future, a percentage of his money should also be invested in an indexed stock fund, which would be expected to earn higher returns than a corporate bond fund. Another percentage should be allocated to a liquid asset class, such as a money market mutual fund, to meet any liquidity needs he might have in the future, given the small amount of his monthly income.

QA13-4   There are several good reasons to have a written investment policy statement, even if the allocator and the client are one and the same. First, more thought will go into it if it is put in writing. Goals will have to be clearly formulated and any conflicting goals will be illuminated so that they can be resolved. A written policy statement also can be revisited easily if there are situational changes that require an adjustment in the goals and/or policies. The written statement can also be used as a standard by which a client can evaluate his asset allocator's performance, or, if the two are one and the same, for the allocator to determine if his chosen portfolio is indeed meeting his goals.

QA13-5   The three approaches to financial analysis are fundamental analysis, technical analysis, and risk-return analysis. In fundamental analysis, the analyst studies the financial ratios of the firm, the firm's products, the competition, and any other relevant facts about the company and the industry in which it operates. Based on this analysis, the analyst makes forecasts about each firm in which he is considering investing. A technical analyst relies on historical market data to make his forecasts. Often called a "chartist," the technical analyst plots graphs of historical stock prices over time in hopes of discerning a pattern that he believes will repeat itself in the future. The analyst produces a graph for each individual stock or market index. The analyst who takes the risk-return approach studies historical means and variances and the correlations between different investments. The analyst usually updates these historical statistics to convert them into expected returns, variances, and correlations. Most asset allocators use this type of analysis on stock indexes, bond indexes, and other asset category indexes rather than on individual assets. They believe that allocating the investment funds to asset categories is more productive than trying to time the market (as technical analysts do) or trying to search for undervalued securities (as fundamental analysts do). It is a fast and economical method.

QA13-6   No. First of all, Jim might have a greater level of risk tolerance than his parents, especially since he has many years of producing income ahead of him while his parents have only a few productive years remaining, assuming they plan to retire by age 65. Secondly, younger people are able to accept greater investment risk because of their longer investment horizon. The longer horizon gives them the ability to offset unexpected losses from their portfolios by saving more than they had originally planned to save. They are also able to create more income by working harder, if necessary. Older people do not have as much time to offset the losses on their portfolio and do not have as many years to make up for losses on investments.

QA13-7   The four asset allocation strategies are strategic asset allocation, tactical asset allocation, dynamic asset allocation, and integrated asset allocation. Strategic asset allocation (SAA) involves driving long-run asset allocation weights that are not changed when capital market conditions experience temporary changes. SAA is also referred to as **policy asset allocation**, the **normal asset mix**, or **long-run asset allocation**. Tactical asset allocation (TAA) involves an attempt to time the market. Temporary asset allocation weights are assigned in response to temporary changes in capital market conditions. With this strategy, the investor's goals and risk-return preferences are assumed to remain constant, but the weights are revised to help (hopefully) to attain the investor's constant goals. Dynamic asset allocation (DAA) refers to a number of different alterations in the asset weights that are made in response to changes in the investor's circumstances and/or changes in the market conditions. Tactical asset allocation is one type of DAA. Integrated asset allocation gives simultaneous consideration to the investor's goals and policies and the capital market conditions. This data is used to develop an optimizer, which could be some mathematical formula or an optimizing computer program. The actual returns that are generated by the optimizer's solution become the new inputs that are reconsidered, along with the investor's updated goals and policies and current market conditions, in determining a revised asset allocation.

QA13-8   This is a false statement. Most asset allocators, in fact, do not rely heavily on technical analysis and/or fundamental analysis, both of which focus on individual security analysis. They prefer to invest in market indexes instead of selecting individual securities, based on the belief that this is the more productive strategy. To select the market indexes in which to invest, they perform a risk-return analysis on each index. The analysts study the historical means and variances of returns and the correlations between different investments and adjust them to reflect expected returns, variances and correlations. This is one of the quickest and cheapest ways to make a forecast. Empirical research indicates it works. A study by Brinson, Hood, and Beebower, as an example, studied pension funds that used the returns from market indexes to replicate the returns from three different categories of assets. The study involved creating a "shadow asset mix," which involved no security selection skills. The shadow asset mix explained 95.3% of the variation in pension fund returns, measured over 40 quarters. This is strong evidence that passive asset allocation is the main determinant of the returns from large, highly diversified institutional portfolios, and also that ignoring fundamental and technical security analysis in the asset allocation process does not involve discarding large amounts of valuable information.

QA13-9   You should explain that quarterly returns on portfolios rarely hit their expected long-run rates of return. Short-term returns often fluctuate both above and below the long-run return that is expected, so there is really no cause for her to be alarmed.

QA13-10 While both Scott and Sandy probably have similar investment horizons, Scott pays taxes at a much higher rate than Sandy. His portfolio allocation should be weighted heavily in assets that are tax-preferred, such as municipal bond funds and funds that have the objective of maximizing capital gains. Sandy's portfolio should not include any municipal bonds since their lower returns will not offer as high a return as a similar-risk corporate bond fund, even after she pays taxes. Sandy's lower income level probably requires that she needs more invested in liquid assets in the event of an emergency than does Scott, whose income level is sufficiently high to handle any unexpected events.

Problems

PA13-1   The after-tax return on the corporate bond fund = 9%(1 - 0.31) = 6.21%, so Jill is better off investing in the corporate bond fund. Even after paying taxes, she earns a higher return on it than on the municipal bond fund, which is expected to return only 6%.

PA13-2   The purchasing power of the principal = $\dfrac{\$500,000}{(1.04)^n}$, where n is the number of years from today. The real annual interest income is calculated as 5% times the purchasing power in year n.

Time	Purchasing power of $500,000 at a 4% inflation rate	Annual return on investment	Real annual interest income
Today	$500,000	5%	$25,000
10 yrs.	$337,782	5%	$16,889
20 yrs.	$228,193	5%	$11,410
30 yrs.	$154,159	5%	$ 7,708

PA13-3   The cost of living will increase by $(1.035)^{10} - 1 = 41.1\%$. This means that the purchasing power of $1 will decrease by $1 - \dfrac{1}{1.411} = 29.1\%$ by the end of the tenth year.

PA13-4   In an IRA, the money will grow tax-deferred at 8%, whereas in a regular account the money will only grow at a rate of $8\%(1 - 0.28) = 5.76\%$.

Account value in	IRA	Regular account
10 years	$28,973	$26,066
20 years	$91,524	$71,701
30 years	$226,566	$151,594

PA13-5   Your sister's gross wages are $1,200 per month. The TSA option leaves her with $792 of disposable income each month:

Gross wages -	TSA contribution =	taxable income x 0.72 =	after-tax income -	savings after-tax =	disposable income
$1,200 -	$100 =	$1,100 x 0.72 =	$792 -	0 =	$792

Saving for retirement by making deposits into a regular savings account leaves her with only $764 of disposal income each month:

Gross wages -	TSA contribution =	taxable income x 0.72 =	after-tax income -	savings after-tax =	disposable income
$1,200 -	0 =	$1,200 x 0.72 =	$864 -	$100 =	$764

PA13-6 (a)

Years from today	College year	Amount needed
10	1	$20,000(1.03)^{10} = $26,878
11	2	$20,000(1.03)^{11} = $27,685
12	3	$20,000(1.03)^{12} = $28,515
13	4	$20,000(1.03)^{13} = $29,371

(b)   The present value of her cash needs at the end of year ten, assuming a 5% discount rate is

$$\$26,878 + \frac{\$27,685}{(1.05)^1} + \frac{\$28,515}{(1.05)^2} + \frac{\$29,371}{(1.05)^3} = \$104,481.$$

PA13-7   Assuming Larry makes the fund switches, his ending wealth will be $27,967, determined as follows:

Quarter	Investment value	Tax on earnings	Reinvestment amount
1	$25,000(1.03) = $25,750	0.28($750) = $210	$25,540
2	$25,540(1.035) = $26,434	0.28($894) = $250	$26,184
3	$26,184(1.0375) = $27,166	0.28($982) = $275	$26,891
4	$26,891(1.04) = $27,967		

With a buy-and-hold strategy, his ending wealth would be $28,000: $25,000(1.12) = $28,000. (Actually, assuming quarterly compounding, the growth rate in one year would be $(1.03)^4 - 1 = 12.55\%$ and his ending wealth would be $25,000(1.1255) = $28,138. You might also inform Larry that this active switching might lead to a less well-diversified portfolio, thereby leaving him exposed to unnecessary risk.

PA13-8 The real return on the Treasury bill investment will be $\frac{1.06}{1.03} - 1 = 2.91\%$ per year, so Investor A's real dollar return is $50,000(1.0291)^5 = $57,711. The real return on the indexed fund will be $\frac{1.12}{1.03} - 1 = 8.74\%$ per year, so Investor B's real dollar return is $50,000(1.0874)^5 = $76,018.

PA13-9 The after-tax return on the corporate bond fund is $10\%(1 - 0.36) = 6.4\%$, so Rich is better off investing in the municipal bond fund, with a return of 7%.

PA13-10

Short-term gains	$ 8,000	Long-term gains	$62,000
Short-term losses	($11,000)	Long-term losses	($32,000)
Net short-term loss	($3,000)	Net long-term gain	$30,000

Heather's taxable long-term gain is $30,000 - $3,000 = $27,000, so her tax liability on the investment income is 0.20($27,000) = $5,400.

CFA Exam Solutions*

The following are the guideline answers provided by the AIMR for the CFA Exam questions:

1. C

2. C

3. A. An Investment Policy Statement for Fairfax based *only* on the information provided in the Introductory material is shown below.

Overview. Fairfax is 58 years old and has seven years to go until a planned retirement. She has a fairly lavish lifestyle but few money worries. Her large salary pays all current expenses, and she has accumulated $2 million in cash equivalents from savings in previous years. Her health is excellent, and her health insurance coverage will continue after retirement and is employer paid. While Fairfax's job is a high-level one, she is not well versed in investment matters and has had the good sense to connect with professional counsel to get started on planning for her investment future, a future that is complicated by ownership of a $10 million block of company stock that, while listed on the NYSE, pays no dividends and has a zero-cost basis for tax purposes. All salary, investment income (except interest on municipal bonds), and realized capital gains are taxed to Fairfax at a 35 percent rate; this tax rate and a 4 percent inflation rate are expected to continue into the future. Fairfax would accept a 3 percent real, after-tax return from the investment portfolio to be formed from her $2 million in savings (the "Savings Portfolio") if that return could be obtained with only modest portfolio volatility (i.e., less than a 10 percent annual decline). She is described as being conservative in all things.

Objectives

- **Return Requirement.** Fairfax's need for portfolio income begins seven years from now, at the date of retirement when her salary stops. The investment focus for her Savings Portfolio should be on growing the portfolio's value in the interim in a way that provides protection against loss of purchasing power. Her 3 percent real, after-tax return preference implies a gross total return requirement of at least 10.8 percent, assuming her investments are fully taxable (as is the case now) and assuming 4 percent inflation and a 35 percent tax rate. For Fairfax to maintain her current lifestyle, she would have to generate $500,000 \times (1.04)^7$, or $658,000, in annual income, inflation adjusted, when she retires. If the market value of Reston's stock does not change, and if she has been able to earn a 10.8 percent return on the Savings Portfolio (or 7 percent nominal after-tax return = $2,000,000 \times (1.07)^7 = \$3,211,500$), she should accumulate $13,211,500 by retirement age. To generate $658,000, a return on $13,211,500 of 5.0 percent would be needed.

- **Risk Tolerance.** From the information provided, Fairfax is quite risk averse, indicating she does not want to experience a decline of more than 10 percent in the value of the Savings Portfolio in any given year. This would indicate that the portfolio should have below-average risk exposure to minimize its downside volatility. In terms of overall wealth, she could afford to take more than average risk, but because of her preferences and the nondiversified nature of the total portfolio, a below-average risk objective is appropriate for the Savings Portfolio.

It should be noted, however, that truly meaningful statements about the risk of Fairfax's total portfolio are tied to assumptions about the volatility of Reston's stock, if it is retained, and about when and at what price the Reston stock will be sold. Because the Reston holding constitutes 83% of Fairfax's total portfolio, it will largely determine the risk she actually experiences as long as it remains intact.

Constraints

- **Time Horizon.** Two time horizons are applicable to Fairfax's situation. The first is the medium or intermediate term between now and when she plans to retire, seven years. The second is the long time horizon between now and the expected end of Fairfax's life, perhaps 25 to 30 years from now. The first time horizon represents the period during which Fairfax should set up her financial situation in preparation for the balance of the second time horizon, her retirement period of indefinite length. Of the two horizons, the longer term to the expected end of her life is the dominant horizon because it is over this period that the assets must fulfill their primary function of funding her expenses, in an annuity sense, in retirement.

- **Liquidity.** With liquidity defined either as income needs or as cash reserves to meet emergency needs, Fairfax's liquidity requirement is minimal. $500,000 of salary is available annually, health cost concerns are nonexistent, and we know of no planned needs for cash from the portfolio.

- **Taxes.** Fairfax's taxable income (salary, taxable investment income, and realized capital gains on securities) is taxed at a 35 percent rate. Careful tax planning and coordination of tax policy with investment planning is required. Investment strategy should include seeking income that is sheltered from taxes and holding securities for lengthy time periods to produce larger after-tax returns. Sale of the Reston stock will have sizable tax consequences because Fairfax's cost basis is zero; special planning will be needed for this. Fairfax may want to consider some form of charitable giving, either during her lifetime or at death. She has no immediate family, and we know of no other potential gift or bequest recipients.

- **Laws and Regulations.** Fairfax should be aware of and abide by any securities (or other) laws or regulations relating to her "insider" status at Reston and her holding of Reston stock. Although there is no trust instrument in place, if Fairfax's future investing is handled by an investment advisor, the responsibilities associated with the Prudent Person Rule come into play, including the responsibility for investing in a diversified portfolio. Also, she has a need to seek estate planning legal assistance, even though there are no apparent gift or bequest recipients.

- **Unique Circumstances and/or Preferences.** Clearly, the value of the Reston stock dominates the value of Fairfax's portfolio. A well-defined exit strategy needs to be developed for the stock as soon as is practical and appropriate. If the value of the stock increases, or at least does not decline before it is liquidated, Fairfax's present lifestyle can be sustained after retirement with the combined portfolio. A significant and prolonged setback for Reston Industries, however, could have disastrous consequences. Such circumstances would require a dramatic downscaling of Fairfax's lifestyle or generation of alternate sources of income to maintain her current lifestyle. A worst-case scenario might be characterized by a 50 percent drop in the market value of Reston's stock and sale of that stock to diversify the portfolio, where the sale proceeds would be subject to a 35 percent tax rate. The net proceeds of the Reston part of the portfolio would be $10,000,000 x .5 x (1 - .35) = $3,250,000. When added to the Savings Portfolio, total portfolio value would be $5,250,000. For this portfolio to generate $658,000 in income, a 12.5% return would be required.

Synopsis. The policy governing investment in Fairfax's Savings Portfolio shall put emphasis on realizing a 3 percent real, after-tax return from a mix of high-quality assets aggregating less than average risk. Ongoing attention shall be given to Fairfax's tax planning and legal needs, her progress toward retirement, and the value of her Reston stock. The Reston stock holding is a unique circumstance of decisive significance in this situation. Developments should be monitored closely, and protection against the effects of a worst-case scenario should be implemented as soon as possible.

B.   A critique of the Coastal Advisors proposal, created for investment of the Savings Portfolio investment, including three weaknesses related to the Investment Policy Statement in Part A, follows.

Critique. The Coastal proposal produces a real, after-tax expected return of approximately 5.17 percent, which is above the 3 percent level sought by Fairfax. The expected return of the proposal can be calculated by subtracting the tax exempt yield from the total current yield (4.9 percent - .55 percent = 4.35 percent) and converting this to an after-tax yield [4.35 percent x (1 - .35) = 2.82 percent]. The tax exempt income is then added back in (2.82 percent + .55 percent = 3.37 percent). The appreciation portion of the return (5.8 percent) is then added to the after tax yield to get the nominal portfolio return (3.37 percent + 5.80 percent = 9.17 percent). Finally, the 4 percent inflation factor is subtracted to produce the expected real after tax return (9,17 percent - 4.0 percent = 5.17 percent). This result can also be obtained by determining these calculations for each of the individual holdings, weighting each result by the portfolio percentage and then adding to a total portfolio result.

From the data available, it is not possible to determine specifically the inherent degree of portfolio volatility. Despite meeting the return criterion, the allocation is neither realistic nor, in its detail, appropriate to Fairfax's situation in the context of an investment policy usefully applicable to her. The primary weaknesses are the following:

- **Allocation of Equity Assets.** Exposure to equity assets will be necessary to achieve the return requirements of Fairfax; however, greater diversification of these assets among other equity classes is needed to produce a more efficient, potentially less volatile portfolio that would meet her risk tolerance parameters as well as her return requirements. An allocation that focuses the equity investments in U.S. *large-cap* and/or *small-cap* holdings and includes smaller international and Real Estate Investment Trust exposure is more likely to achieve the return and risk tolerance goals. If more information were available concerning the returns and volatility of the Reston stock, an argument could be made that this holding *is* the equity component of her portfolio. But the lack of this information precludes taking it into account for the Savings Portfolio allocation and creates the need for broader equity diversification.
- **Cash Allocation.** Within the proposed fixed-income component, the allocation to cash (15 percent) is excessive given the limited liquidity need and low returns the asset class offers.
- **Corporate/Municipal Bond Allocation.** The corporate bond allocation (10 percent) is inappropriate given Fairfax's tax situation and the superior after tax yield on municipal bonds relative to corporates (5.5 percent vs. 4.8 percent).
- **Venture Capital Allocation.** The allocation to venture capital is questionable given Fairfax's policy statement which reveals that she is quite risk averse and dislikes volatility. Although venture capital may provide diversification benefits, venture capital returns historically have been much more volatile than other risky assets such as large- and small-cap stocks in the United States. Hence, even a small percentage allocation to venture capital may prove vexing.
- **Lack of Risk/Volatility Information.** The proposal concentrates on return expectations and ignores risk/volatility implications. Specifically, the proposal should have addressed the expected volatility of the entire portfolio to see if it falls within the risk tolerance parameters of Fairfax.

4. Maria Barda worries that her assets will be insufficient to support her in her remaining years. She does not want to incur a loss in any of her individual securities. This aversion to losses is a characteristic shared by many investors and differs from the "rational choice" concept of investment decision making as outlined by Alpine's portfolio manager.

The rational choice decision making of modern portfolio theory indicates that investors should

- consider investments on a portfolio basis.
- have expected returns (probability-weighted returns of all possible outcomes) of an investment or a portfolio as their primary return consideration.
- focus on maximizing expected returns for their risk level; and
- assess portfolio gains and losses in an unbiased manner.

In contrast, Barda prefers to

- consider her investments individually instead of as part of a portfolio.

- concentrate on the extreme negative outcomes of an investment rather than the expected return; and
- focus on avoiding any losses.

Barda's attitude toward investments is closer to loss aversion than risk aversion. Her preferences cause her to favor a more conservative investment policy than might be warranted by the purely rational perspective of modern portfolio theory.

5.   Vincenzo Donadoni and Maria Barda differ in each of the following areas of their investment policies.

    i.   *Current income requirement.*

       Donadoni. Donadoni has a minimal need for income. He believes that his current CHF 250,000 a year will rise with inflation. He can use his consulting income of CHF 125,000 a year for the next two years to satisfy a portion of his needs. Donadoni now has a low need for income [CHF 125,000/(CHF 13 million - CHF 1.5 million home renovation) = 1.1%] from his portfolio. At the end of two years, his estimated expenses of CHF 250,000 (adjusted for inflation) still represent a modest need for current income [CHF 250,000/(CHF 13 million - CHF 2 million tax payment - CHF 1.5 million home renovation) = 2.6 percent].

       Barda. Barda has a much greater income requirement than Donadoni. She also expresses concern about the effects of inflation. Her lack of other income sources means that her current income needs from her investment portfolio represent a reasonably large percentage of her asset base (LIT 175 million income needs/LIT 2.86 billion asset base = 6.1 percent requirement).

    ii.   *Total return requirement.*

       Donadoni. Donadoni wants to leave a sizable trust (CHF 15 million) for his children. Reaching this goal will require considerable growth of his current financial assets over his remaining lifetime. Donadoni must realize a return above his income needs to meet his long-term financial goals. He should adopt a total-return approach to the portfolio with long-term capital appreciation as the primary objective.

       Barda. Barda's key objective is to preserve the real purchasing power of her assets for her lifetime. Therefore, an appropriate investment strategy for Barda would be to accentuate real current income.

    iii.   *Willingness to assume risk.*

       Donadoni. Donadoni is a risk taker. Considering his history of taking large bets on short-term opportunities and preferring to take the initiative in financial matters, he has an above-average willingness to assume risk.

       Barda. Barda is cautious. Based on her concern that her assets will be insufficient to support her in her remaining years, she has a below-average willingness to take on risk. She prefers to avoid risk and minimize the chance of loss in any individual security.

iv.   *Ability to assume risk.*

   Donadoni.   Donadoni's long time horizon, relatively low income needs, and large asset base relative to his needs suggest an above-average ability to assume risk.

   Barda.   Barda's age and higher income needs relative to her smaller asset base suggest low financial ability to withstand losses in her portfolio.

v.   *Time horizon.*

   Donadoni.   Donadoni's long-time horizon consists of three major intervals. The first interval is the next two years. At the end of this period, his income circumstances will change because of the expiration of his consulting contract. He will also experience a large outflow of funds because of large tax payments. This change will create a liquidity constraint on the portion of the portfolio needed for the tax payment. Alpine should evaluate both events for their potential effect on Donadoni's current income requirement and risk tolerance. The second interval encompasses the remainder of his lifetime, which is an estimated 20-30 years (based on his life expectancy). The third interval includes the time period when the trust will exist for his children. This interval assumes that Donadoni has achieved his goal of leaving a large trust for his children at his death.

   Barda.   Barda faces a single time horizon encompassing the remainder of her life. This time horizon represents an intermediate time frame of 15-20 years (based on her life expectancy). Thus, the time horizon of her portfolio is shorter than that of Donadoni's. Also, her portfolio's time horizon does not extend beyond her death.

CHAPTER 14: PORTFOLIO ANALYSIS

SOLUTIONS

Questions

QA14-1   (a) Portfolio analysis assumes that the weights of all assets sum to one. The weight of any given asset can assume any positive, zero, or negative value. Mutual funds, for example, must have all weights positive because the law prohibits them from selling short or borrowing. (b) The assumption that all the weights sum to one is essential; it forms the basis for portfolio analysis. The weights must sum to unity (or 100 percent) or all the portfolio's original equity investment has not been accounted for. Essentially, the requirement that all weights sum to one is a balance sheet identity.

QA14-2   (a) Simple diversification can be defined as "not putting your eggs in one basket" or "spreading your risks." It ignores the correlation between different assets' returns. Simple diversification can only be defined vaguely and without rigor because it is a vague and simple-minded approach to diversification. (b) Yes, the risk-reduction power of simple diversification is surprising. Simple diversification can substantially reduce a portfolio's total risk. Simply adding more randomly selected assets to the portfolio will continue to reduce the portfolio's total risk until about 36 different assets have been added to the portfolio. Simple diversification can eliminate as much as half of a portfolio's total risk. However, simple diversification will not usually reduce risk any further after about 36 randomly selected assets have been added to the portfolio. (c) Yes. Simple diversification will typically eliminate the unsystematic (or diversifiable) risk in a portfolio of randomly selected assets after 36 different securities have been added to the portfolio. (d) No. Simple diversification cannot be expected to reduce a portfolio's total risk below the undiversifiable (or systematic) level. Simple (or random) diversification can only reduce diversifiable (or unsystematic) risk. It does this by averaging different assets independent (or unsystematic) variations in return to zero. But, the systematic portion of an asset's total risk is undiversifiable. More sophisticated diversification techniques (namely, Markowitz diversification) must be used to reduce systematic risk.

QA14-3   (a) Superfluous diversification can be defined as holding more assets than are needed for effective diversification--specifically, more than 36 securities usually entails superfluous (or wasteful or counter-productive) diversification. (b) Superfluous diversification lowers the owner's net returns because excessive expenses are incurred in managing large numbers of different assets. These expenses include (i) search costs, (ii) transaction costs, (iii) acceptance of lackluster performers, and (iv) high costs of maintaining current information on all assets that are candidates for the portfolio.

QA14-4   The [total risk, E(r)] curves are all convex toward the E(r) axis because as assets' correlations decrease from the maximum value of positive one ($\rho = +1$), the portfolio possibility line that may be formed can only curve in this direction. Stated more mathematically, it is impossible for the curves to be convex away from the E(r) axis because the efficient frontier is a quadratic function that (for realistic empirical reasons) has its center located in an area that requires the upper left quadrant of the [total risk, E(r)] convex hull of investment opportunities to bend toward the E(r) axis.

QA14-5   Before proceeding directly to the answer to the question, first consider a few crucial facts. Fact 1: The objective of diversification is to reduce variability of return in a portfolio.

Fact 2: The variance of a 2-security portfolio is:

$$Var(r) = x_1^2 Var(r_1) + x_2^2 Var(r_2) + 2x_1 x_2 Cov(r_1, r_2)$$

Fact 3: Diversification is most effective if the analyst can find negatively correlated securities since this would make the covariance negative.

$$Cov(r_1, r_2) = (\sigma_1)(\sigma_2)(\rho_{1,2})$$

Fact 4: Speaking empirically, negatively correlated ($\rho < 0$) securities are rare. Thus, the analyst must usually settle for less effective diversification using securities with correlations (or covariances) that are positive, but as low in value as possible.

Fact 5: (Here we begin to address the question directly.) Since most securities have positive systematic risk that cannot be reduced via diversification, diversification among positively correlated securities must be based on the unsystematic portion of the securities' variability of return, namely, the e_i's in the characteristic regression line: $r_{it} = a_i + b_i r_{mt} + e_{it}$ where E(e) = 0. Var(r_i) not explained by the characteristic regression line is unsystematic risk, denoted Var(e). Unsystematic risk is variability in the random error term "e" in the regression equation. If the analyst finds securities that are positively correlated with each other and with the market but have unsystematic risks that are independent (that is, uncorrelated) or negatively correlated, then at least the unsystematic portion of risk may be eliminated or reduced by randomly combining securities into portfolios and averaging only the independent e_i's.

QA14-6   To analyze a portfolio of N different assets, the analyst needs to estimate the expected returns for each of the N assets, the variances (or standard deviations) of the returns of each of the N assets, and the covariances (or correlation coefficients) for each pair of assets in the portfolio [(N^2 - N)/2 covariances.] The weights to be invested in each asset also need to be known. Of these, the most difficult to estimate empirically are the covariance terms. Covariances, however, are also the most important factor in determining the risk of a well-diversified portfolio since the individual variances become a negligible input as the number of assets, N, increases.

QA14-7   The formula for the risk of a 4-asset portfolio is:

$$Var(r_p) = x_1^2 \sigma_1^2 + x_2^2 \sigma_2^2 + x_3^2 \sigma_3^2 + x_4^2 \sigma_4^2 + 2x_1 x_2 Cov(r_1, r_2) + 2x_1 x_3 Cov(r_1, r_3)$$
$$+ 2x_1 x_4 Cov(r_1, r_4) + 2x_2 x_3 Cov(r_2, r_3) + 2x_2 x_4 Cov(r_2, r_4) + 2x_3 x_4 Cov(r_3, r_4)$$

Mathematical statisticians would call the formula above a 4x4 variance-covariance matrix.

QA14-8   Ivan has the right idea--i.e., he is not putting all his eggs in one basket, and bonds have a relatively low correlation with common stocks. However, with 80% of his funds invested in the stock fund, the majority of the risk and return of his portfolio will be determined by the risk and return of the stock fund.

QA14-9 An investor who is indifferent towards risk has an indifference map made up of horizontal straight lines that are all parallel. A risk-indifferent investor's happiness is unaffected by the level of risk, only by the level of the returns, so this type of investor prefers to be on the highest horizontal line possible, but is indifferent about which risk level is associated with that return. Large corporations sometimes behave as if they are risk indifferent when they seek to maximize the value of the firm without bringing risk explicitly into the decision-making process.

QA14-10 Negative weights designate borrowing. One economic interpretation is that it represents a short sale--i.e., the investor has sold shares of a borrowed stock. The second interpretation is that it represents a margined transaction, wherein the investor has borrowed part of the funds he has invested.

Problems

PA14-1 The variances of the returns for assets 1 and 2 is calculated using the following equation:

$$\text{Var}(r_i) = p_1(r_{i,1} - E(r_i))^2 + p_2(r_{i,2} - E(r_i))^2 + p_3(r_{i,3} - E(r_i))^2$$

where $r_{i,1}$ denotes the return associated with asset i in the 1st state of nature.

The variances of the returns for assets 1 and 2 are, therefore:

$$\text{Var}(r_1) = 1/3(0.15 - 0.30)^2 + 1/3(0.30 - 0.30)^2 + 1/3(0.45 - 0.30)^2 = 0.015$$
$$\text{Var}(r_2) = 1/3(0.15 - 0.12)^2 + 1/3(0.12 - 0.12)^2 + 1/3(0.09 - 0.12)^2 = 0.0006$$

The standard deviations of the returns for the two assets are equal to the square roots of the variances. The standard deviation for asset 1 is 0.12247, and the standard deviation for asset 2 is 0.02449.

The covariance of the returns for assets 1 and 2 is calculated as

$$\text{Cov}(r_1, r_2) = \sigma_{1,2} = p_1(r_{1,1} - E(r_1))(r_{2,1} - E(r_2)) + p_2(r_{1,2} - E(r_1))(r_{2,2} - E(r_2))$$

$$+ p_3(r_{1,3} - E(r_1))(r_{2,3} - E(r_2))$$

$$\sigma_{1,2} = 1/3(0.15 - 0.30)(0.15 - 0.12) + 1/3(0.30 - 0.30)(0.12 - 0.12)$$

$$+ 1/3(0.45 - 0.30)(0.09 - 0.12) = -0.003$$

The variance of a portfolio with equal proportions invested in each of the two assets is calculated using the following equation: $\text{Var}(r_p) = x_1^2\sigma_1^2 + x_2^2\sigma_2^2 + 2x_1x_2\sigma_{1,2}$.
Therefore, $\text{Var}(r_p) = (1/2)^2(0.015) + (1/2)^2(0.0006) + 2(1/2)(1/2)(-0.003) = 0.0024$.

Year	Stock A returns	Stock B returns	Stock C returns
20X1	10%	6%	-5%
20X2	-5	10	15
20X3	-7	12	20
20X4	15	8	25
20X5	20	14	30
20X6	-30	7	-35
20X7	12	8	20
Averages	**2.1429%**	**9.2857%**	**10.00%**

The correlation coefficient is calculated as $\rho_{i,j} = \dfrac{\left[\sum\limits_{t=1}^{n}(r_{i,t} - E(r_i))(r_{j,t} - E(r_j))\right] \div (n)}{\sigma_i \sigma_j}$ and

the standard deviations are calculated as $\sigma_i = \sqrt{\dfrac{\sum\limits_{t=1}^{n}(r_{it} - E(r_i))^2}{n}}$.

This yields the following results: $\sigma_A = 16.084\%; \sigma_B = 2.6573\%; \sigma_C = 21.044\%;$

and $\rho_{A,B} = 0.243; \rho_{A,C} = 0.781; \rho_{B,C} = 0.626.$

PA14-3   Using the formula indicated in PA14-2, the standard deviation of Stock A's returns is 16.084%, of Stock B's returns is 2.6573%, and of Stock C's returns is 21.044%.

PA14-4   The expected return of a portfolio is a weighted average of the expected returns of each asset in the portfolio, so $E(r_p) = 0.2(12\%) + 0.4(8\%) + 0.4(20\%) = 13.6\%.$

PA14-5   The variance of a 3-security portfolio is calculated using the following equation:

$\text{Var}(r_p) =$
$x_1^2\sigma_1^2 + x_2^2\sigma_2^2 + x_3^2\sigma_3^2 + 2x_1 x_2 \rho_{1,2}\sigma_1\sigma_2 + 2x_1 x_3 \rho_{1,3}\sigma_1\sigma_3 + 2x_2 x_3 \rho_{2,3}\sigma_2\sigma_3$

The variance of a portfolio made up of 20% in Stock A, 40% in Stock B, and 40% in Stock C is, therefore,

$\text{Var}(r_p) = (0.2)^2(16.084)^2 + (0.4)^2(2.6573)^2 + (0.4)^2(21.044)^2 +$
$2(0.2)(0.4)(0.243)(16.084)(2.6573) +$
$2(0.2)(0.4)(0.781)(16.084)(21.044) + 2(0.4)(0.4)(0.626)(2.6573)(21.044) = 137.492659$

The standard deviation of the portfolio = $\sqrt{137.492659} = 11.7257\%.$

PA14-6   The arithmetic means of the historical returns can be used to estimate expected returns for stocks A & B. The arithmetic means were computed in PA14-2. The arithmetic mean for Stock A is 2.1429% and the mean for Stock B is 9.2857%. The expected return of a portfolio that has equal amounts invested in stocks A & B is

$E(r_p) = 0.5(2.1429) + 0.5(9.2857) = 5.7143\%.$

PA14-7   The standard deviation of a two-security portfolio is calculated as follows: $Var(r_p) = x_1^2\sigma_1^2 + x_2^2\sigma_2^2 + 2x_1x_2\rho_{1,2}\sigma_1\sigma_2$. The variance of the two-security portfolio with equal weights invested in Stocks A and B is $Var(r_p) = (0.5)^2(16.084)^2 + (0.5)^2(2.6573)^2 + 2(0.5)(0.5)(0.243)(16.084)(2.6573) = 71.63198$. The standard deviation is the square root of the variance and is equal to 8.46%.

PA14-8   The covariance of the returns of two securities is calculated as the product of their standard deviations and the correlation coefficient of their returns, or,

$$Cov(r_A, r_B) = \sigma_{A,B} = \rho_{A,B}\sigma_A\sigma_B$$

Thus, the covariance of the returns for Stocks A and B is $(0.243)(16.084)(2.6573) = 10.386$.

PA14-9   Using the formula supplied in the problem, the appropriate weight to invest in Stock D is $x_D = \dfrac{(30)^2 - 0.1(15)(30)}{(15)^2 + (30)^2 - 2(0.1)(15)(30)} = 0.83$, so 83% should be invested in Stock D. It follows that 17% should be invested in Stock G. The expected return on the portfolio is $E(r_p) = 0.83(10) + 0.17(18) = 11.36\%$.

PA14-10   The slope of the capital allocation line (CAL) is $[E(r_m) - r_f]/\sigma_m = [15 - 8]/20] = 0.35$. The slope of the CAL is sometimes called the market price of risk. It represents an investor's risk-return tradeoff. In this instance it means that for each 1% increase in risk (standard deviation), the investor will receive a 0.35% higher return.

PA14-11 (a)   If everything is invested in the risk-free asset, the return on the portfolio is equal to the return on the risk-free asset, or 8%. The risk, or standard deviation, of a risk-free asset is zero.

   (b)   If the money is spread evenly between the risk-free asset and the risky portfolio M, the $E(r_p) = (0.5)(8) + (0.5)(15) = 11.5\%$. The standard deviation of the portfolio is equal to the weight invested in the risky portfolio times its standard deviation: $\sigma_p = (0.5)(20) = 10\%$.

   (c)   If 50% of the money is borrowed (at the risk-free rate of interest), then the expected return of the portfolio is $E(r_p) = -0.5(8) + 1.50(15) = 18.5\%$. The standard deviation is, again, equal to the weight invested in the risky portfolio times its standard deviation:

   $\sigma_p = 1.50(20) = 30\%$.

PA14-12   Tables showing the data calculated to formulate the graphs of the three portfolio possibility curves are provided below, and the graph follows.

$\rho = +1$

Weight in DI	Weight in UST	$E(r_p)$	$Var(r_p)$	Standard deviation
0	1.00	7%	0.022	14.8%
1.00	0	20%	0.134	36.6%
0.5	0.5	13.5%	0.066	25.7%
0.289	0.711	10.76%	0.044	21.2%

$\rho = 0$

0	1.00	7%	0.022	14.8%
1.00	0	20%	0.134	36.6%
0.5	0.5	13.5%	0.039	19.8%
0.25	0.75	10.25%	0.0208	14.4%
0.75	0.25	16.75%	0.0768	27.7%
0.289	0.711	10.76%	0.0225	15.0%

$\rho = -1$

0	1.00	7%	0.022	14.8%
1.00	0	20%	0.134	36.6%
0.5	0.5	13.5%	0.012	10.9%
0.25	0.75	10.25%	0.0004	2.01%
0.75	0.25	16.75%	0.05635	23.7%
0.289	0.711	10.76%	0	0

Figure PA14-12: Graph of portfolio possibility curves for DI and UST:

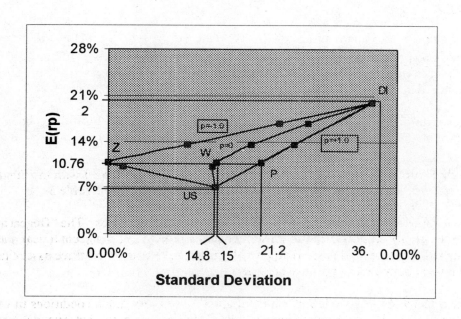

CFA Exam Solutions*

The following are the guideline answers provided by the AIMR for the CFA Exam questions:

1. B
    Solution:
    The formula for the expected return of a portfolio is:

    $$E(R_{port}) = \sum_{i=1}^{n} W_i R_i$$

    where

    W_i = the percent of the portfolio in asset I
    R_i = the expected rate of return for asset I

    So,

    W_X = \$9,000/\$10,000
    = 0.9;

    W_Y = \$1,000/\$10,000
    = 0.1.

    $E(R_{port})$ = 0.9(20%) + 0.1(10%) = 18% + 1%
    = 19%

2. B

3. D

4A. The following shows the calculation of the expected total return associated with the Fund for *each* of the two different asset mixes, given the three scenarios shown in Table 2.

    Table 2 shows projected returns for each of the three economic scenarios. The "Degearing" scenario is for a stable economic environment; economic growth is 2.5 percent a year and the inflation rate is 3.0 percent. This scenario provides positive returns for all three asset classes, and stocks outperform both bonds and Treasury bills.

    The other two scenarios--"Disinflation" and "Inflation"--posit less stable conditions in which stocks do poorly. Bonds also generate losses in the "Inflation" scenario, but provide considerable downside protection under "Disinflation" conditions.

    The calculations for the multiple scenario analysis (see below) show that of the three asset classes, bonds offer the highest expected real returns, 2.25 percent, over the forecast horizon. Over the same horizon, stocks are projected to generate a negative real return of -0.125 percent. Stocks are adversely affected under the "Disinflation" scenario and show losses under the "Inflation" scenario. Given the probabilities assigned to the three scenarios, the stock/bond/cash mix of 40/40/20 provides a superior real return (1.10 percent) to that from the alternative 60/30/10 mix (0.73 percent). This analysis reveals that equities do not automatically produce the highest expected returns even when the preponderant economic probability is for a stable environment accompanied by slow growth. If other less favorable outcomes have a reasonable probability of occurring, higher equity exposures may not produce a commensurately higher return. The multiple scenario forecasting methodology provides a valuable tool for effectively exploring the impact of various possibilities via a "what if" approach.

Real Total Returns

	Degearing		Disinflation		Inflation	Expected return
T-bills	(1.50 x 0.5)	+	(1.5 x 0.25)	+	(0.5 x 0.25) =	1.250%
Bonds	(3.25 x 0.5)	+	(6.5 x 0.25)	+	(-4.0 x 0.25) =	2.250
Stocks	(5.25 x 0.5)	+	(-9.0 x 0.25)	+	(-2.0 x 0.25) =	-0.125

Real Portfolio Returns

	40/20/20 Mix			60/30/10 Mix	
T-bills	1.250 x 0.2 =	0.25%		1.250 x 0.1 =	0.125%
Bonds	2.250 x 0.4 =	0.90		2.250 x 0.3 =	0.675
Stocks	-0.125 x 0.4 =	-0.05		-0.125 x 0.6 =	-0.075
Total		1.10%			0.725%

An alternate calculation approach is set forth below. This approach involves finding the portfolio returns under each scenario and then finding the final expected returns using the probabilities.

Real Returns: 40/40/20 Mix

Degearing:	(5.25 x 0.40) + (3.25 x 0.40) + (1.5 x 0.20) =	3.7%
Disinflation:	(-9.00 x 0.40) + (6.50 x 0.40) + (1.5 x 0.20) =	-0.7
Inflation:	(-2.00 x 0.40) + (-4.00 x 0.40) + (0.5 x 0.20) =	-2.3

Expected Return = [(3.7% x 0.5) + (-0.7% x 0.25) + (-2.3% x 0.25)] = 1.1%

The same alternate procedure applies to the 60/30/10 mix.

B. **Justification:** The answer to Part A provides much of the justification for the Fund's 40/40/20 asset mix. Given the three economic scenarios, each having a reasonable chance of occurring, the expected portfolio real returns are 1.10 percent for the existing mix versus 0.725 percent for the 60/30/10 mix. Therefore, the 40/40/20 mix is superior. Although using the scenarios may fail to capture subsequent events, the 40/40/20 mix provides the lowest risk exposure. The return superiority, if any, represents added value. Perversely, the more stocks in the portfolio, the worse the outcomes under the circumstances captured by the scenarios.

Explanation: The explanation, also captured in the answer to Part A, lies primarily in the fact that stocks generate losses in both the "Disinflation" and the "Inflation" scenarios. Increasing the proportion in stocks increases the portfolio's exposure to their relatively poor performance. Bonds offer the highest expected real returns over the investment horizon, followed by cash equivalents such as Treasury bills, whose return is positive under each scenario. Stocks' superiority of returns under the "Degearing" scenario is insufficient, even with that scenario given a 0.50 probability of being the dominant set of circumstances, to overcome the "Disinflation" outcome for that asset class.

CHAPTER 15: CAPM AND APT

SOLUTIONS

Questions

QA15-1 The capital market line represents the new efficient frontier when the assumption of the existence of a risk-free asset is included. All the portfolios lying on it represent some combination of borrowing or lending at the risk-free rate and investing in the well-diversified market portfolio that contains all risky assets. The capital market line plots expected returns against total risk (i.e., standard deviation) while the security market line depicts the relationship between expected returns and undiversifiable risk (i.e., beta.) In equilibrium, efficient portfolios will plot on both the CML and the SML. Individual securities and inefficient portfolios will never lie on the capital market line. The portfolios lying on the efficient frontier are all well-diversified portfolios that have had all their diversifiable risk eliminated; only non-diversifiable, systematic risk remains. Individual securities and inefficient portfolios have both diversifiable and undiversifiable risk, and, therefore, will not provide the highest return for each unit of total risk, or the lowest risk for any given level of return.

QA15-2 To determine a beta coefficient for a common stock using historical data, you will need to collect the historical returns on the stock for several years and the historical returns on the S&P 500 Index (or some other proxy for the market portfolio) for the same time period. The line that results from regressing the stock returns against the index is called a characteristic line, and the slope of the characteristic line is the stock's beta. The beta coefficient can then be used to determine the expected equilibrium return on the stock, by applying CAPM. Expected returns arrived at by some other type of analysis are compared to this equilibrium return in an attempt to identify overpriced and underpriced securities. If the expected return is greater than the expected return in equilibrium (i.e., the CAPM-suggested return), then the stock is considered to be underpriced. If, however the expected return is less than the CAPM-suggested return, the stock is considered to be overpriced.

QA15-3 One of the assumptions underlying equilibrium portfolio theory is the assumption of homogeneous expectations. In a world of homogeneous expectations, all investors have the same expected return, risk and correlation statistics for any specific asset. The theory also assumes that all investors are only interested in the expected return and risk of an investment when they make their investment decisions, and that all investors are risk-averse--i.e., they want to earn the highest return possible for each unit of risk. In light of these assumptions, all investors will be in complete agreement on the optimal portfolio in which to invest. Therefore, all risky assets must be in that portfolio; no investor will invest in any asset not in the portfolio, so that asset would cease to exist. The investment decision, therefore, is reduced to investing in the optimal portfolio, which contains all risky assets. If an investor wishes to be exposed to less risk, he can divide his funds between the optimal portfolio and investment in the risk-free asset. This reduces his risk and also his expected return. If an investor wishes to accept more risk in exchange for a higher expected return, he can borrow funds at the risk-free rate and invest all the money in the optimal portfolio.

QA15-4   While the assumptions underlying CAPM may not accurately reflect "real world" conditions, the test of whether it is a good model is whether it accurately predicts the relationship between expected return and risk when applied to real world data. (Several studies indicate that it does.) Consider, for example, that a physicist may develop a model regarding the movement of particles in a vacuum. If that model predicts the movement of the particles in the real world atmosphere, then it is a good model. One can think of the CAPM assumptions as creating a "financial vacuum."

QA15-5   When the assumption that investors can borrow and lend at the same risk-free rate of interest is relaxed, a more realistic model evolves. It is assumed that the borrowing rate will be higher than the lending rate. Thus, the intercept of the borrowing CML is higher than that of the lending CML. This results in two different tangency points on the CML, which means that the optimal portfolio held by lenders would be different from the optimal portfolio held by borrowers. Figure 15-3 in the textbook indicates the differing slopes of the two CMLs. Note that the lending CML has a much steeper slope than that of the borrowing CML. This means that borrowers must take on more risk for each unit of expected return that do the lenders. The differing rates assumption also affects the intercepts of the security market line, with the borrowing SML having the higher intercept. The two SMLs will also have different slopes because the variances of the returns on the borrowing portfolio will differ from the variance of the returns on the lending portfolio. Too, since there are two different optimal portfolios involved, the covariance terms will also differ.

QA15-6   EIV refers to the errors-in-variables problem. The problem arises in the studies done on the CAPM because the true beta coefficients are unobservable. Instead, researchers use various ways to estimate betas and use these estimates as proxies for the true beta. This problem leads to an underestimation of the importance of beta as an explanatory variable and the overestimation of the cross-sectional regression coefficients associated with anomalous explanatory variables that *can* be observed without error, such as firm size, book value-to-market value, and the earnings/price ratio.

QA15-7   The market portfolio (hereafter, referred to as m) plays a crucial role in capital market theory. It is assumed to be the portfolio that all investors agree is the optimal portfolio in which to invest. Both the capital market line (CML), a portfolio pricing model, and the capital asset pricing model (CAPM), a pricing model for all assets, are derived from portfolio m. In contrast, m plays no role in APT. The market portfolio, or some surrogate for m, may or may not enter into empirical estimates of the APT model.   APT does not assume the necessary existence of an optimal portfolio.

QA15-8   The risk factors in the APT are unspecified, unidentified, and totally undefined. The only fact we can discern about the APT risk factors is that they involve systematic (or undiversifiable) price variations that can be measured by the factor betas. These factor betas can be statistically estimated by using either regression analysis or factor analysis on empirical data. Different researchers will most probably estimate different factor betas.
              If factor analytic techniques are employed, the factor analysis algorithm that is used will extract its own risk factors from the dependent variables being analyzed. That is, factor analysis creates its own explanatory variables. But the risk factors extracted by factor analysis have no basis in economic theory (unless by coincidence), and they often cannot be identified even by the researcher who used factor analysis to extract them. Furthermore, different factor analysis algorithms (for instance, the Simple Structure, Varimax, Tandem Criteria, etc. approaches to orthogonalizing the errors) will each yield

totally different results when applied to the same set of data. Factor analysis is not inherently part of APT. Factor analysis is merely the statistical algorithm used by some researchers to obtain factor betas from complicated statistical procedures that are unrelated to economic theory.

Our knowledge of financial economics and/or economic intuition can suggest empirically observable variables (such as a market measure like the S&P 500 Index, for instance) that we think should be significant risk factors in APT. Then, regression analysis can be used to test competing hypotheses using classical statistical techniques. For this reason, some researchers think the regression analysis approach is superior to using factor analytic techniques.

QA15-9   The beta coefficient is the regression slope coefficient from the characteristic line for one asset. This beta is estimated for one asset using time-series regression analysis; some surrogate for the market portfolio m is the explanatory variable. In contrast, the factor loadings from factor analysis simultaneously analyze n different assets; returns over T different time periods. No explanatory variables are supplied by the researcher in factor analysis--the factor analysis algorithm extracts its own explanatory variables without the benefit of economic reasoning. In spite of these substantial differences, the beta coefficients in both models are somewhat analogous measures of the systematic risk. In the case of the single-factor APT, the characteristic line beta and the single-factor beta turn out to be identical.

QA15-10   Uncertain. They are similar in some respects and different in other respects. The CAPM is equivalent to the one-factor APT model; therefore, the two theories are not contradictory. However, the CAPM is a more highly specified theory. First, the CAPM can be derived mathematically from either a quadratic utility function, or from several different positive monotone utility functions if a two-parameter probability distribution of returns is assumed. APT requires less rigorous utility foundations; that is one of the reasons that APT is so general. A second way the APT differs from the CAPM is that the APT is a multi-index model in which the indexes are left undefined. In contrast, the CAPM is a single index model with one specific index--the market portfolio, m. A third difference is that recently the CAPM has been extended to be a multi-period model that embraces consumption decisions. But APT is merely a relative pricing model. Later, the APT may be developed to the level of elegance of the CAPM, but that has not yet occurred.

QA15-11   False. Unsystematic risk has no role in either APT or CAPM. Both models assume that unsystematic risk can easily be diversified away to zero. Both models base expected returns only on the undiversifiable risk (i.e., beta and the covariance.)

QA15-12   False. While it is true that the APT uses many factors that are assumed to affect the returns on assets while CAPM assumes only the one factor, namely the return on the market portfolio, the factors for the APT are unknown. It is generally assumed that factors that will affect *all* securities should be included as priced factors while factors affecting only one security (or firm) should not be priced. (They would represent diversifiable risk.) However, there are factors that affect a subset of securities (e.g., industry-related factors), and there has been no clear determination whether or not these should be included as priced factors in the APT. The fact that the factors to use in the APT are unknown is a disadvantage of the model.

Problems

PA15-1   The equation of the security market line is $E(r_i) = RFR + [E(r_m) - RFR]b_i$. The model indicates the return one should expect on a security if it is fairly priced. If an investor expects a return higher than this, the security is underpriced. If her expected return is less than this, the security is overpriced.

Equilibrium expected return	Expected return	
$E(r_A) = 8 + [14 - 8]1.2 = 15.2\%$	17%	**underpriced**
$E(r_B) = 8 + [14 - 8]0.8 = 12.8\%$	14%	**underpriced**
$E(r_C) = 8 + [14 - 8]1.5 = 17.0\%$	15%	**overpriced**
$E(r_D) = 8 + [14 - 8]0.75 = 12.5\%$	16%	**underpriced**

PA15-2 (a)   The portfolio's beta is a weighted average of the betas of each of the individual securities in the portfolio, based on the proportionate investment in each.

Stock	Price	Shares held	Total investment	Weight invested	Estimated beta
Z	$10	1,000	$ 10,000	0.069	0.80
AB	$30	1,000	$ 30,000	0.200	0.90
QZ	$15	4,000	$ 60,000	0.400	1.25
DB	$10	1,000	$ 10,000	0.067	1.05
RST	$ 8	5,000	$ 40,000	0.266	1.15
			$150,000	1.000	

$$\beta_{pf} = 0.067(0.8) + 0.2(0.9) + (0.4)(1.25) + 0.067(1.05) + 0.266(1.15) = 1.11$$

(b)   The CAPM-suggested return is $E(r_{pf}) = 9 + 1.11(16 - 9) = 16.77\%$.

PA15-3   The expected return on the portfolio is a weighted average of the expected returns of each of the securities in the portfolio:

$$E(r_p) = 0.5(14) + 0.5(8) = 11\%$$

The risk of a portfolio is calculated using the following equation:

$$Var(r_p) = x_1^2 \sigma_1^2 + x_2^2 \sigma_2^2 + 2x_1 x_2 Cov(r_1, r_2)$$

Since the variance of a risk-free asset is 0 and the covariance of the returns of a risky asset and a risk-free asset is also 0 (the risk-free asset's returns do not move), the second and third terms of the equation are zero, so the variance of the portfolio in this case is calculated as $Var(r_p) = x_m^2 \sigma_m^2$, and the standard deviation is then $\sigma_p = x_m \sigma_m$. For this portfolio the risk, as measured by the standard deviation, is $0.5(10) = 5\%$.

PA15-4 (a) The relationship between the correlation coefficient and the covariance is given below:

$$\rho_{M,B} = \frac{Cov(r_M, r_B)}{\sigma_M \sigma_B}$$

$$0.5 = \frac{Cov(r_M, r_B)}{(0.1)(0.2)}$$

$$Cov(r_M, r_B) = (0.5)(0.1)(0.2) = 0.0100$$

(b) The equation used to calculate the beta of an asset is as follows:

$$\beta_i = \frac{Cov(r_M, r_i)}{\sigma_M^2}$$

Asset B's beta is $\dfrac{0.0100}{(0.1)^2} = 1.00$.

PA15-5 Applying the CAPM, the expected return on EEUC's stock is $E(r) = 7 + 0.61(11 - 7) = 9.44\%$. If it is returning only 8.5%, the investors have not been receiving enough return on their investments to compensate them for their risk. This means EEUC's stock is overpriced, so its price will be expected to fall unless the investors can receive higher returns as a result of increased electric prices.

PA15-6 (a) $E(r_p) = 6 + 0.90(15 - 6) = 14.1\%$.

(b) The beta of a portfolio is a weighted average of the betas of the stocks held in that portfolio. Since the current portfolio has a market value of $50,000, and the stock Ricardo wants to sell has a market value of $10,000, its weight is 20% ($10,000/$50,000). Using this information, we can obtain the weight of the *remaining portfolio* (rp) as follows:

$$\beta_p = x_1 \beta_1 + (1 - x_1)\beta_{rp}$$

$$0.90 = 0.2(0.75) + 0.8\beta_{rp}$$

$$\beta_{rp} = 0.9375$$

The beta of the *new portfolio* (np) will be the weighted average of the beta of the new stock and the beta of the remaining portfolio.

$$\beta_{np} = 0.2(1.3) + 0.8(0.9375) = 1.01$$

Ricardo's new expected equilibrium rate of return is $E(r_p) = 6 + 1.01(15 - 6) = 15.09\%$. The higher level of systematic risk requires a higher expected equilibrium return.

PA15-7 $E(r) = 5\% + 1.1(4\%) + -0.8(1\%) = 8.6\%$.

PA15-8 $E(r_{GEC}) = 4.0\% + 0.9(5\%) + 1.1(5\%) = 14.0\%$.

PA15-9   The risk-adjusted discount rate that is appropriate of Omega Medical's stock is 16.5%.

$$E(r_{OMC}) = 10\% + 1.5(2\%) + 0.5(7\%) = 16.5\%$$

Using the valuation model, Price $= \dfrac{DIV_1}{k-g} = \dfrac{DIV_0(1+g)}{k-g}$, we find that OMC is worth $18.26 a share.

$$\text{Price} = \frac{\$2(1.05)}{0.165 - 0.05} = \frac{\$2.10}{0.115} = \$18.26$$

PA15-10   The appropriate risk-adjusted discount rate is 14.5% for Titan Trucking Corporation's stock, as shown below:

$$E(r_{TTC}) = 9\% + 1.5(3\%) + -0.5(2\%) + 0.5(4\%) = 14.5\%$$

The forecasted stream of cash dividends is as follows:

Time	Cash dividends per share	
1	$0.25 x (1.25) =	$0.3125
2	$0.3125 x (1.25) =	$0.39
3	$0.39 x (1.25) =	$0.4875
4	$0.4875 x (1.25) =	$0.6094
5	$0.6094 x (1.25) =	$0.7618
6	$0.7618 x (1.05) =	$0.7999

The expected price of Titan Trucking's stock at the end of year 5 is $8.42.

$$\text{Price} = \frac{DIV_6}{k - g} = \frac{\$0.7999}{0.145 - 0.05} = \$8.42$$

Therefore, the price today, calculated as the present value of the expected five-year cash flow stream is:

$$\text{Price} = \frac{\$0.3125}{(1.145)^1} + \frac{\$0.39}{(1.145)^2} + \frac{\$0.4875}{(1.145)^3} + \frac{\$0.6094}{(1.145)^4} + \frac{\$0.7618 + \$8.42}{(1.145)^5} = \$5.92$$

PA15-11   The solution can be found by solving the three equations in three unknowns simultaneously. The problem in matrix form is as follows:

11	1	1	0.6	a_0
13	1	2	0.1	a_1
11	1	2	-0.6	a_2
[R]		[C]		[a]

The MINVERSE option in Microsoft Excel can be used to invert the coefficients' matrix and thereby derive the following solution in matrix form:

2	-2.57142	1.571428	11	5.857142	a_0
-1	1.714285	-0.71428	13	3.428571	a_1
0	1.428571	-1.42857	11	2.857142	a_2
	$[C^{-1}]$		$[R]$		$[a]$

Therefore, the equation for the APT plane is: $E(r_1) = 5.857142 + 3.428571b_{i1} + 2.857142b_{i2}$.

PA15-12   An arbitrage portfolio that duplicates the risk factors of portfolio q can be created by investing equal amounts in the portfolios R and Z from Problem 15-11. We call the new portfolio ss.

$b_{ss1} = 0.5(2) + 0.5(2) = 2$

$b_{ss2} = 0.5(0.1) + 0.5(-0.60) = -0.25$

$E(r_{ss}) = 5.857142 + 3.42857(2) + 2.857142(-0.25) = 12\%$

Therefore, an arbitrageur should buy a long position in q and sell ss short to obtain the arbitrage profits below:

Portfolio	Initial cashflow	Ending cashflow	b_{i1}	b_{i2}
ss = short	+$100	-$112	-2	+0.25
q = underpriced	-$100	+$115	+2	-0.25
Arbitrage	0	+$3	0	0

CFA Exam Solutions*

The following are the guideline answers provided by the AIMR for the CFA Exam questions:

1.   D

2.   B
Solution:
If Portfolio X and Portfolio Y are well diversified, each portfolio should have a beta of about 1.00. According to the capital asset pricing model, the required rates of return on Portfolio X and Portfolio Y are:

$E(R_x) = 0.08 + 1.00(0.16 - 0.08)$
$= 0.16$, or 16.00%.

$E(R_y) = 0.08 + 0.25(0.16 - 0.08)$
$= 0.10$, or 10.00%.
Portfolio X is properly valued because its required and expected rates of return are the same. Portfolio Y is undervalued because its expected return minus its required return (12% - 10%) is positive.

3. **A.** **Security Market Line** (See Figure 15-CFA3 on the following page.)

    i.   ***Fair-value plot.*** The graph on the next page (Figure 15-CFA3) shows, using the **CAPM**, the expected returns, ER, of Stock A and Stock B plotted on the SML.

         The points are consistent with the following equations:

         ER on stock = Risk-free rate + Beta x (Market return - Risk-free rate)

         ER for A = 4.5% + 1.2(14.5% - 4.5%)
                    = 16.5%.

         ER for B = 4.5% + 0.8(14.5% - 4.5%)
                    = 12.5%.

    ii.   *Analyst estimate plot.* Using the analyst's estimates, Stock A plots below the **SML** and Stock B, above the **SML**.

    B.   **Over vs. Undervalue**

Stock A is overvalued because it should provide a 16.5% return according to the **CAPM** whereas the analyst has estimated only a 16% return.

Stock B is undervalued because it should provide a 12.5% return according to the **CAPM** whereas the analyst has estimated a 14% return.

Figure 15-CFA3: Graph of the Security Market Line

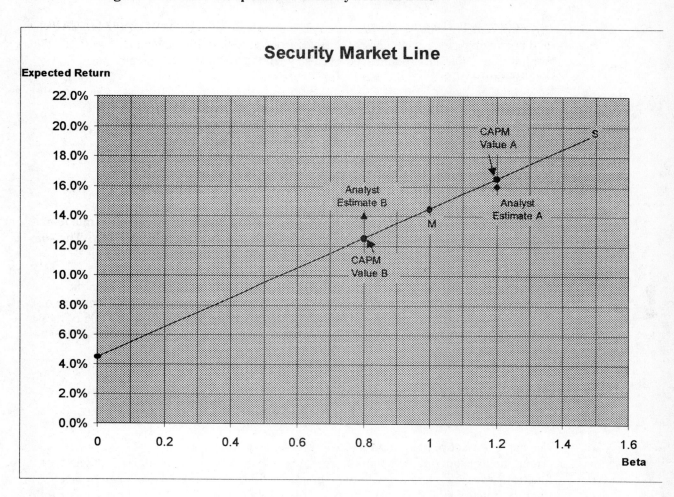

4.

    i.   **Taxes**. MPT assumes that all returns are pretax; it does not take into account the different tax statuses of individuals and institutions. So, MPT assumptions hold for nontaxed portfolios; however, depending on marginal tax rates, different investors with the same pretax returns could face different capital market lines (CMLs) after taxes.

            Nontaxed portfolios/investors are concerned with *gross* returns; taxable investors are concerned with *net* returns. When considering the impact of taxes, the nature of the income (earned income vs. capital gains), the domicile (e.g., U.S. investor), and the individual's marginal rate--all impact the net return. For example, changes in tax laws may *shift* the CML for tax-paying investors.

            Studies have examined the effect of different taxes on capital gains vs. taxes on income/dividends; most indicate that this difference has an impact. With regard to individual marginal rates, for example, the deductibility of interest paid on margin borrowing in conjunction with high marginal income tax rates on dividends may cause investors to move from a lending to a borrowing combination; changes in financing decisions affect the location of the investor's utility curve on the CML.

ii. ***Different lending and borrowing rates.*** The impact of different lending and borrowing rates is to change the CML from a straight line tangent to the efficient frontier to one that incorporates a curved segment connecting two tangent lines representative of the two different interest rates.

Modern portfolio theory assumes that investors can lend and borrow at the risk-free rate. In reality, most investors can probably lend at the risk-free rate (i.e., invest in U.S. T-bills), but the risk-free rate is typically lower than the borrowing rate established by large banks. Investors must typically pay a premium to borrow (as reflected in the prime rate, LIBOR, or broker call rate applied to margin accounts).

Under different rates, the first segment of the CML extends from the risk-free rate to a portfolio on the Markowitz efficient frontier representing the lending portfolio. This line can't be extended any further because of the higher borrowing rate.

The second segment extends from the borrowing rate to a different portfolio on the efficient frontier (to the right and up the curve from the first portfolio) representative of the borrowing portfolio. A curved segment connects these two lines. The slope of the borrowing segment of the line is below that of the original CML emanating from the risk-free rate.

5. **A**

6. **D**

7. **A.** The **capital asset pricing model** (CAPM) is an equilibrium asset pricing theory showing that equilibrium rates of expected return on all risky assets are a function of their covariance with the market portfolio. The CAPM is a single-index (factor) model which defines systematic risk in relation to a broad-based market portfolio (i.e., the market index). This single factor ("beta") is unchanging.

$$R_j = R_f + B_j(R_m - R_f)$$

where:

R_j =   expected return on an asset or portfolio

R_f =   risk-free rate of return

R_m =   expected return on the market

B_j =   volatility of the asset or portfolio to that of the market, m

Arbitrage Pricing Theory (APT) is an equilibrium asset pricing theory derived from a factor model by using diversification and arbitrage. The APT shows the expected return on any risky asset is a linear combination of various factors. That is, the APT asserts that an asset's riskiness and, hence, its average long-term return, is directly related to its sensitivities to certain factors. Thus, the APT is a multi-factor model which allows for as many factors as are important in the pricing of assets. However, the model itself does not define these variables. Unlike the CAPM, which recognizes only one unchanging factor, the key factors in APT can change over time.

$$R_j = R_f + B_{j1}(RF_1 - R_f) + \ldots + B_{jk}(RF_k - R_f)$$

where:

R_j	=	return on an asset
R_f	=	risk-free rate of return
B_{jk}	=	sensitivity of an asset to a particular factor, k
RF_k	=	expected return on a portfolio with an average (1.0) sensitivity to a factor, k
j	=	an asset
k	=	a factor

Research suggests that several macroeconomic factors may be significant in explaining expected stock returns (i.e., these factors are systematically priced):

(1) Inflation;
(2) Industrial production;
(3) Risk premia as measured by a spread between low and high-grade bonds; and the
(4) Yield curve, (i.e., slope of the term structure of interest rates).

Other researchers have identified additional factors which may influence an asset's return:

(5) Real GNP growth;
(6) Rate of growth of real oil prices (i.e., an energy factor);
(7) Real defense spending; and the
(8) Market index.

B.   Because of APT's more general formulation, it is more robust and intuitively appealing than the CAPM. *Many factors, not just the market portfolio, may explain asset returns.* This permits the stock selection process to take into account as many economic variables as are believed to be significant in a valuation context--not only as to individual issues, but also as to groups, sectors, or even the market as a whole. For example, given a forecast of a sudden spurt in the inflation rate, and of the resulting effect on interest rates, the analyst or portfolio manager can, via APT, arrive at an estimate of valuation changes across his/her selection universe and adjust portfolio exposures accordingly. Alternatively, stocks could be selected and portfolios formed based on specific factor-sensitivity criteria set up in advance.

8.   A.   **APT vs. the CAPM**
Arbitrage pricing theory does not include any of the following three assumptions incorporated in the capital asset pricing model (CAPM): noted as parts i, ii, and iii:

i.   *Investor utility function or quadratic utility function.* Capital market theory assumes investors want to maximize utility in terms of risk and return preferences; maximum return per unit of risk or minimum risk per unit of return. From the Markowitz model forward, relevant risk has been measured by variance of returns or standard deviation.

APT makes no assumptions regarding investor preferences; the multifactor model commonly used in APT does not include any exponents higher than 1.

ii.   *Normally distributed returns.* The probability distribution of expected returns of an investment and the associated dispersion or variability of those returns form the basis of Markowitz portfolio theory and the CAPM. Normal or symmetrically distributed security returns enable estimation of a variance term In the CAPM, all investors have identical estimates for the probability distributions of future returns (homogeneous expectations).

APT does not describe or specify or require an assumption about security return distributions of any kind.

iii.   *The market portfolio.* The CAPM assumes that pricing, valuation, risk, and return are solely functions of an asset's relationship to a market portfolio of all risky assets. In practice, the market portfolio is difficult to specify, so a mistakenly specified market portfolio might result. Roll called this misspecification "benchmark error."

APT does not consider or include an assumption of a market portfolio. APT is predicated on a common set of several (macroeconomic) factors.

B.   **Conceptual Difference between APT and the CAPM**
Conceptually, in APT, return is a function of a set of common factors. In the CAPM, return is a function of a market portfolio of all risky assets. Thus, one difference between APT and the CAPM can be described by the fact that APT is a multifactor model that attempts to capture several non-market influences that cause securities or assets to change in price whereas the CAPM is a single-index model that assumes securities or assets change in price because of a common co-movement with one market portfolio of all risky assets.

Another conceptual difference between APT and the CAPM is that, in application of the theory, the market portfolio (or "factor") required by the CAPM is specified. In APT, the common factors are not identified, but the common factors in APT are often described or accepted as including inflation or unanticipated deflation; default risk, government-corporate security spread, risk premiums or interest rate spreads; changes in the term structure of interest rates; changes in real final sales, GDP growth or a similar proxy for long-run profits on an economywide basis; major political upheavals; and exchange rates.

A third difference between APT and the CAPM lies in the incorporation of sensitivity coefficients to measure or describe the risk of assets or securities. APT incorporates a number of sensitivity coefficients. These coefficients determine how each independent variable or macroeconomic factor affects each asset. Different assets are affected to different degrees or extents by the common factors. In the CAPM, the only sensitivity factor is beta, an asset's sensitivity to the changes in the market portfolio (often called an asset's "systematic risk").

CHAPTER 16: PORTFOLIO PERFORMANCE EVALUATION

SOLUTIONS

Questions

QA16-1   Uncertain. Unlike mutual (or open-end funds), most closed-end investment companies do not redeem their shares at net asset value. In fact, most closed-end funds do not redeem their shares at all. The closed-end shares are actively traded in the secondary securities markets such as the NYSE and their market prices are often at a discount from their net asset values. The prices of some of these closed-end fund shares sell at a premium above their net asset values, but discount prices are more common. Any divergence between the net asset value per share and the market price per share of a closed-end fund is interpreted as another anomaly in the efficient markets hypothesis. In recent years, however, some closed-end companies, such as the Eaton Vance Senior Floating Rate Fund and the Oppenheimer Senior Floating Rate Fund, have established a window period each quarter during which the funds will redeem their shares at net asset value.

QA16-2   Both mutual funds and closed-end investment companies are organized under the Investment Company Act of 1940. However, mutual funds have an unlimited number of shares. New shares can be created if an investor wishes to buy into the fund and there are no sellers. In contrast, a closed-end company has a fixed number of shares. In order for an investor to be able to buy shares, another investor must be willing to sell them. Shares of a closed-end company sell on exchange floors whereas the shares of a mutual fund are bought and sold through the fund itself. The market price of closed-end companies is set by supply and demand, as is any corporation's stock, but the price of mutual funds is based on the net asset value of the fund. If the fund is a no load fund, an investor can buy shares of the mutual fund at net asset value. If it is a load fund, the investor must pay net asset value plus a sales charge (i.e., load) for the fund.

QA16-3   The income of an open-end investment company is taxed to the investors of the mutual fund, based on their proportionate ownership of the fund. The fund itself does not pay taxes on the income earned.

QA16-4   Uncertain. While early studies concluded that this statement was false, these studies were tainted by a survivorship bias, which occurs from using a market index for comparison purposes. Market indexes only contain securities that have survived bankruptcy, merger, delisting, and other misfortunes. A study by Goetzman and Ibbotson, published in 1994, mitigated the survivorship bias by comparing the funds' within-sample performance rankings through time. Their results, which are provided in Table 16-8 of the textbook, indicate that if a fund was classified as a winner in a two-year sample, there was a 60-40 chance that it would be a winner or a loser, respectively, in the following subsample. The repeat-winners pattern occurred in four out of the five two-year subsamples. (Note that while the tendency for winners to repeat their good performances is definitely noticeable, it is not guaranteed.) Goetzman and Ibbotson also replicated their study using risk-adjusted returns to defuse the argument that the high-return mutual funds continued to have high rankings simply because they were higher risk funds. The repeat-winner was hypothesis still supported although the results could be due to risk factors that were omitted, timing strategies, or fee-related considerations.

Another researcher, Burton Malkiel, was critical of the Goetzman/Ibbotson study. He conducted his own study using mutual fund data from 1971 through 1991, inclusive. Malkiel concluded that while the repeat-winners phenomenon was observable during the 1970s, it was not present during the 1980s.

QA16-5 A study by Farrar, for which the results are depicted in Figure 16-1 of the textbook, concluded that the average mutual fund did not outperform the market averages. They do not perform any better than a naive buy-and-hold strategy.

QA16-6 To begin with, an investment objective should be set for the fund that will maximize the owners' utility (as much as possible.) If the owners are aggressive, a high-risk, high-return portfolio would be selected. If the majority of the owners are timid, a portfolio that would plot near the bottom of the CML would be the choice. The objective could be advertised and then pursued analytically until the fund is efficient within the desired risk class.

The fund also owns too many securities. With a random selection of securities, the portfolio's diversifiable risk could be reduced to near zero with as few as three dozen securities. Using an analytical selection like Markowitz's portfolio analysis could reduce the number of securities even further. With too many securities, the portfolio would be at a point below the efficient frontier, as depicted in Figure 16-1 of the textbook. Furthermore, a portfolio that is superfluously diversified will yield poor results because it contains too many securities and has high research expenses.

You should also institute portfolio analysis techniques to increase the efficiency of the fund. Portfolio analysis will result in a much smaller number of securities in the optimum portfolio. This will free many analysts who previously were constantly checking over the superfluous number of securities in the firm's portfolio; administrative expenses of keeping track of all of these securities would be cut.

Finally, capital market theory should be utilized to find undervalued securities and overvalued securities. Perform fundamental analysis only on these securities to determine if they can be expected to return to equilibrium on the CAPM. If so, they should be bought long or sold (or sold short), depending on whether they are overvalued or undervalued. This method of directing fundamental analysis will end the aimless exercise of costly fundamental analysis. As a result of this improvement and the reduction in the number of securities held, the less competent analyst may be discharged. Any technical analysts that may be employed should also be discharged since there is strong evidence that markets are, at least, weak-form efficient, and technical analysis is, therefore, a waste of time.

QA16-7 The $b_{i,k}$ coefficients are interpreted to be estimates of the weights that fund i invests in asset category k. The sum of the twelve $b_{i,k}F_{k,t}$ products is interpreted to be a measure of the portfolio manager's style.

QA16-8 Quantitative style analysis is necessary because of the moral hazard inherent in allowing portfolio managers to report their investments months after they are made and to state their investment objectives without verification. Table 16-2 in the textbook shows that a small, but significant majority, of mutual funds do not manage money the way that their legally required written statements stated that they would. Quantitative style analysis tools provide a way to avoid these problems.

A second benefit is the increased explanatory power it provides for mutual fund risk and return statistics. Only subjective, vague categorization is provided by many of the popular financial services firms that rank funds on risk and return.

The use of quantitative management style categories also denies unethical mutual fund managers opportunities to game on their management objective statements at the expense of investors. The definitions of fund categories that are provided by the Investment Company Institute are vague enough to provide a lot of leeway for a mutual fund manager in terms of the types of stocks to hold, the extent of diversification to use, the amount of industry concentration to adopt, and the degree to which sales and purchases are timed, among other things. Fund managers can also utilize the vagueness of the definition if their results do not turn out as well as expected. The manager can indicate that goals were met when they were not.

Lastly, quantitative management style analysis tools make it easier to evaluate a portfolio manager's performance. Using such tools as the SHARPE Index and the TREYNOR Index can determine if one or more of the pre-determined investment goals have actually been attained.

QA16-9 First of all Jensen's alpha cannot be used to rank the performance of different assets unless it is risk-adjusted. The use of the appraisal ratio does this. The appraisal ratio divides Jensen's alpha by the standard error of the estimate, SE(u), to make it suitable for

performance ranking purposes. Appraisal ratio $= \dfrac{A_j}{SE(u)_j}$.

Secondly, one needs to be careful not to confuse the alpha intercept term from the original characteristic line, which is estimated using rates of return rather than risk premiums, with Jensen's alpha The original alpha is different from Jensen's alpha and should not be used for investment performance evaluation; it has no asset-pricing implications.

Lastly, Jensen's alpha is a sample statistic and is, therefore, subject to sampling errors. The alpha term in a regression is dependent on the regression's beta term. If the regression's beta is not statistically significant, the alpha value is meaningless.

QA16-10 The SHARPE Index, developed by William Sharpe, uses standard deviation, a measure of total risk, in ranking portfolios on the basis of risk and return. It measures the additional return (risk premium) over and above the risk-free rate that is paid to investors for each unit of total risk that is assumed. In contrast, the TREYNOR Index, developed by Jack Treynor measures a portfolio's return relative to its systematic risk, i.e., its beta. It measures the risk premium that an investor received for each unit of systematic risk assumed. Both index's assume that funds can be both borrowed and lent at the risk-free rate of interest.

Problems

PA16-1 The SHARPE Index, developed by William Sharpe, is calculated as follows for the two risk-free interest rates specified, 3% and 6%, and the graphs are depicted below:

$$SHARPE_p = \frac{\overline{r}_p - RFR}{\sigma_p}$$

Portfolio	SHARPE for RFR = 3%	SHARPE for RFR = 6%
Alpha	1.333	0.333
Beta	0.875	0.500
Gamma	1.667	1.167
Delta	0.923	0.692
Epsilon	1.000	0.800

When the risk-free rate was 3%, the Beta portfolio performed the worst and the Gamma portfolio performed the best. When the risk-free rate was 6%, the Alpha portfolio performed the worst and the Gamma portfolio performed the best.

Figure P16-1A: Plot of performance using SHARPE

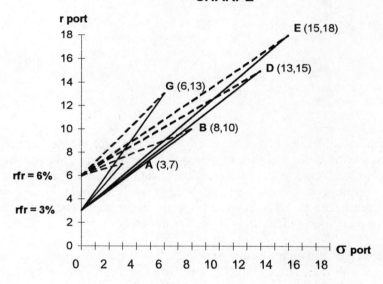

The TREYNOR Index, developed by Jack Treynor, is calculated as follows for the two risk-free interest rates specified, 3% and 6%.

$$TREYNOR_p = \frac{\bar{r}_p - RFR}{Beta_p}$$

Portfolio	TREYNOR for RFR = 3%	TREYNOR for RFR = 6%
Alpha	0.10	0.025
Beta	0.07	0.040
Gamma	0.09	0.064
Delta	0.10	0.075
Epsilon	0.11	0.086

When the risk-free rate was 3%, the Beta portfolio again was the worst performer, but the Epsilon portfolio was the best. At a risk-free rate of 6%, the Alpha portfolio was the worst performer while the Epsilon portfolio was the best.

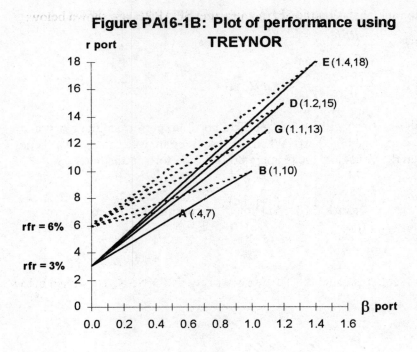

Figure PA16-1B: Plot of performance using TREYNOR

The teaching objectives of this question are to: (1) force the students to calculate the performance measures and thereby internalize the theory, (2) demonstrate that the rankings are sensitive to the risk-free interest rate that is used, and (3) demonstrate that the two seemingly divergent measures tend to result in similar rankings, especially for the best performing assets. The correlation statistics are sophistry; they were included merely to make the student think in a discriminating manner.

PA16-2   The Jensen performance measure ranks portfolios according to the alpha (intercept term) calculated with regression analysis. The funds, ranked from highest to lowest are: $A_C = 4.27\%$, $A_D = 3.46\%$, $A_B = 2.03\%$, $A_E = 1.18\%$, and $A_A = -0.24\%$. As noted in the textbook, however, these alpha values should be risk-adjusted by dividing them by the standard error of the estimate to make them suitable for performance ranking purposes.

PA16-3   Portfolio rankings using the Sharpe measure, SHARPE, are shown below:

$$SHARPE_i = \frac{\bar{r} - RFR_i}{\sigma_i}$$

$$SHARPE_A = \frac{1.71 - 2.52}{7.42} = -0.109 \text{ (5th)}$$

$$SHARPE_B = \frac{3.68 - 2.52}{11.71} = 0.099 \text{ (3rd)}$$

$$SHARPE_C = \frac{6.02 - 2.52}{11.25} = 0.311 \text{ (1st)}$$

$$SHARPE_D = \frac{5.26 - 2.52}{10.78} = 0.254 \text{ (2nd)}$$

$$SHARPE_E = \frac{3.00 - 2.52}{10.64} = 0.045 \text{ (4th)}$$

PA16-4   Portfolio rankings using the Treynor measure, TREYNOR, are shown below:

$$TREYNOR_i = \frac{\bar{r_i} - RFR}{Beta_i}$$

$$TREYNOR_A = \frac{1.71 - 2.52}{1.08} = -0.75 \text{ (5th)}$$

$$TREYNOR_B = \frac{3.68 - 2.52}{1.62} = 0.72 \text{ (3rd)}$$

$$TREYNOR_C = \frac{6.02 - 2.52}{1.45} = 2.41 \text{ (1st)}$$

$$TREYNOR_D = \frac{5.26 - 2.52}{1.36} = 2.01 \text{ (2nd)}$$

$$TREYNOR_E = \frac{3.00 - 2.52}{1.30} = 0.37 \text{ (4th)}$$

PA16-5   Systematic risk is measured by the beta coefficient. Fund B has the largest beta coefficient, 1.62, and therefore, the most systematic risk.

PA16-6   Portfolio E has the lowest coefficient of determination ($R^2 = 0.68$). The coefficient of determination is simply the square of the correlation coefficient, so Portfolio E is the least correlated with the market.

PA16-7   Fund A has the highest coefficient of determination ($R^2 = 0.94$). It moves more closely with the market than the other funds.

PA16-8   The Sharpe performance measure, SHARPE, for the Guardian Fund is

$$SHARPE_G = \frac{\bar{r_G} - RFR}{\sigma_G} = \frac{3.65 - 2.026}{5.97} = 0.272.$$ The Treynor performance measure,

TREYNOR, for the Guardian Fund is $TREYNOR_G = \dfrac{\bar{r_G} - RFR}{Beta_G} = \dfrac{3.65 - 2.026}{0.8} = 2.03.$

PA16-9 The Sharpe performance measure, SHARPE, for the Acorn Fund is

$$SHARPE_A = \frac{\bar{r}_A - RFR}{\sigma_A} = \frac{4.15 - 2.026}{7.36} = 0.29.$$ The Treynor performance measure,

TREYNOR, for the Guardian Fund is $TREYNOR_A = \frac{\bar{r}_A - RFR}{Beta_A} = \frac{4.15 - 2.026}{1.00} = 2.124.$

PA16-10 Jensen's alpha for the Acorn and Guardian Funds are:

Acorn Fund: -0.252%
Guardian Fund: -0.253%

PA16-11 Acorn is more aggressive than Guardian because Acorn has the higher beta (1.0 > 0.8).

CFA Exam Solutions*

The following are the guideline answers provided by the AIMR for the CFA Exam questions:

1.   A

2.   i.   The Sharpe Ratio for Allocation D, using the risk-free rate of 4.5 percent, is: (.144 - .045)/.181 = .547.

     ii. The two allocations with the best Sharpe Ratios are A and E with ratios of 0.574 each.

3.   C

CHAPTER 17: FOREIGN EXCHANGE

SOLUTIONS

Questions

QA17-1   Multinational currency unions that existed prior to the European Monetary Union (EMU) failed because some of the independent central banks of the member nations pursued different monetary policies. For example, one member country's central bank might pursue inflationary monetary policies while another member country's central bank pursued non-inflationary monetary policies, and the conflicting monetary policies undermined the nations' attempt to share a common currency. The European Central Bank, in contrast, can keep the EMU from failing since it has the power to enforce inflation, deficit spending, and currency stability controls on all EMU member countries. The only way a member country can pursue independent economic policies is to withdraw form the EMU.

QA17-2   Abandoning the gold standard allows a government to expand its country's money supply without being encumbered by the need to purchase gold to back the newly created currency. This makes it easier for the government leaders to create enough new money to pay for whatever they want. However, if money supply is increased too rapidly, as has been done in some countries, inflation can result, and inflation erodes the purchasing power of that country's currency. High levels of inflation can negatively affect that nation's economy for years, even after the money supply's rapid growth has been brought back under control.

QA17-3   "Dirty float" refers to a system in which the financial markets determine the exchange rates, but governments are free to intervene and attempt to slow the speed with which exchange rate adjustments take place. Under this system, short-term fluctuations in foreign exchange rates are random and unpredictable.

QA17-4   The total risk faced by an investor who invests directly in a foreign security that is denominated in that same foreign country's currency is determined by three factors: (1) the uncertainty of the returns on the security, which is measured by the variance of the returns on the security; (2) the foreign currency risk; and (3) the comovement between the foreign security's return and the foreign currency's return, which is measured by the covariance between the two returns.

QA17-5   The expectations hypothesis for foreign exchange states that the foreign exchange spot rate that is expected today to exist during the next time period is equal to the value of today's forward rate for delivery at that time. This means that if the 6-month forward rate for British pounds is quoted at $1.6542 per pound today, then the spot exchange rate for the British pound and the U.S. dollar in 6 months is expected to be $1.6542 per pound.

QA17-6   If the inflation rate in the U.S. is 3% and the inflation rate in Denmark is 10%, you would expect the U.S. dollar to appreciate relative to that of the Danish krone (specifically by [(1.10/1.03) - 1.0 = 6.8%]). If this did not occur, then the goods that Denmark exports to the U.S. would be overpriced while exports from the U.S. to Denmark would be underpriced. The value of the Danish krone would be expected to drop since the demand for the overpriced Danish goods would drop. At the same time, the value of the U.S. dollar would be expected to increase as the demand for the underpriced American goods increases.

QA17-7   While uncovered interest rate parity is a useful way to think, it is not used to make predictions for three reasons. First, the difference between two countries' nominal interest rates must be determined based on equally risky assets. This can be problematic if the government bonds of the two countries have different levels of sovereign risk. Secondly, the expected future spot rate term, $E(SP_1)$, in the model is difficult to measure. Third, the foreign exchange adjustments that are required to derive the model in terms of a common currency make using the model cumbersome.

QA17-8   Purchasing power parity (PPP) is an equilibrium economic theory that says that identical goods should sell at the same prices around the world if they are priced in a common currency and if no barriers to trade exists. PPP implies that if the inflation rates in two countries are different, then the value of the currency of the country with the higher rate of inflation must depreciate relative to the value of the currency of the country with the lower inflation rate. Unfortunately, PPP has no ability to explain short-run (monthly) movements in foreign exchange rates and very little ability to explain year-to-year changes. This is due to our inability to measure inflation. There are several reasons for this. First, the items in the basket of goods that is used to calculate a country's price index changes continuously with the passage of time, and it is difficult for government research units to alter the basket of goods used to calculate the price index appropriately. Secondly, the basket of goods used to calculate a country's price index differs among countries. Thirdly, most inflation measures are based on historical data, but decisions are typically based on expectations of inflation, not historical inflation rates.

QA17-9   The Fisher open model explains differences in interest rates between two countries by differences in the countries' real rates and differences in their inflation rates. Therefore, if the real rates of interest for two countries are identical, any difference in their nominal rates of interest is attributed to differences in their expected inflation rates. The model is more useful for analyzing long-run relationships than it is as a forecasting tool due to the problem with measuring expected inflation. Too, if real rates differ from country to country, the model is difficult to use.

QA17-10   Covered interest parity arbitrage implies that the term structure of forward rates will slope upward at a rate equal to the inflation differential between two countries.

Problems

PA17-1   In theory, the futures price is the futures price that offers no opportunity to earn arbitrage profits. In other words, the returns on both currencies must be the same for the same holding period.

Futures price = $\$0.008333 \times (1 + 5\% \times 217/360)/(1 + 3\% \times 217/360) = \$0.00843167$

The day count is an essential part of these solutions. In this problem, there are 18 days from May 14 to 31, 30 days in June, 31 days in July, 31 days in August, 30 days in September, 31 days in October, 30 days in November, and 16 days from December 1 to 16. Thus, $18 + 30 + 31 + 31 + 30 + 31 + 30 + 16 = 217$.

PA17-2   The number of U.S. dollars to be received in exchange for one yen is $1/108.10 =$ $\$0.009251$.

PA17-3   The Swiss franc for delivery in 6 months is selling at a forward discount of 1.1%:
$(FP_1/SP_0) - 1.0 = (1.75/1.77) - 1.0 = -1.1\%$.

PA17-4   The exchange rate that existed when Pete purchased the stock was 1.8655 reals per dollar, so Pete paid $1/1.8655 = \$0.536$ for each share of Itaubanco stock. When he received the dividends and sold the stock, Pete was paid in reals when the exchange rate was 1.7980 reals per dollar, so Pete received $\$0.556$ for each real he received. Pete's rate of return is calculated as follows:

$$r_f = \frac{SP_t P_t - SP_{t-1} P_{t-1} + SP_t CF_t}{SP_{t-1} P_{t-1}} = \frac{0.556(160) - 0.536(153.99) + 0.556(9.50)}{0.536(153.99)} = 14.2\%.$$

PA17-5   The portion of Pete's return that is due to the return on the Itaubanco stock is 10%:

$$r_d = \frac{P_t - P_{t-1} + CF_t}{P_{t-1}} = \frac{160 - 153.99 + 9.50}{153.99} = 10.1\%.$$

The portion of Pete's return that is due to the foreign exchange gain is
$$\frac{0.556 - 0.536}{0.536} = 3.7\%.$$

PA17-6 SP_0 = Current spot rate = (Mexican peso/US\$)

SP_1 = Future spot rate = (Mexican peso/US\$)

INF_f = Inflation rate in Mexico

INF_d = Inflation rate in the U.S.

$$\frac{SP_1}{SP_0} = \frac{1 + INF_f}{1 + INF_d}$$

$$SP_1 = SP_0 \times \frac{1 + INF_f}{1 + INF_d} = 8.466 \text{ peso/US\$} \times \frac{1 + 15\%}{1 + 4\%} = 9.361 \text{ peso/US\$}$$

Thus, a currency with a relatively higher inflation rate tends to depreciate in the future.

PA17-7   In theory, the futures price must be the no-arbitrage futures price. The theoretical non-arbitrage price of four-month Euro futures = US\$1.1567 x (1 + 6% x 120/360)/(1 + 3% x 120/360) = US\$\$1.1682. Since the listed 4-month futures price is higher than the theoretical non-arbitrage price, we can make an arbitrage profit by selling the four-month Euro futures while buying Euro at the spot market.

PA17-8   The total risk faced by the American investor who invests in the Niwot Total
           Stock Index Fund is calculated as follows:

$$VAR(r_f) = VAR(r_c) + VAR(r_d) + \rho_{c,d}\sqrt{VAR(r_c)}\sqrt{VAR(r_d)}$$
$$= (5.81)^2 + (32.57)^2 + (-0.22)(5.81)(32.57) = 1{,}052.93$$

$$\sigma_f = \sqrt{1{,}052.93} = 32.45\%.$$

PA17-9   First, convert the conventional quotation into the quotation we use when applying
           the equation based on the PPP theory. 1.132 US$/Euro equals 0.8834 Euro/US$.

           SP_0 = Current spot rate = (Euro/US$)
           SP_1 = Expected spot rate one year from now = (Euro/US$)$_1$
           SP_2 = Expected spot rate two years from now = (Euro/US$)$_2$
           INF_f = Inflation rate in the Euro Zone
           INF_d = Inflation rate in the United States

$$SP_2 = SP_1 \times \frac{1+INF_f}{1+INF_d} = SP_0 \times \frac{(1+INF_f)^2}{(1+INF_d)^2} = 0.8834 \text{ Euro/US\$} \times \frac{(1+3\%)^2}{(1+2\%)^2} .$$
$$= 0.9008 \text{ Euro/US\$}$$

PA17-10 $SP_1 = SP_0 \times \dfrac{1+INF_d}{1+INF_f} = \text{US\$}0.6105 \times \dfrac{1.032}{1.12} = \text{US\$}0.5625.$ Thus, the dollar will
           appreciate relative to the deutschemark.

CFA Exam Solutions*

The following are the guideline answers provided by the AIMR for the CFA Exam questions:

1.   B
      Solution:

$$F = S \times \frac{1+r_{\$}}{1+r_{DM}} = 1.70x(1.05/1.04)$$
$$= 1.716$$

2.   C

3.   **Part A**

      Purchasing power parity (PPP) is the concept that goods should have equal real prices in any
      country. Thus, the same amount of money should be able to purchase the same basket of goods
      in any country after conversion to that country's currency. If the domestic inflation rate is lower
      than a foreign country's rate then the foreign country's currency must depreciate relative to the
      domestic currency. For a pair of countries, the country with the higher rate of inflation will have
      a depreciating foreign exchange rate. So, if a foreign trading partner's inflation rate is higher than

a domestic trading partner's inflation rate, foreign goods will become more expensive unless the foreign currency becomes "cheaper," declines in value relative to the domestic currency.

Part B

Reasons why PPP might not hold in the short run: (1) The definition and measurement of inflation rates are imprecise because different goods are included in different countries' price indexes or consumption brackets. (2) Suitable substitute goods for imports may not be available domestically; accordingly, there would be no pressure on exchange rates. (3) Transportation costs can prevent arbitrage in the goods market. (4) Changes in the patterns of capital flows can influence exchange rates. (5) Central bank intervention in the foreign exchange market can influence exchange rates. (6) Speculative activity in the foreign exchange market can influence rates. (7) The choice of a base period is important; the initial date selected might not represent an equilibrium position. (8) Government-imposed barriers to trade, including tariffs and quotas, distort prices between countries.

Part C

Empirically, PPP has been shown to hold over longer periods of time. Thus, although deviations from PPP may persist for extended periods, the concept can be used, given assumptions about future inflation differentials, to indicate long-term trends in exchange rates. Having an indication of the potential direction of foreign currency movements might aid an analyst in the evaluation of foreign investments. The information might also be useful in asset allocation decisions and evaluating hedging strategies.

4. **A.** **Relative Purchasing Power Parity**

    i. *Definition.* Purchasing power parity (PPP) is a well-known relation in international finance. PPP comes in two versions: absolute PPP and relative PPP. Absolute PPP asserts the "law of one price"' that is, the real price of any good must be the same in all countries. Relative PPP focuses on overall inflation rates in two countries and claims that exchange rate movements should offset any inflation differential in the two countries. It states that the spot, or immediate delivery, exchange rate adjusts perfectly to inflation differences between two countries.

    Algebraically, relative PPP can be summarized as

$$\frac{S^1}{S^0} = \frac{1+I_F}{1+I_D}$$

    where S^0 is the spot exchange rate (the foreign price of one unit of domestic currency) at time zero, S^1 is the spot exchange rate at time 1, I_F is the foreign inflation rate, and I_D is the domestic inflation rate.

    If relative PPP holds in the short run, the real return on an asset the foreign investor can expect to (and will) receive will be the same real rate of return as the domestic investor receives on the same asset. This is because PPP implies that the differences in inflation rates between countries are offset by appreciation or depreciation of the currency of the foreign investor. Thus, both domestic and foreign investors achieve the same equalized real rate of return because the currency adjustment offsets any inflation differential. Exchange rate movements mirror inflation differentials and equalize returns on assets across countries for both the foreign and the domestic investor.

ii.   *Reason why assumption that relative PPP holds leads to same returns.*
If relative PPP holds in the sort run, the real return on an asset the foreign investor can expect to (and will) receive will be the same real rate of return as the domestic investor receives on the same asset. This is because PPP implies that differences in inflation rates between countries are offset by appreciation or depreciation of the currency of the foreign investor. Thus, both domestic and foreign investors achieve the same equalized real rate of return because the currency adjustment offsets any inflation differential. Exchange rate movements mirror inflation differentials and equalize returns on assets across countries for both the foreign and domestic investor.

B.   Interest Rate Parity

i.   *Definition.* The interest rate parity relation states that the interest rate differential between two countries must equal the forward discount (or premium) in the currency market. In other words, the forward exchange rate is equal to the spot exchange rate multiplied by any interest rate differential.

Algebraically, interest rate parity can be summarized as

$$\frac{F}{S^0} = \frac{1+r_F}{1+r_D} \text{ or } F = \frac{1+r_F}{1+r_D}(S^0),$$

where F is the current forward exchange rate, S^0 is the current spot exchange rate, and r_F and r_D are the current foreign and domestic interest rates, respectively.

ii.   *Why interest rate parity must hold.* If interest rate parity does not hold, a riskless arbitrage opportunity will exist. Here is an example of how covered interest arbitrage would take place to exploit the discrepancy in the asset pricing:

Suppose: Spot exchange rate FF/US$ = 8
                1-year French interest rate = 14%
                1-year U.S. interest rate = 10%

A speculator could immediately borrow dollars at 10 percent and convert them to French francs at 8 to the U.S. dollar. The investor would then invest the francs at 14% and earn a profit of 4% but would run the risk of franc depreciation. The transaction could be turned into a riskless interest rate arbitrage by simultaneously purchasing a forward exchange contract to convert francs to dollars at a known forward rate in one year. However, the implied forward exchange rate should adjust so that it squeezes out any riskless arbitrage opportunity.

If markets are free and available to speculators, interest rate parity must hold after taking into account transaction costs.

CHAPTER 18: GLOBAL INVESTING

SOLUTIONS

Questions

QA18-1   Since foreign securities are usually denominated in foreign currencies, one foreign investment involves two separate investments. The foreign investor must first buy the foreign currency that is needed. Then, the foreign currency is used to purchase the foreign security. When the investment is liquidated, the foreign security is sold and foreign currency, which must be exchanged for the domestic currency of the investor, is received. Thus a foreign investment is actually an investment in the foreign security *and* an investment in the foreign currency at the same time.

QA18-2   There are several additional risks that are peculiar to international investing, namely (a) country (or sovereign) risk, (b) foreign exchange risk, and (c) the risk that the foreign investor cannot obtain the needed investment information as readily as domestic investors in the foreign country. This latter risk, the information risk, puts the foreign investor at a competitive disadvantage relative to the domestic investors in the foreign country--after all, information has value. Finally, (d) there is international liquidity risk. Foreign markets are frequently inefficient, thin, illiquid, and they sometimes get manipulated (since security price manipulation is not illegal in some foreign countries.)

QA18-3   The correlation coefficients between securities markets in different countries are typically lower than the correlations attainable by investing in domestic markets. Markowitz portfolio analysis, when viewed in an international context, demonstrates that low inter-country correlations are the key to risk-reducing international diversification. See Figure 18-2 in the textbook. The international efficient frontier becomes more dominant as the investment opportunities were expanded to include more countries.

QA18-4   Not every international market is worthwhile to enter. The efficient frontier, depicted in Figure 18-2, shows that investing in the emerging markets was a lucrative opportunity at the time of the investigation. Any investment must offer (i) a good rate of return, or, (ii) good risk reduction possibilities, and/or (iii) some combination of both (i) and (ii) to be desirable.

QA18-5   Different countries have political systems that differ substantially (for example, capitalism versus socialism), different currencies (such as Mexican pesos and Japanese yen), different foreign exchange regulations (for example, fixed versus floating exchange rates), different trade restrictions (such as import and export limitations and tariffs), different political alliances (such as several emerging market countries versus the developed market countries), and various other kinds of barriers to international trade. Furthermore, different countries may be at different phases in their business cycles. (For example, the U.S. may be starting a recovery just as some other countries are in the trough of a recession.) They may also be in differing military postures (such as peace versus cold war versus hot war) at the same time. As a result of all of these important differences, the different countries' security markets are not expected to be highly synchronized or highly positively correlated. Stated differently, the differences listed above cause international financial markets to be at least partially segmented rather than fully integrated (homogeneous).

QA18-6 Myron can invest in Toyota American Depository Receipts (ADRs). Toyota ADRs are traded in the U.S. security markets; the Toyota stock prices are listed in American newspapers such as the WALL STREET JOURNAL (see the ADR Section) daily in U. S. dollars; and all of Toyota's cash dividends will be paid in U. S. dollars so that Myron will not have to bother with foreign exchange transactions.

QA18-7 Yes, Ralph (or anyone else) can buy shares in international investment companies that own diversified portfolios of foreign investments. The shares in these funds are actively traded in liquid U.S. markets. For example, the Japan Fund, the Thai Fund and the Korea Fund are all closed-end investment companies that own diversified portfolios of stocks in the countries after which they are named. In addition, there are several dozen mutual funds in the U. S. and in other countries that specialize in particular kinds of international investments.

QA18-8 Increasing integration among the countries of the world should cause a slow increase in the inter-country correlations between security markets and other economic measures with the passage of time. Specific factors contributing to this trend are the following: (a) increased international lending by banks, (b) the expansion of the multinational operations of the large companies, (for example, Coca-Cola and Ford Motor Company make more sales outside the U.S. than within the U.S., and many large firms around the world are increasing their international investments), (c) more foreign companies investing in the U.S., (d) a few powerful financial centers (such as New York City, London, and Tokyo), which are each dominated by a handful of large companies, exerting increasing influence on the world's economy, (e) the political moves away from communism toward increasingly capitalistic systems, (Russia initiated this in the 1990s and started a swing to the right politically that might have affected other nations similarly.)

QA18-9 Unfortunately, researchers have concluded that investments in multinational corporations (MNCs) such as AT&T do not provide as much international diversification as investing in an internationally diversified portfolio of securities. The variability in an MNC's stock returns are largely determined by variations in the MNC's domestic stock markets. An investigation of nine countries showed that between 69 and 93 percent of those countries' MNC's variability could be explained by simultaneous variability in the headquarters countries' stock market indexes. (A related study did indicate that as the percentage of an MNC's sales that occur outside of its domestic market increase, the MNC's dependency on (or correlation with) its domestic stock market tends to decrease.) Susan would be better off buying shares in an investment company that specializes in investment in foreign companies. She would not have to worry about exchange rate risk in that case, either. Investing through an ADR would be another option for Susan, but since this would represent an investment in just one company in one foreign country, she would not achieve as much international diversification benefits as she could with an investment company.

QA18-10 ADRs on stocks that are issued by large, well-known international corporations, sponsored by the issuer, and listed on an organized stock exchange in the U.S. are highly liquid. Those issuers that sponsor their own ADR issues provide complete financial statements in foreign languages and even pay the ADRs' fees. Unfortunately, many ADRs are unsponsored. In this case, the ADR investors must pay the ADR fees. The investor in an unsponsored ADR may not be provided a complete set of financial statements that are neatly translated into English, either. Many ADRs are not listed on organized exchanges, instead trading in the over-the-counter (OTC) market. Some of these are traded in an inactive part of the OTC market by being listed on pink sheets that are updated weekly. Unsponsored ADRs that are issued by obscure corporations and are traded in this manner are not very liquid. (However, some well-known, large corporations whose ADRs are liquid prefer to have them traded via the pink sheets instead of being listed on an organized exchange in order to avoid costly disclosure requirements and stringent accounting conventions that exist in the U.S.) A second problem is that the investor in an ADR may not get any voting power. Some depository banks are allowed to vote on behalf of the ADR shareholders under certain circumstances.

Another problem that the investor in an ADR can face is high price volatility in the country in which the issuing firm of the ADR is headquartered. This is a problem that frequently exists in emerging market countries where the securities' markets are small, illiquid, and unregulated. There may also be more complicated tax regulations to which the foreign income is subject, and it is also more difficult for an investor to follow the news about a foreign security than it is to follow the domestic news.

Problems

PA18-1   The currency statistics are below:

Correlation Matrix				Standard deviations
	U.S.	U.K.	Japan	
U.S.	1.000			21.843%
U.K.	0.659	1.000		46.754%
Japan	0.389	0.152	1.000	43.092%

Note: The standard deviation formula is given in the solutions to the portfolio analysis chapter -- Chapter 14.

PA18-2   The correlation of the returns for Australia and Canada is 0.747. The standard deviations for the returns of Australia and Canada are 28.867% and 21.407%, respectively.

PA18-3   The expected return from the 25-25-50 portfolio is 17.894%, and the standard deviation is:

$$\sigma = \sqrt{136.5392 + 116.0468 + 119.2464 + 38.39238 + 168.1516 + 91.52058}$$
$$= \sqrt{669.897} = 25.88\%.$$

PA18-4   The 60-40 portfolio's expected return is 13.95%, and the standard deviation is:

$$\sigma = \sqrt{133.3563 + 165.0197 + 221.6284}$$
$$= \sqrt{520.0044} = 22.80361\%.$$

PA18-5   The standard deviation of the 50-50 portfolio is:

$$\sigma = \sqrt{119.2464 + 114.597 + 169.7368}$$
$$= \sqrt{403.5802} = 20.08931\%.$$

PA18-6   Last year, an American dollar would purchase 1.6224 deustchemarks , or $0.61637 = 1DM. This year it will buy 1.8342 deustchemarks, or $0.54520 = 1DM. Therefore, the loss on the German currency was $\dfrac{0.54520 - 0.61637}{0.61637} = -11.5\%$. The total gain is calculated as (1 + return on stocks)(1 + return on currency) - 1 = (1.17)(1 + -0.115) - 1 = 3.5%.

PA18-7   Bob earned a rate of return equal to $\dfrac{\text{price change}}{\text{purchase price}}$ = (price change)/(purchase price), or

¥310/¥2,680 = 11.6% on his 3-month investment in AIWA. However, Bob earned a negative return on his investment in yen for the 3-month period. When he bought AIWA 1 yen was worth 1/117.60 = $0.0085034, but when he sold AIWA 1 yen was worth only 1/123.50= $0.0080971. The rate of return on the yen was ($0.0080971 - $0.0085034)/$0.0085034 = -4.78%. His total return was, therefore, (1.116)(1 + -0.0478) -1 = 6.27%.

PA18-8 An exchange rate of 117.60 yen per dollar means that 1 yen is worth 1/117.60 = $0.008503. If Nissan was selling for 441 yen, then the price per share in U.S. currency was 441 x $0.008503 = $3.7498. The discrepancy in the price of the Nissan ADR and the price of Nissan on the Tokyo exchange is not necessarily indicative of a market inefficiency. There are several explanations for this. First, an ADR is not always issued for one share of the issuing firm's stock. It may be for more than one share. Secondly, since dividends on an ADR are paid in dollars, the investor does not have to bother with foreign exchange transactions. This benefit is priced into the ADR. ADRs also reduce some other risks associated with foreign investments, such as fraud, and this would also be reflected in the price of the ADR.

PA18-9 An American investor in a British stock like Barclay's would be a foreign investor who must exchange dollars for British pounds in order to complete the transaction. The return is calculated as (1 + return on stock)(1 + return on currency) - 1 = (1.10)(1.05) - 1 = 15.5%.

PA18-10 (a) Rolf had to pay 26,990 x $0.1800 per share of the Swiss stock, or $4,858.20.

(b) Rolf earned $\dfrac{(\$0.175)(28,100) - \$4,858.20}{\$4,858.20} = \dfrac{\$59.30}{\$4858.20} = 1.22\%$ on his investment.

(c) Rolf's gain on his investment in the stock was $\dfrac{SF\,28,100 - SF\,26,990}{SF\,26,990} = 4.11\%$, but he lost

$\dfrac{\$0.1750}{\$0.1800} - 1 = -2.78\%$ on his investment in Swiss francs over the same period.
R = (1.0411)(1+ -0.0278) - 1.0 = 1.22%.

CFA Exam Solutions*

The following are the guideline answers provided by the AIMR for the CFA Exam questions:

1. D

2. A

3. A. The consultant is alluding to the behavior of cross-country equity return correlations during different market phases, as reported in various research studies. Specifically, the consultant is referring to the fact that correlations in down markets tend to be significantly higher than correlations in up markets. In other words, equity markets appear to be more correlated when they are falling than when they are rising.

One of the reasons why investors invest in equity markets abroad is to reduce the risk of large losses. That is, when the domestic market is expected to fall, some other market may be expected to rise, thus reducing the impact of price declines in the overall equity portfolio. Unfortunately, the evidence referred to above suggests that global equity investing may not prove to be very helpful in terms of avoiding large losses in the total equity portfolio (i.e., when protection is needed the most). If markets are highly correlated when they are falling, then it will be unlikely for foreign equity markets to rise when the U.S. market is expected to fall. In such a situation, benefits from international diversification are likely to be substantially reduced. The implication is that in the short run, average historical correlations will overestimate investment performance if the equity markets happen to be in a down-market phase.

B.   Although cross-country equity return correlations can vary significantly in the short run, they remain surprisingly low when measured over long periods of time. This implies that, from a policy standpoint, international investing still offers the potential to construct more efficient portfolios, in a risk-return trade-off sense, than ones constructed using domestic assets only. This is so because global investing has the *potential* to reduce risk without sacrificing returns, even with adverse short-run outcomes.

For example, Odier and Solnik show that the average correlation of the U.S. equity market with 16 other equity markets was only slightly higher than the correlation of U.S. stocks with U.S. bonds. Yet research on past data show the potential for achieving higher returns is much larger with 16 foreign stock markets than with U.S. bonds.

4.   Expected Return

	Germany	Japan	United States
Return Premium	6% - 4% = 2%	7% - 6% = 1%	8% - 7% = 1%
Currency Premium	2% + 4% = 6%	-1% + 6% = 5%	7%

or

	Japan Local	DM Exchange		DM Yield	Yen Yield	
Green	7%	+ 2%	+	(4%	- 6%)	= 7%

	German U.S. Local	Exchange		U.S. Yield	DM Yield	
Advisor	6%	+ 0%	+	(7%	- 4%)	= 9%

- Complete return includes the return on the local market, the expected return on currency, and the cost/benefit of holding that currency.

- The cost is the differential of the respective one-year Eurodeposit yields.

- Green forgot to include the cost of holding currency in his assessment.

5.   An allocation to emerging markets can reduce the overall risk of a portfolio that is invested in developed markets because of two characteristics of cross-country return correlations. First, emerging markets need not have high volatility. For example, according to Divecha, Drach, and Stefek, the volatility of the BARRA Emerging World Universe from February 1986 to March 1991 was only 28 percent although markets in many individual countries in this universe had volatilities above 50 percent in the same period. Second, emerging markets individually and as a group have had low correlations with developed markets. For instance, the correlation between

the International Finance Corporation's Emerging Markets Composite Index and the Financial Times/Standard & Poor's Actuaries World Index was only 0.35 in the February 1986-March 1991 period.

CHAPTER 19: GLOBAL BOND MARKETS

SOLUTIONS

Questions

QA19-1(a)   **OATS** are bonds issued by the French government. OATS stands for Obligations Assimilables du Tresors.

(b)   **Bunds** are bonds issued by the German government's Deutsche bank.

(c)   **Yankee bonds** are bonds issued by a foreign entity, denominated in U.S. dollars, and sold in the United. States. American investment bankers register the issue with the SEC.

(d)   **Shogun bonds** are bonds issued in Japan by non-Japanese borrowers that are denominated in non-yen currencies.

(e)   **Bulldog bonds** are bonds issued by non-British entities that are sold in Britain and denominated in British pound sterling.

QA19-2   Not quite. The ABS bond prices are not market prices that are determined by the natural forces of supply and demand as are the prices of stocks trading on the NYSE. Matrix prices are used for most of the bonds in the ABS. These are estimates of bond prices, which are based on quotations from bonds that have similar coupon rates, maturities, quality ratings, and indenture provisions. The ABS provides neither a liquid market nor a market that is free from internal arbitrage opportunities. Large orders to buy or sell a particular bond will be unlikely to be executed in full at the posted prices.

QA19-3   The two types of political risk faced by international bond investors are repatriation-of-funds risk and sovereign risk. **Repatriation-of-funds risk** is the risk that a government will block payments of principal or interest that is owed to foreign creditors. **Sovereign risk** is the risk that a government will refuse to honor its debts.

QA19-4   **Domestic bonds** are bonds that are issued by a domestic firm, are denominated in the domestic currency, and are regulated by the government of the country in which they are issued. **Foreign bonds** are issued in one country and currency by a bond issuer from another country. They are usually traded in the country of issuance and are regulated by the country of issuance. **Eurobonds** are underwritten by an international investment banking syndicate and are issued in several national markets simultaneously. The currency of denomination for these bonds may or may not correspond to the issuer'' home currency.

QA19-5   Yankee bonds are issued by non-U.S. firms and sold in the U.S. They are denominated in dollars. These bonds are underwritten by American investment banking firms and are registered with the SEC. They are taxed and regulated by the U.S. government. Eurodollar bonds are, in contrast, underwritten by an international investment banking syndicate. They are also denominated in dollars, but are issued into several national markets simultaneously. They are neither taxed nor regulated by any government entity.

QA19-6   Eurodollar bonds are neither taxed nor regulated by any government entity. An American issuer, therefore, can often obtain the proceeds from a Eurodollar bond issue much faster than from a domestic bond issue since domestic bonds have to be registered with the SEC. Due to the lack of regulation, an American firm may find the administrative costs associated with the issuance of a Eurodollar bond to be less as well. An American investor might prefer a Eurodollar bond because the income is not taxed. While this is reflected in lower yields offered by a Eurodollar bond, an investor who wishes to evade taxes might prefer a Eurodollar bond to a domestic bond.

QA19-7   Its yield-to-call is more relevant under the circumstances. If the bond is selling at a premium, then market rates have fallen since its initial issue. If you expect the current rate to remain fairly stable, the issuing firm will, in all likelihood, call in the bonds at the first opportunity, perhaps replacing it with new, lower coupon bonds.

QA19-8   The yield-to-maturity calculation assumes that the coupon payments will be reinvested at that same rate. Since Tzu-chia accumulated her payments in a savings account that paid only 5% interest, she did not earn the 10% yield-to-maturity on this investment. She earned a lesser return.

QA19-9   Brady bonds were created to allow emerging countries to finance their debt until they were able to pay it off. The banks in emerging countries could exchange their illiquid defaulted bank loans for the more liquid Brady bonds. The **discount bonds** are usually floating rate coupon bonds with maturities of 25 to 30 years. These bonds are issued at a deep discount from the par value of the defaulted debts they replace, but are not themselves original issue discount bonds. The **par bond**, on the other hand, has a face value that is equal to the par value of the defaulted debts. They are long-term bonds that typically pay coupon interest, but the coupon rate of the par bonds is set well below current market rates, thus providing for the debt reduction. As a result, these bonds do sell at an original issue discount. **Debt-conversion bonds (DCBs)** and **new-money bonds (NMBs)** are usually floating rate bonds that are amortized progressively over 20 to 25 years. These are typically issued in conjunction under the Brady plan's new-money option to motivate debt holders to invest new money into the emerging country. The DCBs have features that make them more attractive than other types of Brady bonds, but still less attractive than other competitive bonds. Each dollar invested in an NMB can typically be converted into $5 worth of the more desirable DCBs. This provides an incentive to investors to purchase the NMBs. **Front-loaded interest-reduction bonds (FLIRBs)** are usually 19-year bonds that pay low coupons during their early years, thus providing a front-loaded debt forgiveness feature. After several initial years of low fixed coupons, the coupon rate is increased to a higher fixed rate for a period of several additional years. In the final years, FLIRBS usually pay floating rates. Principal repayments are made continually over the life of the bond, and a rolling-interest guarantee is provided during the early years of the bond's life. **Past-due interest bonds (PDIs)** are issued to pay interest payments that were left unpaid in the past. Some PDIs are called floating rate bonds and others are called interest due and unpaid bonds.

QA19-10   Investing in a bond that is denominated in a foreign currency involves two separate transactions. First, the investor must purchase the foreign currency, and then the foreign currency is used to buy the bond. If the foreign currency component is to be hedged, the investor must take a short position in the foreign currency. Then, if the foreign currency depreciates in value, the loss will be offset by the investor's gain from the short position. The short position typically is taken in the forward market at the same bank and at the same time that the foreign currency is purchased. Whether or not such a hedge is worthwhile is an issue that is hotly debated. Many economists argue that the foreign currency prices already reflect the expected average movement of the foreign exchange prices, making it impossible to capture any long-run average gains from unhedged currency trading. On the other hand, if the foreign currency rates include an embedded risk premium or discount, it may be possible to capture some small additional returns from unhedged foreign exchange transactions. In practice, the decision to take an unhedged position or a hedged position depends on the currency involved and the particular period of time.

Problems

PA19-1(a)   The first interest payment is 3 months away, so it gets discounted for only one-half of the 6-month period. The final coupon and principal payment is 4.5 periods from today. Therefore, the clean price is calculated as follows:

$$\text{Clean price} = \frac{\$50}{(1.04)^{0.5}} + \frac{\$50}{(1.04)^{1.5}} + \frac{\$50}{(1.04)^{2.5}} + \frac{\$50}{(1.04)^{3.5}} + \frac{\$1,050}{(1.04)^{4.5}}$$

$$= \$49.029 + \$47.143 + \$45.330 + \$43.587 + \$880.115$$

$$= \$1,065.20.$$

(b)   The dirty price is equal to the clean price plus the accrued coupon payment. The accrued coupon payment is calculated as follows:

$$\left(\begin{array}{c} \text{coupon payment} \\ \text{for relevant period} \end{array} \right) \left(\frac{\begin{array}{c} \text{number of days} \\ \text{since last coupon} \end{array}}{\begin{array}{c} \text{number of days between} \\ \text{scheduled coupon payments} \end{array}} \right) = \$50(0.5) = \$25.$$

The dirty price = $1,065.20 + $25.00 = $1,090.20.

PA19-2(a)   The bond equivalent yield involves solving the following equation for the ytm:

$$PV = \frac{\frac{coupon_1}{2}}{(1 + \frac{ytm}{2})^1} + \frac{\frac{coupon_2}{2}}{(1 + \frac{ytm}{2})^2} + \ldots \frac{\frac{coupon_{2T}}{2} + par\,value}{(1 + \frac{ytm}{2})^{2T}}$$

$$\$770.60 = \frac{\$40}{(1 + \frac{ytm}{2})^1} + \frac{\$40}{(1 + \frac{ytm}{2})^2} + \ldots + \frac{\$1,040}{(1 + \frac{ytm}{2})^{20}}$$

Using trial and error or a financial calculator, we determine that $\frac{ytm}{2} = 6\%$; therefore, ytm = 6% x 2 = 12%.

(b)   The effective yield to maturity is calculated using the following equation:

$$PV = \frac{\frac{coupon_1}{2}}{(1+EYTM)^{0.5}} + \frac{\frac{coupon_2}{2}}{(1+EYTM)^{1.0}} + ... \frac{\frac{coupon_T}{2}+par\,value}{(1+EYTM)^{T}}$$

$$\$770.60 = \frac{\$40}{(1+EYTM)^{0.5}} + \frac{\$40}{(1+EYTM)^{1.0}} + ... + \frac{\$1,040}{(1+EYTM)^{10}}$$

Using a financial calculator, EYTM = 12.36%.

PA19-3(a)   The bond equivalent yield is calculated using the following equation to solve for ytm:

$$PV = \frac{\frac{coupon_1}{2}}{(1+\frac{ytm}{2})^{1}} + \frac{\frac{coupon_2}{2}}{(1+\frac{ytm}{2})^{2}} + ... \frac{\frac{coupon_{2T}}{2}+par\,value}{(1+\frac{ytm}{2})^{2T}}$$

$$\$1,058.26 = \frac{\$45}{(1+\frac{ytm}{2})^{1}} + \frac{\$45}{(1+\frac{ytm}{2})^{2}} + ... + \frac{\$1,045}{(1+\frac{ytm}{2})^{16}}$$

Using trial and error or a financial calculator, we determine $\frac{ytm}{2} = 4\%$, so ytm = 4% x 2 = 8%.

(b)   The effective yield-to-maturity is calculated using the following equation:

$$PV = \frac{\frac{coupon_1}{2}}{(1+EYTM)^{0.5}} + \frac{\frac{coupon_2}{2}}{(1+EYTM)^{1.0}} + ... \frac{\frac{coupon_T}{2}+par\,value}{(1+EYTM)^{T}}$$

$$\$1,058.26 = \frac{\$45}{(1+EYTM)^{0.5}} + \frac{\$45}{(1+EYTM)^{1.0}} + ... + \frac{\$1,045}{(1+EYTM)^{8}}$$

Using a financial calculator, we determine EYTM = 8.16%.

PA19-4(a)   The yield-to-maturity for the Eurodollar bond, which makes annual interest payments is calculated as follows:

$$PV = \frac{coupon_1}{(1+ytm)^{1}} + \frac{coupon_2}{(1+ytm)^{2}} + ... + \frac{coupon_T+par\,value}{(1+ytm)^{T}}$$

$$\$1,071.60 = \frac{\$100}{(1+ytm)^{1}} + \frac{\$100}{(1+ytm)^{2}} + ... + \frac{\$1100}{(1+ytm)^{12}}$$

Solving for ytm, using either trial and error or a financial calculator, results in a yield-to-maturity of 9%.

(b)

(i) At a reinvestment rate of 0%, the investor will receive simply $1,200 in coupons, with no interest earned on interest, and $1,000 face value at maturity, so his realized yield is calculated as follows:

$$\$2,200 = \$1,071.60(1+r)^{12}$$

$$r = \sqrt[12]{\frac{\$2,200}{\$1,071.60}} - 1 = 6.18\%.$$

(ii) At a reinvestment rate of 5%, the future value of the coupons will be $\$100\sum_{t=1}^{12}(1.05)^{12-t} = \$1,591.71$. Therefore, the value of his investment at the end of year twelve is $\$1,000 + \$1,591.71 = \$2,591.71$. The realized return is

$$\$2,591.71 = \$1,071.60(1+r)^{12}$$

$$r = \sqrt[12]{\frac{\$2,591.71}{\$1,071.60}} - 1 = 7.64\%.$$

PA19-5(a) There are 19 years left to maturity when Rosemary plans to sell the bond. The price she can expect to receive is determined by a potential buyer's expected cash flows from this point on, discounted at the new required rate of return of 10%.

$$\text{Price} = \$90\sum_{t=1}^{10}\frac{1}{(1.10)^t} + \$1,000\left(\frac{1}{(1.10)^{19}}\right) = \$916.35$$

(b) Rosemary's holding period return is calculated as follows:

$$r = \frac{(P_1 - P_0) + CF}{P_0} = \frac{(\$916.35 - \$1,000) + \$90}{\$1,000} = 0.635\%.$$

PA19-6(a) The yield-to-maturity is calculated as follows:

$$PV = \frac{\dfrac{coupon_1}{2}}{(1+\dfrac{ytm}{2})^1} + \frac{\dfrac{coupon_2}{2}}{(1+\dfrac{ytm}{2})^2} + \ldots \frac{\dfrac{coupon_{2T}}{2} + par\,value}{(1+\dfrac{ytm}{2})^{2T}}$$

$$\$1,153.72 = \frac{\$60}{(1+\dfrac{ytm}{2})^1} + \frac{\$60}{(1+\dfrac{ytm}{2})^2} + \ldots + \frac{\$1,060}{(1+\dfrac{ytm}{2})^{30}}$$

Using trial and error or a financial calculator, $\dfrac{ytm}{2}$ is determined to be 5%, so ytm = 5% x 2 = 10%.

(b) The yield-to-call is calculated using the following equation:

$$PV = \frac{\dfrac{coupon_1}{2}}{(1+\dfrac{ytc}{2})^1} + \frac{\dfrac{coupon_2}{2}}{(1+\dfrac{ytc}{2})^2} + ... + \frac{\dfrac{coupon_{time\ of\ 1st\ call}}{2} + call\ price}{(1+\dfrac{ytc}{2})^{number\ of\ periods\ to\ first\ call}}$$

$$\$1,153.72 = \frac{\$60}{(1+\dfrac{ytc}{2})^1} + \frac{\$60}{(1+\dfrac{ytc}{2})^2} + ... + \frac{\$60 + \$1,120}{(1+\dfrac{ytc}{2})^{14}}$$

Using a financial calculator, $\dfrac{ytc}{2}$ is determined to be 5.05%, so ytc = 5.05% x 2 = 10.10%.

PA19-7(a) The current yield on the bond is calculated by dividing the annual interest income on the bond by its current market price:

$$Current\ yield = \frac{\$100}{\$1,081.11} = 9.25\%.$$

(b) The yield-to-maturity on the bond is calculated using the following equation:

$$PV = \frac{\dfrac{coupon_1}{2}}{(1+\dfrac{ytm}{2})^1} + \frac{\dfrac{coupon_2}{2}}{(1+\dfrac{ytm}{2})^2} + ... \frac{\dfrac{coupon_{2T}}{2} + par\ value}{(1+\dfrac{ytm}{2})^{2T}}$$

$$\$1,081.11 = \frac{\$50}{(1+\dfrac{ytm}{2})^1} + \frac{\$50}{(1+\dfrac{ytm}{2})^2} + ... + \frac{\$1,050}{(1+\dfrac{ytm}{2})^{10}}$$

Using trial and error or a financial calculator, we determine $\dfrac{ytm}{2}$ = 4%, so ytm = 4% x 2 = 8%.

PA19-8(a) The price Jason paid should be equal to the present value of his expected future cash flows, discounted at the bond's yield-to-maturity of 6%.

$$Price = PV = \$70 \sum_{t=1}^{10} \frac{1}{(1.06)^t} + \$1,000\left(\frac{1}{(1.06)^{10}}\right) = \$1,073.60.$$

(b) The current yield is the annual interest income divided by the price Jason paid for the bond:

$$Current\ yield = \frac{\$70}{\$1,073.60} = 6.52\%.$$

(c)   One year later, the bond will have 9 years remaining to maturity. At the new yield of 8%, the price that Jason could receive for the bond is calculated as follows:

$$Price = \$70 \sum_{t=1}^{9} \frac{1}{(1.08)^t} + \$1,000 \left(\frac{1}{(1.08)^9} \right) = \$937.53.$$

His one-year holding period return is calculated as follows:

$$r = \frac{(P - P_{01}) + CF}{P_0} = \frac{(\$937.53 - \$1,073.60) + \$70}{\$1,073.60} = -6.15\%$$

PA19-9(a)   Since you purchased the bond for its par value, its yield-to-maturity is equal to the coupon rate on the bond, or 8%.

(b)   The future value of the coupon payments, including the interest earned on interest, is FV $= \$40 \sum_{t=1}^{16} (1.06)^{16-t} = \$1,026.90$, so the future value at the end of 8 years is $2,026.90, the sum of the value of the coupon payments and the face value of the bond. Therefore, the realized annual return on this investment is:

$$\$2,026.90 = \$1,000 \left(1 + \frac{r}{2} \right)^{16}$$

$$\frac{r}{2} = \sqrt[16]{\frac{\$2,026.90}{\$1,000}} - 1 = 4.51\%$$

$$r = 4.51\% \times 2 = 9.02\%.$$

PA19-10(a)   Using annual payments, the yield-to-maturity is calculated using the following equation:

$$PV = \frac{coupon_1}{(1 + ytm)^1} + \frac{coupon_2}{(1 + ytm)^2} + ... + \frac{coupon_T + par\,value}{(1 + ytm)^T}$$

$$\$1,050 = \frac{\$120}{(1 + ytm)^1} + \frac{\$120}{(1 + ytm)^2} + ... + \frac{\$1,120}{(1 + ytm)^5}$$

Using a financial calculator, we determine the ytm to be 10.66%.

(b)   If payments are made semiannually, the yield-to-maturity is calculated using the equation below:

$$PV = \frac{\frac{coupon_1}{2}}{(1 + \frac{ytm}{2})^1} + \frac{\frac{coupon_2}{2}}{(1 + \frac{ytm}{2})^2} + ... \frac{\frac{coupon_{2T}}{2} + par\,value}{(1 + \frac{ytm}{2})^{2T}}$$

$$\$1,050 = \frac{\$60}{(1 + \frac{ytm}{2})^1} + \frac{\$60}{(1 + \frac{ytm}{2})^2} + ... + \frac{\$1,060}{(1 + \frac{ytm}{2})^{10}}$$

A financial calculator indicates that $\dfrac{ytm}{2} = 5.34\%$, so the ytm $= 5.34\% \times 2 = 10.68\%$.

(c) If payments are made monthly, the yield-to-maturity is calculated using the following equation:

$$PV = \frac{\dfrac{coupon_1}{12}}{(1+\dfrac{ytm}{12})^1} + \frac{\dfrac{coupon_2}{12}}{(1+\dfrac{ytm}{12})^2} + ... \frac{\dfrac{coupon_{12T}}{12} + par\,value}{(1+\dfrac{ytm}{2})^{12T}}$$

$$\$1,050 = \frac{\$10}{(1+\dfrac{ytm}{12})^1} + \frac{\$10}{(1+\dfrac{ytm}{12})^2} + ... + \frac{\$1,010}{(1+\dfrac{ytm}{12})^{60}}$$

A financial calculator indicates that $\dfrac{ytm}{12} = 0.893\%$, so ytm $= 0.893\% \times 12 = 10.72\%$.

CFA Exam Solutions*

The following are the guideline answers provided by the AIMR for the CFA Exam questions:

1. C

2. B

3. B

4A. Both national and local government credits technically have sovereign powers. Therefore, an analyst must have an understanding of the rules and tools that government officials (the "management") use. The following are political risk factors that relate to the analysis of both sovereign and municipal debt:

1. **Political system of government.** A system that allows a smooth transition of power and a consistent approach to executing laws provides confidence in the strength of any agreements and continuity in the payment of debt service. A streamlined system with a clear delineation of power assures effective decision making when adverse conditions occur.

2. **Consistency of political ideologies.** A record of consistency in the basic ideologies suggests predictable future actions that allow making education assumptions about the continued payment of debt. This issue addresses political tendencies and the records of both those in power and their opponents.

3. **Cooperation within the community of governments or integration into political and financial arrangements with other governments.** Integration into the community of related governmental units enables a government to maximize its economic strengths by allowing free flow of commerce and investment and providing peaceful grounds on which to arbitrate disputes.

4. **Power of the people.** The power to vote gives people the ability to change laws, which affects a government's ability to generate revenues for the payment of debt. Racial, ethnic, labor, political, or religious instability can hurt regional security, adversely affect the economy, and reduce the government's ability to pay debts. Factors contributing to political and economic growth are the standard of living, income distribution, and education of the people.

5. **Political longevity and the mechanisms of succession.** Determining whether a government can succeed, prove its ability to maintain order and inspire economic growth, and withstand change takes time. Therefore, a history of success is a credit strength.

6. **Politics dictates the economic system.** The economic system is the basis for generating and distributing wealth. Those in power define and implement economic systems such as capitalism and socialism.

7. **Competency and integrity of leadership.** A government's creditworthiness is only as good as its leadership.

B. The following are economic risk factors that affect the ability of a government unit to pay its debt service:

1. **Endowment of natural resources.** Natural resources provide a means of generating revenues. For a national credit, they protect against large swings in currency valuation and ensure the availability of necessary raw materials.

2. **A well-diversified economy with a significant private sector**. A diversified industrial and commercial base cushions a government's revenues against adverse impacts from cyclical factors or declines in separate sectors of the economy.

3. **Prospects for economic growth and development.** The access to resources (e.g., human and natural), infrastructure (e.g., roads and ports), and laws conducive to capital investment enhance the prospects for economic growth. Therefore, a government with strong economic growth and development is likely to have the ability to pay debt service.

4. **Fiscal performance and monetary management.** A government with sound fiscal performance and monetary management is likely to meet its debt obligations. Large budget deficits create instability and may increase inflationary pressures and drain financial resources. Financial flexibility, including the ability to tax, affects a government's ability to generate revenues to pay its debts.

5. **Employment and cost of living (inflation).** The prospects of employment and a high standard of living generate confidence in the economy and a willingness to invest capital and labor to generate additional wealth. These factors are also a source of social stability associated with a better quality of life.

6. **Trade structure.** The nature of trade partly determines economic stability. Several factors affect the long-term ability to meet financial obligations, including the openness to trade, the diversification and competitiveness of exports, and sources of foreign exchange.

C. The following three factors contribute favorably to the ability of a nation to pay its external debts:

(i) **Sources of foreign exchange.** Diversified sources of foreign exchange provide stability to the flow of foreign exchange earnings. The goods offered for export must be in demand and competitively priced. Other sources of foreign exchange that strengthen a nation's credit are service revenues and transfers from workers who are abroad. Foreign direct and portfolio investments also generate foreign exchange.

(ii) **Composition of imports.** Imports of intermediate goods and goods that can be used to produce other goods provide the opportunity to generate additional exports, which generate additional earnings. The import of goods and services that add to the nation's infrastructure (e.g., materials for roads and ports) enhances a nation's ability to export more efficiently.

(iii) **Composition of exchange partners.** The reliability of suppliers and customers is crucial. A diversity of trade partners provides flexibility to sustain exchange earnings. Diversification of trade reduces risk.

5. **Part A**

The issue of whether to hedge the currency risk inherent in non-domestic investment exposures is a complex and hotly debated one. Good arguments exist on both sides of the issue. Because individual investors' goals, circumstances, and preferences vary, it is not possible to pronounce a final answer that will hold in all situations.

Arguments in favor of hedging:

1. Hedging can reduce international equity risk (volatility) by 19-25 percent.
2. Hedging can reduce international bond risk by 50-60 percent.
3. Hedging allows larger international allocations to be made, improving the diversification value of such investing.
4. Hedging allows larger equity allocations to be made, both domestic and international, providing higher expected returns and lower risk levels.
5. Hedging can maintain the match between FPI's non-domestic assets and its U.S.-dollar pension liability because, ultimately, benefits are paid in U.S. dollars.
6. A currency strategy can be overlaid on the hedging, creating an opportunity for additional returns (tactical or dynamic strategies).
7. Hedging allows a focus on security, industry, or country selection rather than currency movement.
8. A considerable portion of past good returns on international assets has been derived from weakness in the dollar, and hedging can protect against a secular reversal in the dollar's trend (i.e., strengthening of the dollar versus foreign currencies).
9. Hedging currency risk is important for a company with an underfunded pension plan and a weak balance sheet, such as FPI, because currency-related losses aggravate the financial position of such a company.
10. Hedging reduces the correlation between hedged foreign bonds and hedged foreign equities, allowing a greater allocation to these sectors.

Arguments against hedging:]

1. The costs of hedging (ranging between 20 and 100 basis points) can seriously reduce realized investment returns.
2. The cost is particularly high for bonds, which typically get about half their return from currency.
3. Hedging increases the correlation between domestic and foreign markets; consequently, it reduces the diversification benefit of international investing.

4. Some foreign currency exposure is desirable to protect against imported inflation from imported goods, which represent about 10 percent of total U.S. GDP.

5. Because pension funds have a long investment horizon and currency movements tend to revert or cancel out over time, currency hedging is unnecessary.

6. Hedging may not be worthwhile when the allocation to foreign securities is relatively small.

Part B

The chairman is wrong: Everything will not be working in FPI's favor because the stronger the dollar becomes relative to the currencies of other countries represented in the investment portfolio, the more the investment returns in dollar terms will be reduced.

Part C

In time, past relationships will indeed change as the committee member suggests they will. In particular, the following will almost certainly be noted:

1. Intercountry correlations will tend to rise, reducing the diversification benefit to be derived by a domestic investor as to specific other countries.

2. As these correlations rise among countries, the value of global investment in general as a diversifier for domestic portfolios will decline.

3. As investors become more active across country boundaries, information flows will increase and markets will become more efficient, possibly reducing the value of research seeking to exploit market inefficiency.

4. Increased efficiency within and across markets will act to reduce the risk premium for global investment in general and, possibly, reducing it significantly in particular (formerly the most inefficient) markets.

CHAPTER 20: MARKET INTEREST RATES

SOLUTIONS

Questions

QA20-1 One-year bonds should be affected only by expectations of inflation for one year ahead because one-year bonds will have matured by the end of the year. In contrast, the inflationary expectations for each of the next 20 years should concern the buyers of 20-year bonds because the purchasing power of their income and principal will be affected over this longer horizon.

 The phrase <u>level of interest rates</u> refers to whether interest rates are at a high level or a low level. In contrast, the <u>term structure of interest rates</u> refers to the shape of the yield curve. Studies of the term structure of interest rates have revealed that changes in interest rates associated with level changes have, historically, been greater than changes in interest rates due to changes in the term structure. This difference in magnitude is the main difference between level and structure changes. Changes in both the level and the structure tend to be related to the stages of the business cycle.

 The investor in the 20-year bonds should be concerned with both the level and the structure of interest rates since both will have an impact on the market value of his investment. In contrast, the investor in 1-year bonds cannot be affected much by changes in the term structure. Changes in the level of interest rates can have a larger effect, but even this effect is modest because a 1-year bond will soon mature and repay its face value regardless of the level or structure of market interest rates.

QA20-2 The yield curve might slope upward most of the time if (a) expectations of rising interest rates are more common than expectations of falling interest rates; and, (b) liquidity premiums tend to give the yield curve an upward slope. The yield curve might slope downward most of the time if (a) expectations of falling interest rates became prevalent; and, (b) demands for bonds in the long-term segment of the yield curve is stronger than demand for short bonds, as suggested by the segmentation theory.

QA20-3 Each Treasury issue used when attempting to draw a Treasury yield curve is riskless; this holds default risk constant throughout the time over which the yield curve is depicted. If different default risk premiums were present within one yield curve, it would be so difficult to interpret that it would be rendered meaningless. However, even a yield curve that is constructed using a sample composed exclusively of U.S. Treasury securities, deviations from a smooth curve can result.

 Two factors that cannot be held constant when drawing a Treasury yield curve explain why deviations from a smoothly drawn yield curve are inevitable. First, market participants tend to act so as to equalize the after-tax yields between similar bonds. For example, consider two Treasury issues with the same maturity. If one issue is selling at a discount and the other at par, then the issue selling at a discount will have a lower yield-to-maturity since it has a tax advantage (if income from price gains is taxed at a different tax rate from coupon income.) Second, some issues are also callable. The issue with the call feature will have a higher yield-to-maturity, ceteras paribus, to attract investors. These two factors explain why data points lay off of the yield curve and why this does not detract from the validity of the expectations theory. The problems they cause can be overcome by constructing a Treasury yield curve using non-callable bonds and tax-adjusting the bonds' YTMs.

Treasury bonds furnish a simple example; corporate bonds are even more heterogeneous than Treasury bonds. As a result, fewer factors can be held constant if a large sample of corporate bonds is being assembled with which to draw a yield curve. For example, in addition to the factors that can make U.S. Treasury bonds different, a corporate bond may or may not have a sinking fund requirement, may or may not be collateralized, may or may not be subordinated to another issue of bonds issued by the same firm, ad infinitum.

QA20-4   Investors receive two types of income from their bond investments: coupon interest and price gains or losses. The coupon payments are usually fixed and never vary unless the bond issuer defaults. So, when market interest rates rise or fall, the associated changes in the bonds' yields-to-maturity (YTMs) must all be accomplished through changes in the market prices of the bonds. These price changes must be larger for long-term bonds than for short-term bonds that experience the same change in their YTM because the price change for the long-term bonds must cover a larger number of years. As a result, long-term bond prices are always more volatile than the prices of short-term bonds. Nevertheless, the market interest rates always fluctuate more for short-term bonds than for long-term bonds.

It helps to remember that the length of the average business cycle in the United States measures seven years from peak to peak, or from trough to trough. The YTMs of short-term bonds are more volatile than long-term bond YTMs because short-term yields extend only one or two years into the future, and thus over either a booming or a recessionary portion of the business cycle, but typically not both. In contrast, the long-term bond's life extends over one or more complete business cycles, and thus, must equal long-run average interest rates in order to induce investors to buy. Still, the average of many short-term interest rates will not vary as much as the individual short-term rates.

More concisely, it is clear that as we move through time, $Var(ar) < Var(r_t)$, where ar is the moving average defined below:

$$ar = \frac{r_1 + r_2 + \ldots + r_T}{T}$$

A moving average of the high and the low interest rates like ar smoothes out the extreme values and never reaches the highest or lowest levels attained by the shorter-term interest rates that make up the average.

QA20-5   A bond dealer who had to carry an inventory of bonds and expected interest rates to rise would expect to profit from a bear hedge. The long-term bonds would fall in price as interest rates rose, and the dealer would profit on the short position. However, the prices of the short-term bonds that are nearing maturity are not as affected by changes in the interest rates, so little or no loss could be realized on the long position in short-term bonds. This is called a bear hedge because it is based on the bearish assumption that the level of interest rates will rise, causing all bond prices to fall. The aggressiveness of a bear hedge varies directly with the length of time between the maturities of the short-term bond and the long-term bond. As a result, a bear hedge involving a short position in 30-year bonds and a long position in 2-year bonds is riskier than a bear hedge involving a short position in 3-year bonds and a long position in 2-year bonds.

QA20-6   The solution from the CFA Institute to the CFA Exam question about market interest rates is below. As you read the answer below, bear in mind that the stage of the business cycle may be different from what it was at the time the answer was written.

(a)   The term structure of interest rates refers to the relationship between yields and maturities for fixed income securities of the same or similar issuer. Expectations regarding future interest rate levels give rise to differing supply and demand pressures in the various maturity sectors of the bond market. These pressures are reflected in differences in the yield movements of bonds of different maturities.

        The "term structure of interest rates," or "yield curve," will normally be upward sloping in a period of relatively stable price expectations. The theoretical basis for the upward sloping yield curve is the fact that investors generally demand a premium, the longer the maturity of the issue, to cover risk through time.

(b)   According to the expectations theory of yield curve determination, if borrowers prefer to sell short maturity issues at the time lenders prefer to invest in longs, as in the case when interest rates are expected to fall, longer maturity issues will tend to yield less than shorter maturity issues. The yield curve will be downward sloping. This generally occurs in periods such as the past several years when restrictive monetary policy by the Federal Reserve System, in an attempt to control inflation and inflation expectations, resulted in very high short-term interest rates. In these circumstances, demand for longer-term maturities is severely dampened.

(c)   The "real" rate of interest is simply the difference between nominal interest rates and some measure of inflation, such as the current consumer price index or GNP deflator. In other words, it is inflation-adjusted interest rates.

(d)   The market for U.S. Treasury securities is very large and highly liquid as a result of the huge cumulative debt of the United States Government over time. Features of Treasury securities tend to be fairly standardized and, by definition, all from one issuer. AAA corporate bonds, on the other hand, are issued by hundreds of different corporations and there are unique features to every different issue even from the same corporation. Thus, their marketplace is much more complex in terms of assessing individual securities.

        Some corporate issues are large and trade in very liquid markets. Others, however, are much smaller and tend to have much more restricted marketability. With so many issuers as well as issues, there is more room for inefficiencies to exist for short periods of time, given the diversity of the market place.

        Any market that is less than efficient offers arbitrage opportunities. Because of these inefficiencies, issues of comparable quality, maturity, and other features can be priced differently, offering swap opportunities for bond traders or portfolio managers. Also, bonds that otherwise appear identical may, for various reasons, have better trading characteristics and perhaps may warrant a certain premium because of this.

(e)   Over the past several years, fairly wide spreads have existed between AAA-corporates and Treasuries. Investor preference for Treasuries stems from several factors. Treasury securities are extremely liquid and provide investors with more flexibility. Secondly, Treasury securities do not have the kinds of restrictive call protection generally encountered with high-grade corporates. Thus, in a period of high interest rates, investors purchasing long-term securities anticipate an eventual decline in inflation and interest rates and thus prefer to lock in higher long-term yields.

QA20-7   A quality spread is also referred to as a credit-risk premium or default-risk premium. It measures the additional yield that the market requires riskier bonds to pay to induce investors to buy them rather than the high-quality U.S. Treasury bonds. A quality spread is calculated by subtracting the yield on a U.S. Treasury bond from the yield on a risky bond of the same maturity.

A horizon spread is also known as a maturity-risk premium. It measures the additional yield that the market requires longer bonds to pay to induce investors to buy them rather than shorter-term bonds. The horizon spread reflects the slope of the yield curve. It is calculated by subtracting the yield on a short-term Treasury bond from that of a long-term Treasury bond.

QA20-8   The Federal Reserve uses its monetary policy tools to control interest rates. If the Federal Reserve wants to keep interest rates low, it may pursue an expansionary monetary policy. However, if the U.S. government runs a deficit, it must borrow money as we all do if we spend more than what we have. The government competes against private businesses for the available funds, and this competition drives the interest rates, which reflect the price of credit, up. Furthermore, if the Federal Reserve were to become even more expansionary to meet the demand for credit in an attempt to keep interest rates low, foreign investors, who invest in Treasury securities, may find them less attractive than bonds issued by some other government, such as the German government, which are considered to be just as default-free as the U.S. government bonds, if those bonds (referred to as bunds) offered higher yields. In order to compete for the funds supplied by foreign investors, the yields on the U.S. Treasury securities would have to increase. It is also the case that too much expansion by the Federal Reserve can result in inflation, which would result in higher interest rates.

QA20-9   The three major yield curve theories are the horizon (or liquidity) premium theory, the segmentation theory, and the expectations theory. The horizon premium theory asserts that, on average, yields on long-term bonds should be higher than yields on short-term bonds. This theory maintains that the yield curve should normally be upward sloping. The rationale underlying this theory is that investors must be paid a premium to induce them to "lend long" and face the higher interest rate risk associated with longer-term bonds.

The segmentation theory asserts that the yield curve is composed of a series of somewhat independent maturity segments; that is, some lenders like to lend for short periods, some for intermediate periods, and others for long periods. Therefore, the yield curve is determined by the supply and demand for funds in each of these maturity segments. For example, if there are more investors who want to lend long than there are borrowers who want to borrow long and more borrowers who want to borrow for the short-term than there are lenders who want to lend for the short-term, then interest rates on short-term bonds would be higher than those on long-term bonds.

The expectations theory asserts that long-term yields are the average of the short-term yields expected to prevail during the intervening period. Thus, if all investors expect interest rates to rise, the yield curve would be upward-sloping; if they expect rates to fall, the yield curve would be downward-sloping; and if they expect no change in interest rates, a flat yield curve would be observed.

QA20-10   The current yield spread is 80 basis points and you are expecting it to decrease to 50 basis points. This means that either the higher quality bond, Bond 1, will have an increase in yield or the lower quality bond, Bond 2, will have a decrease in yield, or both. Since bond prices move inversely with yields, you would want to hold Bond 2. If it does have a decrease in yield, its price should increase. You might also consider shorting Bond 1. If it experiences an increase in yield, its price will fall.

Problems

PA20-1   The problem assumes that $_0S_4 = 7\%$ and $_0S_3 = 6\%$. Using Equation 20-9,

$$1 + {_tF_{t+n}} = \frac{(1 + {_0S_{t+1}})^{t+1}}{(1 + {_0S_t})^t}, \text{ so}$$

$$1 + {_3F_4} = \frac{(1.07)^4}{(1.06)^3} = \frac{1.311}{1.191} = 1.10, \text{ and } {_3F_4} = 10\%.$$

PA20-2   The yield-to-maturity on a zero coupon bond is the interest rate that equates the price paid with the discounted expected future cash flows, so

$$\$880 = \frac{\$1,000}{(1 + ytm)^5}$$

$$ytm = \sqrt[5]{\frac{\$880}{\$1,000}} - 1 = 2.59\%.$$

PA20-3   The price of a bond is equal to the present value of its expected future cash flows:

$$Price = \frac{\$900}{(1.08)^1} + \frac{\$900}{(1.08)^2} + \ldots + \frac{\$10,900}{(1.08)^7} = \$10,520.64.$$

The bond will sell at a premium price of $10,520.64.

PA20-4   Using Equation 20-9,

$$1 + {_tF_{t+n}} = \frac{(1 + {_0S_{t+1}})^{t+1}}{(1 + {_0S_t})^t}, \text{ so}$$

$$1 + {_3F_2} = \frac{(1.09)^2}{(1.08)1} = 1.10, \text{ and } {_1F_2} = 10\%.$$

PA20-5   Using Equation 20-9,

$$1 + {_tF_{t+n}} = \frac{(1 + {_0S_{t+1}})^{t+1}}{(1 + {_0S_t})^t}, \text{ so}$$

$$1 + {_2F_3} = \frac{(1.105)^3}{(1.09)^2} = 1.1356, \text{ and } {_2F_3} = 13.56\%.$$

PA20-6   Using Equation 20-10, we can determine the implicit future rates for multi-period bonds:

$$1 + {_tF_{t+n}} = \left[\frac{(1 + {_0S_{t+n}})^{t+n}}{(1 + {_0S_t})^t} \right]^{1/n}$$

$$\sqrt[3]{\frac{(1.12)^4}{(1.08)}} - 1 = 13.37\%.$$

PA20-7   Using Equation 20-10, we can determine the implicit future rates for multi-period bonds:

$$1 + {}_tF_{t+n} = \left[\frac{(1 + {}_0S_{t+n})^{t+n}}{(1 + {}_0S_t)^t} \right]^{1/n}$$

$$\sqrt{\frac{(1.12)^4}{(1.09)^2}} - 1 = 15.08\%.$$

PA20-8   Using Equation 20-10, we can determine the implicit future rates for multi-period bonds:

$$1 + {}_tF_{t+n} = \left[\frac{(1 + {}_0S_{t+n})^{t+n}}{(1 + {}_0S_t)^t} \right]^{1/n}$$

$$\sqrt[10]{\frac{(1.12)^{15}}{(1.08)^5}} - 1 = 14.06\%.$$

PA20-9 (a)   The yield-to-maturity is the discount rate that makes the present value of the expected future cash flows equal to the price of the bond. Therefore, for zero coupon bonds, the yield-to-maturity can be determined as follows:

$$\text{Price} = \frac{\text{Face value}}{(1 + \text{ytm})^{\text{number of years to maturity}}}$$

$$so\ \text{ytm} = \sqrt[\text{number of years to maturity}]{\frac{\text{Face value}}{\text{Price}}} - 1$$

The yield-to maturity for each bond is given below:

Bond price	Years to maturity	Yield-to-maturity
$935	1	6.95%
$870	2	7.21%
$800	3	7.72%
$750	4	7.46%

     (b) $\dfrac{(1.0772)^3}{(1.0721)^2} - 1 = 8.75\%.$

PA20-10   To lock in the 1-year forward rate for year three at the start of year one, an investor should buy a 3-year bond (long position) and sell a 2-year bond (short position).

Action	Beginning of year 1	End of year 2	End of year 3
*Buy 1.10875			
3-year bonds	-$870	0	+$1,087.50
*Sell one			
2-year bond	+$870	-$1,000	0
Totals	0	-$1,000	+$1,087.50

*870/800 = 1.0875, so the return at the end of year 3 is 8.75%.

PA20-11 $\sqrt[3]{\dfrac{(1.0746)^4}{(1.0695)}} - 1 = 7.63\%.$

PA20-12

Years to maturity	YTM	Real rate	Implied inflation*
1	6.95%	3%	3.84%
2	7.21%	3%	4.09%
3	7.72%	3%	4.58%
4	7.46%	3%	4.33%

*This is calculated by solving for INF (inflation) in the Fisher equation.

$$(1 + RR) = \frac{1+r}{1+INF}, \text{ so } INF = \frac{1+r}{(1+RR)} - 1 \quad \text{For example, in year 1, INF} =$$

$$\frac{1.0695}{1.03} - 1 = 3.835\%.$$

PA20-13 $\dfrac{(1.0721)^2}{(1.0695)} - 1 = 7.47\%.$

PA20-14 $\dfrac{(1.105)^{10}}{(1.1025)^9} - 1 = 12.78\%.$

PA20-15 $\sqrt{\dfrac{(1.106)^{11}}{(1.1025)^9}} - 1 = 12.19\%.$

CFA Exam Solutions*

The following are the guideline answers provided by the AIMR for the CFA Exam questions:

1.   **D**

2.   **D**
        Solution:

$$_{t+2}r_1 = \frac{(1+R_3)^3}{(1+R_2)^2} - 1$$

$$= \frac{(1+0.065)^3}{(1+0.060)^2} - 1$$

$$= 0.0751$$

$$= 7.51\%$$

3.   A.   The significance is to show the **downward slope** of the yield curve
                in the first year coinciding with the 50 bp change in six months and 50 **bp in one year**.

The yield curve is steeply inverted (downward sloped), at least to the first year to reflect the two 50 bp adjustments, then becomes slightly inverted through the 2 1/2 year mark, and is basically flat by three years.

B.   The shape of the yield curve is explained by the Expectations Theory or the Liquidity Preference Theory. Expectations Theory postulates that the shape of the term structure is determined by market participants' expectations of future interest rates, which allow the accurate prediction of future spot rates from the current term structure.

The Liquidity Preference Theory postulates that whatever risk-averse investors' expectations are about rates, because they prefer to hold short-term maturity bonds, they require a yield premium to buy longer term bonds. When the market anticipates lower rates, the liquidity premium will dampen the downward slope of the yield curve.

Alternative approach to the answer: Spot rates are a geometric average of forward rates. When rates are expected to fall, investors will require higher yields to hold shorter maturities (because of the lower yields expected when the short maturities must be reinvested), and the term structure will slope downward. The small term premiums will modify the slope of the curve but are not enough to make the slope of the curve upward sloping in the early years.

Forward rates and spot rates are related according to the following formula:

$$(1 + R_t)^t = (1 + R_{t-j})(1 + f_{j, t-j})^j$$

Under the Liquidity Preference Theory, the relationship between spot and forward rates is somewhat different:

$$(1 + R_t)^t = (1 + R_{t-j})[1 + E(R_{j, t-j}) + L]^j$$

4.   A.   The <u>forward rate</u> is the expected yield during some future period--e.g., the forward rate for year three is the one year rate expected to prevail in year three (three years from now).

To calculate the forward rate for a three-year bond two years from now, you would use the following formula:

$$(1 + {}_{t+m}r_{n-m,t})^{n-m} = (1 + {}_tR_n)^n/(1 + {}_tR_m)^m$$

where: r =   the forward rate for the period n - m
         R_n =   the observable yield for a security with maturity n
         R_m =   the observable yield for a security with maturity m

In this case, we are looking for the forward rate for a three-year bond, two years from now (i.e., the forward three-year rate for the period from two to five years). Therefore, the computation would be as follows:

$$(1 + {}_{t+2}r_{3,t})^3 = (1 + {}_tR_5)^5/(1 + {}_tR_2)^2$$

$$= (1 + 0.077)^5/(1 + 0.079)^2$$

$$= 1.2446$$

$$_{t+2}r_{3,t} = 7.566\%$$

B.   The January 19XX term structure indicates an upward sloping yield curve. The <u>pure expectations hypothesis</u> would contend that investors are expecting higher short-term rates in the future and, therefore, the forward rate curve would be even steeper than the currently prevailing yield curve which is the geometric average of these future short-term rates. The <u>market segmentation hypothesis</u> would contend that there is greater demand for short-term securities by those who have an interest in this segment of the market. Put another way, those institutions that tend to invest in the short-term segment of the yield curve have greater funds at the present time compared to those who have an interest in long-term securities. The <u>liquidity hypothesis</u> would imply that this upward sloping yield curve is a natural by-product of the risk averse investors who require a higher yield to invest in longer term securities because of the higher risk involved--i.e., the greater volatility of longer maturity securities.

C.   The term structure over this period experienced what is referred to as a "snap down" in that the short-term rates went up, but the long-term rates went down substantially. As a result, a portfolio with a maturity of two years (and a duration of less than two) would have experienced a fairly small price decline because the yields for one and two year bonds went up. Therefore, this portfolio would have experienced an increase in value.

D.   In January 19XX, the spread between short-term and long-term was about 135 basis points compared to the normal spread of 170 basis points. Under these conditions, you would expect this spread to increase during the ensuing period, and this could happen in several ways. Assuming no change in the general level of rates, you could either expect short rates to decline or long rates to increase. Alternatively, if you expected an increase in rates, you would envision that long rates would experience a larger increase in order to reestablish the normal spread. Finally, if you expected a decline in rates, you would expect long rates to decline by less than short rates to reestablish the norm. The point is, in all scenarios, you would expect the change in long rates to be less than optima. Put another way, this set of expectations would discourage you from aggressively investing in long-term securities. Obviously, this portfolio decision would have been suboptimal based upon what happened because the long bonds had the very best performance because of the "snap down" in the yield curve. This example reflects the point made in the Meyer article that when making a decision with regard to yield spreads, it is also necessary to have some expectations regarding the future level of interest rates. If you really expected that interest rates would decline substantially in the future, you would have possibly anticipated the change in the shape of the yield curve or have been willing to invest in long bonds simply because of the greater volatility during a period of declining interest rates.

5.   The essence of the answer is to price each bond's cash flows using the spot curve (Table 2). The nonarbitrage price of bond A is

$$\frac{10}{1.05} + \frac{10}{(1.08)^2} + \frac{110}{(1.11)^3} = 98.53.$$

The market price of bond A is 98.40, 13 cents (13.2 basis points of market price) less than the nonarbitrage price.

The nonarbitrage price of bond B is

$$\frac{6}{1.05} + \frac{6}{(1.08)^2} + \frac{106}{(1.11)^3} = 88.36.$$

The market price of bond B is 88.34, only 2 cents (2.3 basis points of market price) less than the nonarbitrage price.

Conclusion. Despite having the lower yield to maturity (10.65 percent versus 10.75 percent), Bond A is the better value because the excess of its nonarbitrage price over market price is greater than for Bond B.

CHAPTER 21: HORIZON RISK AND INTEREST RATE RISK

SOLUTIONS

Questions

QA21-1   For perpetual bonds (such as British consols), the coupon rate does not affect the bond's duration, but, for bonds with finite lives, a larger coupon rate shortens the duration. This is because more of the cash flows from the bond are received earlier in the bond's life than is the case with smaller coupon bonds.

QA21-2   The longer a bond's term to maturity, the longer is its duration. This is because it takes longer for an investor to receive all his cash flows from an investment in a longer term bond, and duration is the weighted average number of time periods till the investor's cash flows occur.

QA21-3   A bond's duration moves inversely with its yield-to-maturity (and also with its coupon rate, for that matter).

QA21-4   The overall quotation is false, even though the first sentence in the quotation is true. Although a bond's duration does not measure the time until any actual cash flow, it is still a valuable measure of the time structure of the bond's entire set of cash flows. The duration measures the average length of time the invested funds remain invested, considering all cash flows. In addition, it is a measure of interest rate risk.

QA21-5   The Modified duration (MOD) is calculated as $\dfrac{dP/P}{d(YTM)}$. It measures the percentage price change in a bond that occurs in response to a small change in the market interest rate; the denominator represents this change (d(YTM).) MAC's denominator is d(YTM)/(1 + YTM), however, so MAC measures the percentage change in a bond's price that results from a *percentage* change in the market interest rate.

QA21-6   If the portfolio expects interest rates to increase, then he expects bond prices to fall since prices move inversely with interest rates. Therefore, he would want to have the bond that would experience the smallest price decrease. Bond 3 will have the smallest price decrease since it has the shortest duration; it has a higher coupon rate and less time to maturity than the other two bonds.

QA21-7   The equation that is used to calculate a limiting value for a bond's Macaulay duration is $MACLIM = \dfrac{1.0}{YTM} + 1.0$. If the bond is a perpetual bond, its Macaulay duration will be equal to this number. If a coupon bond is selling at or above its par value, its Macaulay duration increases with the bond's term to maturity and converges on MACLIM as the term to maturity approaches infinity. If a coupon bond is selling at a discount, its Macaulay duration will be at its highest at some maturity that is less than infinity, and then declines toward the limiting value of MACLIM.

QA21-8   Horizon analysis involves computing a horizon return for each bond that is an investment candidate. A bond's horizon return is its total return, which includes cash flows and price changes, over whatever investment horizon is relevant. By comparing horizon returns, an investor can evaluate several different potential bond candidates, bond swaps, and investment strategies. Different scenarios can be analyzed to develop a probability distribution of returns over the investment horizon. The major difficulty in performing this type of analysis is that the computation of horizon returns requires forecasts about future yield and reinvestment rates. For this reason, many investors prefer to use the YTM to compare different bond investments since it is more easily obtained.

QA21-9   While duration is the first derivative of the bond price-yield curve, convexity is the second derivative. Thus, it measures the change in duration that occurs when interest rates change. Bonds with positive convexity experience decreases in their durations when interest rates rise and vice-versa. So, if interest rates rise, resulting in lower bond prices, the duration of a bond with positive convexity will shorten, and the bond's price will fall at a decreasing rate. Likewise, if interest rates fall, resulting in higher bond prices, the duration of a bond with positive convexity will lengthen, causing the bond's price to rise at an increasing rate.

QA21-10   Contingent immunization combines active bond portfolio management and immunization. Its purpose is to ensure that the fixed income assets earn at least some minimum safety net return or, if possible, a higher return. With contingent immunization the bond portfolio manager is given discretion to actively manage his portfolio so long as it earns a return that exceeds the safety net return. If the safety net return not achieved, active management is terminated abruptly, and the remaining assets are immunized in order to assure that the safety net return is not violated.

Problems

PA21-1   A perpetual bond with a yield-to-maturity (YTM) of six percent would have a duration of 17.667 years, regardless of its coupon rate. Only the YTM affects Macaulay's duration (MAC) for perpetuities. For finite-life bonds, a larger coupon rate would shorten the maturity.

$$MAC = \frac{1.0}{YTM} + 1 = \frac{1.0}{0.06} + 1 = 17.667.$$

PA21-2   If the bond's yield-to-maturity (YTM) is 9.0 percent, its present value and Macaulay's duration (MAC) can be calculated as follows:

(1) Year	(2) PV of cashflow	(3) PV as proportion of bond's price	(4) equals (1) x (3)
1	$73.36	0.0777	0.0777
2	67.36	0.0713	0.1426
3	61.76	0.0654	0.1962
4	56.64	0.0600	0.2400
5	52.00	0.0550	0.2750
6	47.68	0.0505	0.3030
7	43.76	0.0463	0.3241
8	542.16	0.5739	4.5912
PV=	$944.72		MAC = 6.1498 years

Column 2 shows that the bond's present value (PV) is $944.72. And column four indicates that its MAC is 6.1498 years. The bond's interest rate elasticity (EL) is the same as its duration; more concisely, MAC = EL = 6.1498 when YTM = 9.0%.

PA21-3   If the bond's yield-to-maturity (YTM) is 8.0 percent, its present value would equal its face value of $1,000 since the bond's coupon rate is also 8.0 percent. The bond's present value (PV) is calculated below.

(1) Year	(2) PV of cashflow	(3) PV as proportion of bond's price	(4) equals (1) x (3)
1	$74.07	0.0741	0.0741
2	68.59	0.0686	0.1371
3	63.51	0.0635	0.1905
4	58.80	0.0588	0.2352
5	54.45	0.0545	0.2725
6	50.41	0.0504	0.3024
7	46.68	0.0467	0.3269
8	583.49	0.5832	4.6656
PV =	$1,000.00		MAC= 6.2043

The bond's interest elasticity (EL) would be the same as its MAC, namely, MAC = EL = 6.2043. A comparison of the YTMs and MACs in the answers to problems 21-2 and 21-3 suggests that YTMs and MACs move inversely. More generally, we can conclude that interest rate risk and YTM move inversely since MAC is a measure of interest rate risk. (Note: This is true for bonds that have positive convexity. Some bonds, particularly those with a call feature, have negative convexity, and the opposite is true.)

PA21-4 (a)   The Macaulay's duration for the three bonds, two of which paid semi-annual coupons, are as follows:

MAC for A is 1.86 years.
MAC for B is 2.66 years.

MAC for C is 3.0 years (since MAC = T for zero-coupon bonds.)

(b)   Bond C has the longest duration because the investor must wait the full three years before getting back any of his investment. Bonds A and B return some of the funds sooner than 3.0 years and, therefore, have MACs that are shorter than 3 years. Bond A returns more of the investor's money sooner and, therefore, it has the shortest duration.

PA21-5   This problem can be solved with a financial calculator, such as the Texas Instrument Student Business Analyst or Hewlett-Packard Model HP12C.

(a)   Treat this bond as if it had 13 years to maturity, or, 26 half years. The HP12C solution for the present value is:

$n = 26$ $i = 6$ PV = ?   PMT = 50   FV = 1000
Press PV
Price = PV = $869.97

(b)   The duration was calculated for the bond with 13 years left to maturity and found to be MAC = 7.15 years

PA21-6 (a)   The HP12C solution for the present value of a bond that has 10 years, or 20 half-years, till maturity is:

$n = 20$ $i = 4$ PV = ?   PMT = 50   FV = 1000
Press PV
Price = $1,135.90

(b)   The duration is MAC = 6.77 years.

PA21-7 (a)   This can be solved easily by using a financial calculator. The HP12C solution to calculate the YTM is :

$n = 28$ $i = ?$ PV = -856   PMT = 60   FV = 1000
Press i (= 7.21%)
YTM = 2 x 7.21% = 14.42% per year. Alternatively, the effective YTM = $(1.0721)^2 - 1 =$ 14.94%.

(b)   The HP12C solution for the $1,150 price is as follows:

$n = 28$ $i = ?$ PV = -1150   PMT = 60   FV = 1000
Press i (= 4.99%)
YTM = 2 x 4.99% = 9.98%. Alternatively, the effective YTM = $(1.0499)^2 - 1 =$ 10.23%.

PA21-8   Using an HP12C, the YTMs can be calculated as follows:

Bond 1: $n = 6$ $i = ?$ PV = -1000 PMT = 100 FV = 1000
Press i
YTM = 10%
Bond 2: $n = 6$ $i = ?$ PV = -1000   PMT = 0   FV = 1700
Press i
YTM = 9.25%

The Macaulay durations for the two bonds are:
Bond 1: MAC = 4.791 years.
Bond 2: MAC= 6.0 years. Since this is a zero-coupon bond, its duration is equal to its time to maturity of 6 years.

PA21-9   An ending value of the bond must be calculated as well as the future value of all interest payments.

   (Step 1) Using an HP12C, the FV of the interest payments is calculated as follows:
        $n = 10$ $i = 6$ $PV = 0$ $PMT = 50$ $FV = ?$
        Press FV(= $659.04)

   (Step 2) Using an HP12C, the price of the bond at the end of 5 years can be determined as follows:
        $n = 10$ $i = 6$ $PV = ?$ $PMT = 50$ $FV = 1000$
        Press PV (= $926.40)

   (Step 3) Using an HP12C, the return over the 5-year period is calculated as follows:
        $n = 5$ $i = ?$ $PV = -1000$ $PMT = 0$
        $FV = (\$926.40 + \$659.04 = \$1,585.44)$
        Press i
        The annual return is 9.66%.

PA21-10 (Step 1) Using an HP12C, the FV of the interest payments is determined as follows:
        $n = 6$ $i = 6$ $PV = 0$ $PMT = 50$ $FV = ?$
        Press FV(= $348.77)

   (Step 2) Using an HP12C, the price of the bond at the end of 3 years is calculated as follows:
        $n = 14$ $i = 6$ $PV = ?$ $PMT = 50$ $FV = 1000$
        Press PV(= 907.05)

   (Step 3) Using an HP12C, the return over the 3-year period is calculated as follows:
        $n = 3$ $i = ?$ $PV = -1000$ $PMT = 0$
        $FV = (\$348.77 + \$907.05 = \$1,255.82)$
        Press i
        The annual return is 7.89%.

PA21-11 (Step 1) Using an HP12C, the FV of the interest payments is determined as follows:
        $n = 10$ $i = 4$ $PV = 0$ $PMT = 50$ $FV = ?$
        Press FV(= $600.31)

   (Step 2) Using an HP12C, the price of the bond at the end of 5 years is calculated as follows:
        $n = 10$ $i = 4$ $PV = ?$ $PMT = 50$ $FV = 1000$
        Press PV(= $1,081.11)

(Step 3)   Using an HP12C, the return over the 5-year period is calculated as follows:

n = 5   i = ?   PV = -1000   PMT = 0

FV = ($600.31 + $1,081.11 = $1,681.42)

Press i

The annual return is 10.95%.

PA21-12   Duration was found to be equal to (a) 6.54 years at 10 percent, and (b) 6.31 years at 12 percent.

CFA Exam Solutions*

The following are the guideline answers provided by the AIMR for the CFA Exam questions:

1.   C

2.   A

Solution: Modified duration equals Macaulay duration, divided by 1, plus the current yield to maturity, divided by the number of payments in a year.

D_{mod} $= 9/(1 + 0.10)$
$= 9/1.1$
$= 8.18$ years.

3.   B

4.   An informed manager will recommend purchase of Aaa bonds over Aa bonds for an investment with a one-year horizon. Although the Aa bonds show the largest *indicated incremental return*, based on the initial spreads of expected return over governments, the Aaa bonds can be expected to produce the largest *realized incremental return*, as shown by the following calculation:

Incremental return   = Initial spread - (Change in spread x Duration)
Aaa bonds   =   31 bp - (0 bp x 3.1 years) = 31 bp
Aa bonds   =   40 bp - (10 bp x 3.1 years) = 9 bp

Realized spreads are dependent on the interaction of the three elements (initial spread, horizon spread, and horizon duration) and can differ substantially from initial indications of relative return and relative attractiveness.

5.   Assume that the expected 50 bp declines in Federal Funds rates in 6 and 12 months are both delayed by 6 months and that the Federal Funds rate is now expected to increase by 100 bp in 2 1/2 years (when no increase was previously expected).

If you agree with the new interest rate forecast, you should select the two-year benchmark U.S. Treasury (bullet) instead of the cash/three-year U.S. Treasury barbell.

The delayed 50 bp drops in future rates and the 100 bp increase both cause current cash or spot rates to increase, implying an upward shift of the yield curve, which will occur in two weeks. Both investments have the same duration, but the barbell, which has the greater convexity, might be expected to have the smaller decline in value in two weeks when the market shares your view.

However, the yield curve shift is nonparallel. A steepening occurs, where the three-year rate increases more than the two-year rate. Such a steepening increases the value of a bullet relative to a barbell. In this example, the steepening is sufficient for the bullet to experience a lower decline in value that the barbell.

Alternative justification. Given the new expectations about future interest rates, the two-year interest rate will increase approximately 25 bp and the three-year rate will increase approximately 33 bp. Given prevailing U.S. Treasury rates, increases of this size will cause the three-year Treasury to decline much more than the two-year (the three-year falls roughly twice as much). Even though the barbell invests only about two-thirds of its value in the three-year (and the rest in cash), the total dollar decline in the barbell will be more than the total dollar decline in the two-year bullet.

CHAPTER 22: CREDIT RISK

SOLUTIONS

Questions

QA22-1   Home mortgages are like collateralized bonds with sinking funds in several respects. First, both securities are backed by real estate collateral. Second, both securities are marketable debt securities (unless the mortgage has a clause specifically forbidding its resale, which is rare.) Third, both securities require periodic payments to amortize the debt. There are several differences, too, however. First, the home mortgage's quality depends on both the home owner's income and the resale value of the home. In contrast, the collateral bond issue's quality depends on the earning power of the issuing corporation and, in addition, on the value of the collateral assets. The second difference is that the collateralized bond issue may have provisions in the indenture for a blanket mortgage, a closed-end or open-end mortgage, a call provision, an after-acquired clause or other considerations that are unusual in home mortgages. Third, the denominations differ substantially. The typical home mortgage is a security that has a face value of from $50,000 to $150,000, whereas the typical corporate bond has either a $1,000 or a $100 face value.

QA22-2   False. Weinstein's results showed no significant bond price reaction after the announcement of the rating change. What little abnormal (or unsystematic) price change occurred after the rating change was not sufficient to pay the broker's buy-sell commissions to consummate the trade. Most bond price declines were spread over a period of months that preceded the announcement of a rating decrease. Thus, if bond trading gains are to be made from the changing financial health of corporate issuers, the gains will have to come from far-sighted financial research and not from simple-minded reactions to publicly announced rating changes.

QA22-3   The same factors (namely, profitability, liquidity, competition, etc.) that the bond rating agencies consider in determining a corporation's bond rating also affect the firm's overall desirability as a common stock investment. Therefore, anything that affects a corporation's bond rating should also be observed by common stock analysts and, as a result, be reflected in the stock's market price without delay.

 The research results of Dr. Weinstein on bond prices and Professors Griffin and Sanvicente on common stock prices reported that the market prices of both stocks and bonds anticipated the rating change approximately one year prior to its announcement. These findings suggest that the rating agencies might be relying on the research of other stock and bond analysts as it is reflected in the market prices as cues to revise the bond ratings. In contrast, virtually no price reaction occurred after the rating agency announced the rating changes. This implies that if bond trading gains are to be made from changes in the financial health of corporations, the gains will have to come from far-sighted financial research and not from reactions to publicly announced rating changes.

QA22-4   The Federal Reserve's monetary policies constantly affect all market interest rates in various ways. However, these fluctuating market interest rates should not influence the bond quality rating agencies when they assign grades to bond issues. The bond rating agencies observe financial ratio guidelines and the issuer's competitive position. These factors are averaged and evaluated over the complete business cycle rather than being measured at a single point in time, which would ignore the never-ending string of constantly changing ratios and facts that are needed to gain a broader perspective.

QA22-5 If the bankruptcy court believes the insolvent firm is having difficulties that are temporary, the court will grant the troubled firm additional time in which to pay its liabilities in order to avoid bankruptcy. Bankrupt firms will be liquidated only if the court feels that the liquidation value of the firm is greater than the value of the firm as a going concern. The objective of U.S. bankruptcy law is to save the firm, if possible. Therefore, many bankruptcies result in the reorganization of the firm rather than the liquidation of it.

QA22-6 If the firm's managers increase the debt level of the firm, with no change in the firm's assets, in order to improve the return on equity, and if the new debt has the same seniority as the firm's old debt, the old debtholders will lose. The value of the old debt will decrease since its risk is increased due to the fact that more creditors will have claims against the firm's cash flows and assets. It is possible that the stockholders will be winners in this scenario. Although their risk is also increased (increased debt increases the systematic risk of the firm), the increase in the return on their equity may more than compensate them for the increased risk level. Restrictive bond covenants would, of course, prevent this scenario from occurring.

QA22-7 The priority claims are as follows:

1. The attorney's fees and court costs associated with the bankruptcy proceedings.
2. Any expenses incurred between the time of the filing of an involuntary bankruptcy petition and the appointment of the trustee
3. Employee back wages, up to a maximum of $2,000 per worker.
4. Past-due contributions that the bankrupt firm owes to its employee pension plan
5. Any just consumer claims that might be outstanding
6. Back taxes to federal, state, and/or local governments.
7. Unsecured general creditors.
8. Preferred stockholders.
9. Common stockholders.

QA22-8 The key questions that the Standard and Poor's raters ask deal primarily with the borrowing firm itself and are as follows:

1. Does the company have a large enough portion of the market share to influence industry dynamics significantly? Does it have the opportunity to exercise price leadership? Does it offer a full range of products or have proprietary products or a special niche in the market?
2. Is the company a leader or a follower in the industry? How do its research and development expenditures compare with the industry average?
3. Is the company a relatively low-cost producer? Are its facilities newer or more advanced than average? Is it more or less vertically integrated than average? Has the company complied with any mandated expenditures to a greater or lesser degree than average? Is the company facing a more onerous labor situation that its competitors?
4. How does the firm's use of leverage and the various types of financing vehicles compare with others in the same industry?

QA22-9　　　The after-acquired property clause states that if an issuer acquires additional assets after a first collateralized bond is outstanding, the new assets will automatically become part of the collateral pledged to support the first bond. Since this provides greater security to the bondholders, you would expect this bond to offer a lower yield than a similar bond that has no such provision.

QA22-10　　Interest rates were extremely volatile in the early 1980s, and investors, therefore, were very reluctant to lend money at a fixed rate. (Floating rate bonds became popular during this time.) In order to induce investors to do so, the put option was written into the indentures of many bonds. This allowed investors to sell the bond back to the issuing firm in the event that interest rates rose. Investors could then use the proceeds received to invest in new, higher yielding bonds for the same level of risk. Although a bond with a put feature would offer a lower yield than a similar bond that did not have this feature, investors obviously felt that the lower yield was worth it in order to limit their exposure to interest rate risk.

Problems

PA22-1　　　The total liabilities and preferred stock of the firm is $150 million, which is just equal to the estimated value of the firm, so the existing common shareholders will receive nothing. Senior claims are honored in full before junior claims receive anything. Therefore, the distribution of the new securities is as follows:

Old claimant	Received under reorganization
Secured bondholders	$ 40,000,000 in debentures
	$ 20,000,000 in subordinated debt
General unsecured creditors	$ 20,000,000 in subordinated debt
	$ 20,000,000 in preferred stock
Preferred shareholders	$ 50,000,000 in common stock
Common shareholders	$ 0
Total	$150,000,000

PA22-2　　　The notes are subordinate to the bank loans, and therefore, the bank loans are paid before the subordinated note holders receive anything. The general creditors are unaffected by the subordination agreement and receive [$7,000,000 general creditor debt/$22,000,000 total firm debt] x [liquidation proceeds] = 0.318 x liquidation proceeds, but no more than $7 million.

	Face value of debt	Liquidation value = $15 million
Bank notes	$10 million	$ 10 million
Subordinated loans	$ 5 million	$ 0.23 million
General creditors	$ 7 million	$ 4.77 million
Common shareholders		$ 0
Total		$15 million

PA22-3　　　The notes are subordinate to the bank loans, and therefore, the bank loans are paid before the subordinated note holders receive anything. The general creditors are unaffected by the subordination agreement and receive [$7,000,000 general creditor debt/$22,000,000 total firm debt] x [liquidation proceeds] = 0.318 x liquidation proceeds, but no more than $7 million.

	Face value of debt	Liquidation value = $25 million
Bank notes	$10 million	$10 million
Subordinated loans	$ 5 million	$ 5 million
General creditors	$ 7 million	$ 7 million
Common shareholders		$ 3 million
Total		$25 million

PA22-4

Year-end Quality Rating	Probability of state	New bond value + coupon	Probability-weighted value	Difference of value from mean	Probability-weighted difference squared
AAA	0.0005	$1,059.03	0.530	23.43	0.274
AA	0.0155	$1,050.84	16.288	15.24	3.600
A	0.8500	$1,037.40	881.79	1.80	2.754
BBB	0.1320	$1,024.20	135.194	(11.40)	17.155
BB	0.0010	$ 952.53	0.953	(83.07)	6.901
B	0.0006	$ 896.58	0.538	(139.02)	11.596
CCC	0.0003	$ 817.06	0.245	(218.54)	14.328
Default	0.0001	$ 628.73	0.063	(406.87)	16.554
	1.0000	Mean =	1,035.60	Variance = Standard Deviation =	73.162 $8.55

PA22-5 Using the annual discount rates for the BBB-rated bond, we get

$$\text{Price} = \frac{\$90}{(1.078)^1} + \frac{\$1,090}{(1.081)^2} = \$1,016.26.$$

PA22-6 The Z-score is calculated by using the following formula:

$$Z_i = 0.033\left(\frac{\text{EBIT}}{\text{Total assets}}\right)_i + 0.999\left(\frac{\text{Sales}}{\text{Assets}}\right)_i + 0.006\left(\frac{\text{Aggregate market value of all equity}}{\text{Book value of debt}}\right)_i$$

$$+ 0.014\left(\frac{\text{Retained earnings}}{\text{Total assets}}\right)_i + 0.012\left(\frac{\text{Working capital}}{\text{Total assets}}\right)_i + e_i$$

$$= 0.033\left(\frac{\$4,000,000}{\$25,000,000}\right) + 0.999\left(\frac{\$40,000,000}{\$25,000,000}\right) + 0.006\left(\frac{(3,000,000 \times \$12)}{\$14,000,000}\right)$$

$$+ 0.014\left(\frac{\$6,000,000}{\$25,000,000}\right) + 0.012\left(\frac{\$2,000,000}{\$25,000,000}\right)$$

$$= 0.033(16) + 0.999(1.6) + 0.006(257) + 0.014(24) + 0.012(8) = 4.10.$$

The average Z-score for non-bankrupt firms was 5.02. Roche-Haight's score is slightly below average, but the firm does not seem to be in any real immediate danger, and it is out of the range of erroneous classifications.

PA22-7   The solution to Altman's MDA problem is based on the table of values below:

Ratio	Bain	Smith	Upson
Working capital/Total assets	- 6%	41%	10%
Retained earnings/Total assets	-63%	36%	14%
EBIT/Total assets	-32%	15%	-20%
Equity market value/Book value of total liabilities	40%	248%	150%
Sales/Total assets	1.5X	1.9X	1.7X
Z score	-0.2715	4.8771	2.2543

The Z-scores for the three firms are calculated as shown below:

$$Z_i = 0.033\left(\frac{EBIT}{Total\ assets}\right)_i + 0.999\left(\frac{Sales}{Assets}\right)_i + 0.006\left(\frac{Aggregate\ market\ value\ of\ all\ equity}{Book\ value\ of\ debt}\right)_i \quad \textbf{Eqn.(22-1)}$$

$$+ 0.014\left(\frac{Retained\ earnings}{Total\ assets}\right)_i + 0.012\left(\frac{Working\ capital}{Total\ assets}\right)_i + e_i$$

$$Z_{Bain} = 0.033(-32) + 0.999(1.5) + 0.006(40) + 0.014(-63) + 0.012(-6) = -0.2715$$
$$Z_{Smith} = 0.033(15) + 0.999(1.9) + 0.006(248) + 0.014(36) + 0.012(41) = 4.8771$$
$$Z_{Upson} = 0.033(-20) + 0.999(1.7) + 0.006(150) + 0.014(14) + 0.012(10) = 2.2543$$

Interpreting the three Z-scores above in terms of Figure 22-3, we can conclude that Bain Corporation is likely to go bankrupt. Smith Incorporated will probably be solvent. Since the Z-score of Upson Limited falls between 2 and 3, it will unclear whether Upson will be bankrupt or solvent. In other words, Upson is unclassified by Altman's MDA equation.

PA22-8   The EBIT interest coverage ratio for Pioneer is calculated as

$$\frac{EBIT}{Interest} = \frac{\$12,800,000}{\$1,650,000} = 7.76.$$

The EBITDA interest coverage ratio for Pioneer is calculated as

$$\frac{EBITDA}{Interest} + \frac{\$12,800,000 + \$1,200,000}{\$1,650,000} = 8.48.$$

Based on the median values provided in Table 22-9, we might expect Pioneer's bonds to receive an A rating since the median EBIT interest coverage ratio for A-rated bonds is 6.26 and the EBITDA interest coverage ratio for A-rated bonds is 8.51.

PA22-9   For Pioneer, the funds from operations/ total debt ratio is

$$\frac{\$12,800,000 + \$1,200,000}{\$37,550,000} = 0.37.$$ Since it is less than 1.00, it is questionable whether

Pioneer can maintain solvency in the long-run.

PA22-10   Pioneer's long-term debt to capitalization ratio is $\dfrac{\$16,000,000}{\$67,000,000} = 23.9\%$, and its total

debt to capitalization ratio is $\dfrac{\$37,550}{\$67,000} = 0.56 = 56\%.$

Pioneer is slightly more leveraged than the industry average (56% > 50%), but it uses less long-term debt (23.9% < 28.2%.) Assuming that the majority of the short-term debt is non-interest bearing, Pioneer may be better able to cover its interest expense than the average firm in the industry, even though it has more total debt on its books. Hopefully, Pioneer has not put itself in the position of inciting the ire of its suppliers and other short-term creditors, however.

Cases

1.   The part-by-part solution to the CFA exam question about the Georgia-Pacific case follows. The solution below is the official CFA exam grading committee solution.
   (a)   At least 15.87%, the yield to maturity of the current outstanding fixed rate issue.
   (b)   Floating rate notes may not sell at par for any of the following reasons:
      (i)   The yield spread between 6-month Treasury bills and other money market instruments of comparable maturity could widen, that is, competition from other money market instruments.
      (ii)   The credit standing of Georgia-Pacific may have eroded relative to Treasury securities which have no credit risk. Therefore, the 0.75 per cent premium would become insufficient to sustain the issue at par.
      (iii)   The coupon increases are implemented with a lag, i.e., once every six months. During a period of rising interest rates, even this brief lag will be reflected in the price of the security.
      (iv)   The bond market may be perfectly efficient, especially with respect to small and nonseasoned issues.
   (c)   The risk of call is low. Intermediate-term interest rates would have to decline by more than a third (15.87% to 10.10%) by 6-15-86 to make call of the fixed rate issue attractive.
   (d)   The fixed rate issue has the most appeal for active bond portfolio management since a change in interest rates downward from present levels could produce a substantial gain in principal value in addition to the coupon interest and interest-on-interest returns. By contrast, floating rate notes lack significant capital gain or loss potential because the changing coupon interest tends to stabilize principal values; hence, the opportunity to maximize total return based on a forecast of declining interest rates is less than in the case of fixed rate obligations.
   (e)   Yield-to-maturity incorporates the return from a fixed stream of coupon interest payments and the accretion or depreciation between the present price of the bond and its par value to be received at maturity. Because the floating rate note consists of a variable stream of interest payments to maturity, the effective maturity for comparative purposes with other debt securities is closer to next re-coupon date than the final maturity date.

Therefore, yield-to-maturity is an indeterminable calculation for a floating rate note, with "yield-to-recoupon" date a more meaningful measure of total return.

(f) The floating rate note will give the higher realized compound yield (includes reinvestment rate on the coupon interest payments) in a period of stable or risking interest rates because the coupon interest is higher than the fixed rate issue and will be adjusted upward regularly, thereby providing the opportunity for reinvestment of the income stream at progressively higher rates.

2. If the Apex Tobacco Company case is assigned, the instructor might find it useful to explain that bankruptcy courts can declare (a) an arrangement, (b) a reorganization, or (c) a bankruptcy, listed in order of the severity of the problem, when a trouble firm comes before the court.

After a reorganization, if Apex's earnings can be restored to $125,000 per year, the firm's total common stock outstanding will have a market value of $1 million (assuming the price-earnings ratio of 8 times, mentioned in the case.) This requires $300,000 additional capital, however. Thus, the old common stockholders would wind up holding stock with a $350,000 total market value. (This is equal to half of the $1 million less $300,000, or 1/2 x $700,000.) If the old stockholders' outstanding shares are worth less than $350,000, they will presumably support the reorganization (or at least not fight it.)

The unsecured creditors with claims of $675,000 ($450,000 current liabilities plus long-term debt of $225,000) would share equally in the $600,000 liquidation value. This equals ($600/$675) 0.888 or $0.89 for each dollar of debt owed them. This is probably a worse settlement for the long-term debt holders than having their holdings converted to common stock with an anticipated market value of $500,000 (1/2 x $1 million.) It is a better deal for the current debt holders, who would not get their full payment under the reorganization. The final solution will be determined at a meeting of all stockholders and creditors--it is both emotional and political, and therefore, impossible to foretell. However, rational stockholders and creditors would probably vote for the reorganization.

CFA Exam Solutions*

The following are the guideline answers provided by the AIMR for the CFA Exam questions:

1. C

2. A. The total debt to total capital ratio measures the degree of leverage of the firm. Leverage is the relationship of debt owed to the company's total resources as valued on the balance sheet. An analyst would evaluate the absolute leverage and the change in the use of leverage for a firm and compare the level of leverage to that of other companies in the same industry. A firm with a high total debt-total capital ratio will be perceived as having a higher level of credit risk. By comparing this ratio to its competitors' ratios, an analyst can judge the prudence of such leverage for a company in the particular industry. A firm increases it financial leverage when it takes on more debt in proportion to its total capitalization (resources). The change in financial leverage may indicate a change in the company's attitude towards risk taking. The firm will lose some financial flexibility--financing alternatives and ability to access funds--and will generally pay a higher price to acquire funds than a lower-leveraged company. Higher financial leverage may also reduce the firm's choices for financing future growth and paying dividends. Covenants may restrict the company's ability to use its financial resources as it sees fit when this ratio becomes too high.

The pretax interest coverage ratio measures the annual interest burden (the amount the firm must pay its creditors) placed on a firm relative to its earning capacity. This coverage ratio is important because it looks at the firm's ability to pay its annual interest expense from pretax earnings (EBIT). A high coverage ratio is considered positive; a low coverage ratio may indicate more risk, which is a financial constraint. The ratio also suggests the protection afforded creditors to continue to receive interest income, despite a business downturn or an increase in leverage by the firm. Although this ratio indicates the ability of the company to pay cash to its creditors, the numerator includes non-cash earnings and is reduced by non-cash expenses. Finally, the comfort level of coverage should be based on the expected consistency of earnings (an industry issue) and with consideration given to the firm's access to cash.

Cash flow as a percent of total debt focuses not only on earnings, but also on the firm's ability to generate the cash needed to service its debt. "Earnings" can be deceptive because of non-cash items used to get earnings. Analyzing cash flow is critical because it provides insight into a firm's ability to cover debt with internally generated funds. By relating cash flow to total debt, the analyst can make a judgment about the firm's ability to repay the principal-creditor's original investment and debt service (principal and interest). The ratio suggests the amount of time needed for a firm to pay off the original borrowings from internally generated cash.

B.   PowerTool's capitalization ratio, after the acquisition, would continue to allow the company to repurchase dividends or buy stock. By increasing this ratio as a result of the acquisition, the company has reduced its financial flexibility. This is because any such payment of dividends or stock repurchase would be more limited than before the acquisition. The firm's ability to pay dividends adds to its flexibility when issuing common or preferred stock and to the value placed on the new stock. Increasing capitalization without adding debt improves the ratio. The company still has flexibility to issue debt--this covenant does not restrict the amount of debt.

With a put option covenant, the bondholders have the option to keep or put the bonds if the rating drops. If, for this definition, "A-" officially falls outside of the "A" category, then the company may already be in this situation. At the very least, the debt rating is so close to being "A-" and on its way to being "BBB+" that further debt issuance is restricted. At this point, the company should have a provision for paying off the debt, if put, such as a line or letter or credit. Such action would add to the company's financial flexibility in two ways. It would give the firm the ability to buy back the debt and indicate to potential investors the willingness of an outside source to lend money to the company.

Whether or not investors choose to exercise the put option after a downgrade depends largely on the current market price of the bonds. If the bonds are trading at a price below 105, exercise of the put is probable. At prices near 105, investors may consider retaining their holding if they perceive that the company is leveraging for the right reasons and that the company will be stronger in the long run.

If the put is exercised by bondholders, the company may have to issue new debt at a lower price and higher interest cost. This action would add to the cost of doing business and reduce the firm's financial flexibility.

C.   **Industrial Tool Business**

From the perspective of PowerTool bondholders, there are several advantages to the Fenton acquisition with regard to the industrial tool business.

Advantages

1.   The industrial tool market is mature. This business has little growth potential except by acquiring market share or buying share through price competition, which erodes margin and financial strength in the short run. PowerTool is already the largest in this no-growth industry. It can control its market share to provide a "cash cow" for growth outside that market. It should be able to concentrate on the success of the new product. The acquisition of Fenton will provide growth and improve profitability of PowerTool.

2.   PowerTool bought a company in a related business, in an industry with significant growth prospects. Fenton's R&D has produced a patented new line that has tested positively. All of these aspects of Fenton are good reasons for the acquisition. The R&D may provide growth opportunities in the industrial tool market by making a new market or "improved" replacement product to sell to existing customers.

3.   Although a large company buying a small, innovative company can often result in conflict because of differences in management style, this is not likely to be the case with Fenton. The retirement of Jerry Fenton could ease the transition. The larger company may be able to offer employees benefits that the smaller, highly leveraged company could not, which may inspire employees to stay on.

4.   PowerTool has a strong sales force, and Fenton needs a sales force to sell its new product. This also gives the sales force an opportunity to see both its sales and its employee income grow. Income growth will contribute to bondholder protection.

Disadvantages

1.   The tactics for prospering in a mature market and buying competition require financial flexibility. PowerTool has reduced its financial alternatives through this costly acquisition. The cost includes not only the cost of buying the company but also the resources needed to make Fenton grow.

2.   Fenton's retail market may not be compatible with PowerTool's industrial line. PowerTool's new power tools also may not be compatible with Fenton's current line. If the new business detracts from the industrial business, PowerTool could lose important market share, and profits may decline, causing bond rating to decline.

3.   The lack of marketing strength of both PowerTool and Fenton makes this a poor match. A strong sales force at PowerTool may be insufficient to satisfy the marketing needs of the industrial tool business. In retail, marketing is even more important than in industrial sales, and, in this area, Fenton is also weak.

4. PowerTool must invest funds in the market areas for both companies and probably in manufacturing facilities for the new power tools. The leveraging up of PowerTool may reduce the financial flexibility necessary to produce, market, and sell the product. Increased leverage may also affect the firm's ability to maintain the dominant position in industrial tools.

Retail Tool Business

From the perspective of PowerTool bondholders, there are several advantages and disadvantages to acquiring Fenton regarding the retail tool business.

Advantages

1. The patent on the new Fenton product gives the company the marketing opportunity of not having a directly competitive product in the market. The uniqueness reduces the competition based on price because there is no duplicate product. Otherwise, pricing can be a strong competitive tool in retail. Price competition comes with products that can be interchanged or substituted for one another with relative indifference. Fenton has created a product that test markets suggest will address customers' needs. Thus, the company is buying into a growth market with a new protected product that looks like a winner. Such products inspire investors to provide capital to such a firm, thus adding to financial flexibility. PowerTool has bought new, innovative products that should boost its growth above the industry'' growth prospects.

2. PowerTool's distribution system and sales force may help solve the marketing shortcomings regarding the sale of the new product line. This may be accomplished by getting the product to the geographic locations on a timely basis and by providing the people to spread the word about the new products.

3. After the acquisition, the financial position of PowerTool is still much better than Fenton's financial position. PowerTool may not have to spend much money expanding facilities and markets for its industrial tools. Yet, the growth opportunities at Fenton are much better than those at PowerTool.

4. PowerTool's market recognition in the tool business should help market the retail line. The name and size of the company can add credence to the quality of the retail products and influence shelf location.

5. Fenton has proven technological and innovative strengths that PowerTool may lack. Innovation is important for the company to stay competitive in the retail market. Thus, PowerTool is staying in a related business and buying much-needed growth potential through innovation. R&D-intensive firms are likely to have future staying power and a competitive edge.

6. Diversifying the product mix can reduce the volatility of earnings and help insure positive returns. Diversification of product may provide pricing flexibility. For example, one product can compete on price (slim margins) without affecting the profit margins of the other. PowerTool has added a product line that may be able to use the existing production capacity. Diversification will therefore reduce bondholder risk.

Disadvantages

1. Fenton's new product needs marketing expertise, and so does PowerTool's old product. Marketing is critical in the retail business. PowerTool's reduced financial flexibility will limit the potential strength of the new product if it cannot be properly marketed.

2. The growth in the retail market may not be large enough to affect PowerTool's returns because PowerTool is a large company and Fenton is a small company.

3. Fenton's new product has shown promise only in test markets. It has no track record, yet it is projected to account for 50 percent of the business in five years. Any uncertainty about the success of the new product adds uncertainty about the success of the acquisition and increases risk for bondholders.

4. Management of both companies is in transition. If Jerry Fenton were the innovator at Fenton, this transition would affect the value of the company because he has retired. The old Fenton employees are now subject to a more mature management style. Whether the mix works is always uncertain in these situations. The expectation is that the old management style at PowerTool will continue; if it does not, confusion will replace the clear direction this acquisition needs.

D. Reason supporting a *hold* of PowerTool bonds.

1. PowerTool management has a proven track record, little turnover, and is well respected. Despite its marketing problems, PowerTool has the ability to stay competitive. Management judgment seems to be good. Although the CEO retired, there seems to be continuity. Management is experienced and can generally make a profit and maintain adequate financial flexibility.

2. In the industrial tools business, it would probably take a technical breakthrough such as Fenton's to grow unless management wanted to compete on price or acquire the competition. Buying Fenton is a logical alternative to fighting in a no-growth business. PowerTool bondholders may benefit by the innovative expertise of Fenton and diversify out of a no-growth business.

3. PowerTool is buying its way into a new segment of its existing business, which adds customer diversification without straying far outside its realm of expertise. The potential for using the existing facilities for the production of retail hand tools (a growing business) adds financial flexibility because PowerTool can transform production for a best use. This also helps ensure customer satisfaction regarding delivery time and the filling of quantity orders.

4. Fenton needs PowerTool's financial flexibility and management expertise to take advantage of its innovative strength. PowerTool will use its strong sales force to market the new product and increase profitability, which will be positive for its bonds.

5. The put option covenant provides downside risk protection to its bondholders in case the acquisition does not succeed and the bond rating declines below A.

6.   The dividend covenant imposes discipline on the managers and prevents them from distributing cash to shareholders to the detriment of bondholders.

Reason supporting a *sell* of PowerTool bonds.

1.   PowerTool is the largest company in a no-growth industry. Its marketing skills are not up to customer standards already. PowerTool is leveraging itself into a credit downgrade to buy a small company in a different market. Fenton has its own marketing failings, but its "hot new product" will require a successful market introduction.

2.   Credit deterioration and stringent new covenants reduce the financial flexibility of the company. The firm needs to overcome its deficiency in the marketing area, including the ability to counteract any offensive moves by competitors in the no-growth industrial tool business. Debt will cost more in the future. It will be harder to draw equity investment with the covenants that now exist. If the covenants in Part B are not attached to the bonds, other bondholders have a superior claim on corporate assets.

3.   PowerTool may have paid too big a premium for Fenton.

4.   The test marketing for the new product may be a gamble. This is especially true if the marketing is done by a company without marketing resources. PowerTool has a sales force that is seen as strong, yet customers complain about marketing. This is even more important in the retail market. Without good marketing, the new product's success is in jeopardy. It seems that the new product was the reason for the acquisition, given that the product is expected to be 50 percent of Fenton's sales in a mere five years. This product has no track record.

5.   PowerTool was between ratings classes before the acquisition and was given the lower rating. The company may receive an A- or lower rating, which would trigger the exercise of the put option by some debt holders. If PowerTool has to refinance the debt at a higher interest rate, this would affect the price of debt and might result in further downgrading. Also, PowerTool might not be able to respond immediately to a sudden exercise of the options, causing a delay in the return of bondholders' principal.

6.   The bonds are currently trading as A-rated bonds, which may imply a price that is higher than the underlying credit quality of the company (A-) warrants.

3.   Jane Berry should buy the **Patriot Manufacturing bond.**

Table 5 factors. Table 5 shows that Patriot is less risky than Sturdy Machines. First, the pretax interest coverage of Sturdy Machines is just over one vs. Patriot's at 6.1 times. Second, Patriot's cash flow/total debt is higher than Sturdy Machines and is improving faster. Finally, Patriot's total debt/capital is lower than Sturdy Machines and is decreasing.

Qualitative factors. The qualitative factors supporting this recommendation include, first, the fact that Patriot is an improving credit, as evidenced by the recent rating upgrade. Sturdy Machines, on the other hand, is a deteriorating credit, as evidenced by the recent rating downgrade. Second, given that the credit-rating changes were recent, one would expect no change (or continued increases) in the rating of the Patriot bonds and no change (or continued decreases) in the rating of the Sturdy Machines bonds. Finally, Berry can anticipate that the Patriot bonds will fall in yield (rise in price). Sturdy Machines' bonds appear to be riskier than Patriot's bonds.

CHAPTER 23: EQUITY VALUATION--A MICROVIEW

SOLUTIONS

Questions

QA23-1   The perpetual constant growth DDM allocates the firm's earnings per share, EPS, between two components. First, part of the earnings are used to pay cash dividends per share of [(1 - RR)(EPS)] = DIV dollars. Second, the remainder of the earnings per share are the retained earnings of [(RR)(EPS)] dollars that are used to finance future growth internally. In other words, on a per share basis: EPS = [(1 - RR)(EPS)] + [(RR)(EPS)] = DIV + [(RR)(EPS)] = (Dividends) + (Retained earnings). Each year's retained earnings of [(RR)(EPS)] dollars are reinvested in the firm to earn that year's internal rate of return of ROE percent. As a result, the firm's equity will grow at a rate of g = [(ROE)(RR)]. If part of the firm's retained earnings were held in cash that earns a zero return, or, if some of the retained earnings were invested to earn less than the firm's ROE, then the firm would return less than g = [(ROE)(RR)]. But, without external financing, it is impossible for the firm to sustain growth at a rate greater than g = [(RR)(ROE)]. Summarizing, in an all-equity firm, reinvested earnings can finance the maximum sustainable growth rate symbolized by g in Eqn. (23-10).

$$EPS_t = EPS_0(1 + g)^t = EPS_0[1 + RR(ROE)]^t \qquad \textbf{Eqn.(23-10)}$$

Assets, earnings, and dividends all grow at the same sustainable growth rate of g in an all-equity firm.

QA23-2   The required rate of return is the minimum return necessary to induce the investor to accept the risks associated with the investment. In addition to considering the riskiness of the investment, the required rate of return also considers the opportunity cost that the investor could have earned on alternative investments. These considerations determine the investor'' minimum required rate of return. It is appropriate to use this required rate of return as the discount rate in computing the present value of an investment.

QA23-3   No, not every dollar of retained earnings will necessarily lead to a dollar of price appreciation (capital gains.) If a corporation invests its retained earnings in unprofitable projects, its common stockholders will receive no payback from earnings retention. The analysis of growth stock investing showed that no matter how much of a firm's earnings are retained to finance internal growth, the value of the corporation's equity shares will not appreciate unless those earnings are invested in projects that have positive NPVs. See the discussion surrounding Eqn.(23-12e) in the textbook. This finding could explain why many growth firms are observed to grow physically larger as they use retained earnings to buy more assets, but they do not appreciate much in value because their new projects have low NPVs.

   In contrast to the growth firms that grow physically larger as they use retained earnings to buy new assets, but appreciate in value at an unimpressive rate because the acquired assets have zero net present values (NPVs), some corporations are adept at using retained earnings to enrich their shareholders. Microsoft, for example, has always retained 100% of its earnings, and it uses these retained earnings to buy projects with high positive NPVs. As a result, the common stock of Microsoft appreciates rapidly. In other words, for every dollar of Microsoft earnings that are retained, Microsoft's shareholders get more than a dollar in capital gains income.

QA23-4   No. The price that an investor should be willing to pay for a stock does not depend on his expected holding period. This is first demonstrated by examining the perpetual constant growth model:

$$P_0 = \frac{DIV_1}{k - g}$$

Note that none of the variables in the model reflect an investor's holding period. The expected price at the end of the holding period implicitly reflects the expected dividends from that time forward. For example, if an investor expects to hold the stock for only four years, the price he can expect to sell the stock for at the end of the fourth year implicitly reflects the expected dividend stream from that point on as indicated below:

$$P_4 = \frac{DIV_5}{(1+k)^1} + \frac{DIV_6}{(1+k)^2} + \frac{DIV_7}{(1+k)^3} + \ldots$$

QA23-5   A growth stock is defined as one for which ROE > k. If all new investment is financed internally, one might expect the price of the growth stock to increase with an increase in the retention rate. This can be seen by examination of Eqn.(23-12d):

$$P_0 = \frac{EPS_1}{k} + \frac{1}{(1+k)}\left[\frac{EPS_1(ROE)(RR)}{k} - (RR)(EPS_1)\right]$$

As RR, the retention rate, increases, so will P_0, if ROE > k. In a normal firm, ROE = k. Note that under this condition, the last term in the equation under this condition is equal to zero. Therefore, the price of the firm will be unaffected by the retention rate of the firm.

QA23-6   Since the spread between the required rate of return and the growth rate, k - g, is equal to the dividend yield on the stock, an increase in the spread implies an increase in the dividend yield on the stock. The required rate of return is the sum of the dividend yield on the stock and the expected capital gains on the stock. If the required rate of return remains constant, then the increase in dividend yield must be accompanied by a decrease in the expected capital gains on the stock for the mathematical relationship to hold.

$$P_0 = \frac{DIV_1}{k - g}$$

$$k - g = \frac{DIV_1}{P_0} = \text{dividend yield}$$

k = required rate of return = dividend yield + g
where g represents the capital gains yield.

QA23-7   Yes, this assumption is a logical one. It is realistic to assume that the issuer's risk-adjusted discount rate exceeds its growth rate. The markets recognize the fact that an issuer's growth rate and its riskiness increase together, and that growth firms are riskier than no-growth firms. As a result, the market prices adjust so that the risk-adjusted cost of capital for a firm rises with its growth rate. Therefore, it is reasonable to assume that k and g fall and rise together and to assume that k is larger than g.

QA23-8   False. While it may be true that a forecast of dividends 50 to 100 years, into the future, which the perpetual constant growth model implicitly does, is very unreliable, the present value of those dividends is so small that it makes a negligible difference in the price of the stock. Additionally, smaller firms, for which dividends well into the future are most difficult to forecast, are generally riskier, commanding a higher discount rate. The higher the discount rate, the lower the present value of expected future cash flows, and the more negligible distant dividends are in determining the price of the stock of the firm.

QA23-9   Cash dividend payments by growth stocks may be attributed to market imperfections. For example, some states have laws that forbid such institutional investors as life insurance companies, commercial banks, pension funds, and other financial intermediaries from investing in common stocks that have not paid cash dividends consistently in recent years. This may encourage growth firms to pay cash dividends when paying them is suboptimal economic behavior.

QA23-10   Stock Z is a true growth stock since its ROE > the required rate of return, k. Stock X is an example of a normal firm where ROE = k.

Problems

PA23-1   The perpetual constant growth DDM can be used to determine the price of this firm's stock.

$$P_0 = \frac{DIV_0(1+g)}{k-g} = \frac{\$0.70(1.08)}{0.20-0.08} = \$6.30$$

PA23-2   The expected dividend stream for the investor must first be determined:

$DIV_1 = \$0.70(1.08) = \$0.756$
$DIV_2 = \$0.756(1.08) = \$0.816$

Next the dividend at the end of year three must be calculated in order to determine the expected price of the stock at the end of year two since prices are based on *expected* dividends.

$DIV_3 = \$0.816(1.08) = \$0.882$

This implies a price at the end of year two of $P_2 = \dfrac{\$0.882}{0.20-0.08} = \$7.35$. This investor should pay a price today equal to his discounted future cash flow stream:

$$P_0 = \frac{\$0.756}{(1.20)^1} + \frac{\$0.816}{(1.20)^2} + \frac{\$7.35}{(1.20)^2} = \$6.30$$

This is identical to the price calculated in PA23-1, demonstrating that an investor's expected holding period does not affect the price he should pay for the stock.

PA23-3   The dividend stream for the first growth rate is determined. Then the holding period price implied by the second growth rate is calculated. These cash flows are then discounted back to determine a fair market price for the stock today.

$DIV_1 = \$0.30$
$DIV_2 = \$0.30(1.30) = \$0.39$
$DIV_3 = \$0.39(1.12) = \$0.44$

$$P_2 = \frac{DIV_3}{k - g} = \frac{\$0.44}{0.18 - 0.12} = \$7.33$$

$$P_0 = \frac{\$0.30}{(1.18)^1} + \frac{\$0.39}{(1.18)^2} + \frac{\$7.33}{(1.18)^2} = \$5.80$$

PA23-4   Stock M will be more sensitive. It has the larger growth rate in dividends, given the same required rate of return, where g = ROE x RR.

$g_m = 12\% \times 0.6 = 7.2\%$
$g_N = 12\% \times 0.3 = 3.6\%$

Because of this, Stock M can be thought of as having a longer duration since more of its return (from dividends) is expected in the future. Longer duration securities are more sensitive to changes in interest rate. To prove this to yourself, consider the following:

Price calculated for current required rate of return:

Stock M

$$P_0 = \frac{\$1.00}{0.12 - 0.072} = \$20.83$$

Stock N

$$P_0 = \frac{\$1.75}{0.12 - 0.036} = \$20.83$$

Price if k is increased to 15%:

$$P_0 = \frac{\$1.00}{0.15 - 0.072} = \$12.82$$

$$P_0 = \frac{\$1.75}{0.15 - 0.036} = \$15.35$$

PA23-5   Fledgling's imputed P/E ratio can be backed out of the following equation:

$$P/EPS = \frac{\dfrac{DIV_1}{EPS_1}}{k - g}$$

$$10.52 = \frac{payout\ ratio}{0.30 - 0.21}$$

$payout\ ratio = 10.52(0.30 - 0.21) = 0.9468 = 94.68\%$

PA23-6   The price-earnings ratio for Fledgling would increase from 10.52 to 47.34 as calculated below:

$$P/EPS = \frac{\dfrac{DIV_1}{EPS_1}}{k-g} = \frac{0.9468}{0.30-0.28} = 47.34$$

PA23-7   Pliant's estimated value per share can be calculated using the following equation:

Estimated value per share = (Estimated EPS)(Estimated price-earnings ratio)
Estimated value per share = $2.25 x 15 = $33.75

PA23-8   Since CellOptics is all-equity financed, Total assets = Total equity = $15 million.
$$ROE = \frac{net\ income}{total\ equity} = \frac{12\ million}{15\ million} = 8\%.$$ The retention rate = 1 - 0.2 = 0.8, so g = ROE x RR = 8% x 0.8 = 6.4%.

PA23-9   The perpetual constant growth DDM can be used to calculate the price for the stock as follows:

$$P_0 = \frac{EPS(dividend\ payout\ ratio)}{k-g} = \frac{\$3.50}{0.16-0.12} = \$35.00$$

PA23-10 (a)   The growth rate for Trimark must be determined first.

g = ROE x RR = 15% x 0.4 = 6%

Since $P_0 = \dfrac{DIV_1}{k-g}$, $k = \dfrac{DIV_1}{P_0} + g = \dfrac{\$3.00(0.6)}{\$20} + 0.06 = 15\%.$

(b)   Since the required rate of return, k, is equal to the ROE (k = ROE = 15%) for Trimark, the NPV of future investment opportunities is equal to zero; therefore, the price is unaffected by the dividend payout ratio.

CFA Exam Solutions*

The following are the guideline answers provided by the AIMR for the CFA Exam questions:

1.   C

2.   C
      Solution:
      $8,500,000 x 5.4%
      = 459,000/120,000
      = $3.83.

3.　　C

Solution:

X = 43.50 x 26

4.　　**A.　　Possible Valuation Decrease**

The constant-growth-rate version of the DDM is often expressed as

$$P = \frac{D_1}{K-g} \text{ and also } P = \frac{D_0(1+g)}{K-g}, \text{ in that } D_1 = D_0(1+g),$$

in which D_1 is next year's dividend per share, K is the required rate of return (sometimes called the internal rate of return), and g is the dividend growth rate.

Soft Corporation's acquisition of a slower-growth competitor might decrease its valuation based on a constant-growth DDM because

- SC's $300 million in new long-term debt and related interest costs decreases the likelihood that the dividend will be increased next year (D_1);
- the acquisition of a slower-growth company reduces the acquirer's long-term growth rate for dividends;
- the higher financial leverage resulting from the acquisition will increase the perceived riskiness of SC, raising investors' required rate of return (K);
- everything else being equal, these factors (lower dividend growth rate and higher required rate of return) **could** interact to increase the denominator and decrease the numerator of the DDM.

B.　Possible Increase in P/E Multiple

The acquisition might increase the P/E multiple investors will be willing to pay for SC for the following reasons:

- The acquisition could provide internal sources of growth. *Synergies* (the opportunity for cost cutting, economies of scale, etc.) from the combination might well emerge in time, which would increase the earnings growth rate in the intermediate term. Investors might anticipate this improved growth rate, which would enhance the P/E multiple.
- The acquisition could provide external sources of growth. Particularly if the acquired company is an important direct competitor, investors' perceptions of *reduced competition* and *improved pricing* in the future could lead to a higher multiple on the stock on current earnings.
- The acquisition will add value if returns exceed costs. The use of debt to finance the acquisition will enhance the ROE of SC *if* the incremental profitability exceeds the after-tax cost of debt capital. If investors perceive this higher ROE to be *sustainable*, their expectations for growth and, consequently, the multiple they are willing to pay for the stock are likely to increase.
- Investors may decide that the external sources of growth (see above) justify *viewing the riskiness of the combined entity as less than that of SC alone*, which would justify a higher P/E multiple.
- Short-term EPS may drop because of the expenses related to the acquisition, but investors looking beyond this short-term drop may believe that *longer-term earnings growth* prospects have improved. The multiple on current earnings may rise as a result of this expectation.
- If SC is currently underleveraged, the debt load taken on in this acquisition may actually *optimize SC's leverage*, which would produce a lower overall cost of capital and justify a higher P/E multiple.

5.　　A.　　**Constant growth dividend discount model:** $D_1/(k-g) = P_0$
　　　　　　Litchfield:　　　$0.90/(0.10 - 0.08) = $45.00
　　　　　　Aminochem:　　$1.60/(0.11 - 0.07) = $40.00

B.   **Expected return:** $R_f + \beta (R_m - R_f) = k$
Litchfield: 5% + 1.2(20% - 5%) = 23%
Aminochem: 5% + 1.4(20% - 5%) = 26%

C.   **Internal growth rate:** $[(E - D)/E][E/BV] = g$
Litchfield: [($4.00 - $0.90)/$4.00]($4.00/$30) = 10.3%
                    BV = $300/10 = $30
Aminochem: [($3.20 - $1.60)/$3.20]($3.20/$16 = 10.0%
                    BV = $320/20 = $16

D.   **Recommendation:** Aminochem (AOC) is a more attractive investment than Litchfield (LCC) based on the answers to parts A, B, and C, and the information provided in Table 1.

       Justification: Using the constant growth dividend discount model (DDM) (computed in Part A), the stock price of AOC is more attractive at a price of $30 (well below its DDM value of $40) than LCC at a price of $50 (above the DDM value of $45).

       AOC has the higher expected return (computed in Part B) because it has a higher beta and the market (S&P 500) is expected to rise.

       LCC's internal growth rate (computed in Part C) is higher than that of AOC, but LCC's higher price-to-earnings ratio of 12.5 ($50/$4) versus 9.4 ($30/$3.20) for AOC is not justified by the small difference in growth rate.

6.   The first explanation of the value-versus-growth effect is that the empirically observed positive return spread between value and growth stocks represents a *risk premium*. That is, investors expect the positive return spread as a reward for taking on higher risk. This explanation is consistent with the efficient market hypothesis. According to some researchers, a characteristic of low price-to-book (P/B) or low price-to-earnings (P/E) stocks is that they have poor earnings growth prospects. Also, investors do not highly regard low-expectation firms. Therefore, investing in such stocks represents a risk (distress) and presents discomfort for some investors. Consequently, investors require a higher expected return to entice them to invest in these securities. The *ex post* positive return spread between value and growth stocks represents nothing more than the realization of an expected risk premium.

      The second explanation of the value-versus-growth effect is that the *ex post* positive return spread between value and growth stocks represents a *surprise* caused by mispricing of securities. This explanation is inconsistent with the efficient market hypothesis. According to some researchers, the mispricing occurs because stock markets are initially slow to react and then overreact to information about earnings. Inertia and positive momentum characterize short-run price behavior. The market seems to price growth stocks as if their above-average relative earnings growth will continue for a very long time in the future and price value stocks as if their earnings will continue to be depressed for a long time. Earnings have a tendency to revert to the mean, however, in a short time span (four to five years). When the reversion happens, the market is surprised and returns from growth (value) stocks tend to be low (high).

CHAPTER 24: MEASURING EARNING POWER

SOLUTIONS

Questions

QA24-1   Uncertain. While a study by Paul Healy and Krishna Palepu revealed that when an announcement was made that a firm planned to omit a regular cash dividend payment, the stock price dropped by an abnormal 9.5%, on average, and when an announcement was made that a firm planned to increase its dividend payment, the price had an abnormal increase of 4%, there is a problem in the cause and effect relationship. Dividend announcements provide information to the market, and the announcement of a dividend decrease is generally taken to mean that the firm's management is concerned about the firm's long-term financial position. It is this information that causes the stock price to fall, and not the mere announcement. Consider a situation in which a pharmaceutical company announces that it plans to suspend a dividend payment in order to reinvest all their earnings so that it might beat a competitor to the market with a cure for AIDS. It is extremely unlikely that one would observe that firm's stock price to fall with the announcement. On the other hand, when IBM announced a decrease in its long-standing dividend in the late 1980s, its stock price did drop. The markets were aware of IBM's financial problems at the time, and its price had already plummeted, but the announcement was interpreted as a statement by management that the financial problems of "Big Blue" would not soon be solved. Similarly, when management announces an increase in a regular cash dividend, the announcement is interpreted as a statement by management that it expects a higher level of earnings to be sustainable in the future since management would not increase dividends only to have to cut them in the near future, and it is this information content, not the announcement itself, that contributes to the price increase. Otherwise, any time management wanted to bolster its firm's stock price, it could announce a dividend increase. Investors are not that dumb.

QA24-2   During a period of inflation, LIFO will result in a higher cost of goods sold and a lower taxable income since the inventory that has been most recently purchased, at higher prices, is considered to be the first sold.

QA24-3   False. Although it is true that a depreciable asset will be fully depreciated over its useful life to zero, the method of depreciation that a firm chooses is not irrelevant. Using the accelerated depreciation method allowed by the IRS--MACRS or ACRS as the case may be--allows a firm to report lower taxable income in the early years of the asset's life than it would if it had chosen to use straight-line depreciation. Since money has time value, the lower taxes paid in the early years will increase the shareholder wealth.

QA24-4   Goodwill can be amortized over a period of up to 40 years. However, the situation that contributes to the goodwill may exist for a shorter period of time, in which case it would be a truer reflection of the firm's financial condition if it were amortized only over the number of years for which the goodwill is expected to contribute to higher profits for the firm than it might otherwise have.

QA24-5   Primary EPS is simply the earnings per share based on the actual number of shares outstanding at the time of the report. If, however, a firm has such things as convertible bonds, convertible preferred stock, executive stock options, employee stock options, and/or warrants outstanding, the exercise of these will increase the number of shares outstanding, thus diluting the earnings per share. If the effect of the dilution is a decline in EPS of less than 3%, it need not be reported. However, if it is greater than 3%, a fully diluted EPS, which indicates what the earnings per share would be if these options were exercised, thus increasing the number of shares outstanding, must be reported.

QA24-6   According to APB rules, the items are classified as follows:

(a)   Bad debt losses: ordinary
(b)   Write-off of obsolete inventory: ordinary
(c)   Destruction of a building by a hurricane: extraordinary
(d)   Loss from the sale of a division: ordinary
(e)   Expropriation of the assets of a business by a foreign government: extraordinary
(f)   Loss due to foreign currency translations: ordinary

QA24-7   Because firms use an accrual basis when accounting for revenues and expenses, sales that have been made on credit, for which no cash has yet been received, are included in a firm's revenues. Therefore, subtracting any increases in accounts receivable and adding any decreases in accounts receivable, adjusts revenues for actual cash flows. Likewise, when a firm purchases goods on credit from its suppliers, the expense is included in the cost of goods sold when the inventory is sold, even though the firm has not had a cash outflow. To adjust for this, an increase in accounts payable is added back and a decrease in accounts payable is subtracted.

QA24-8   The economic income of a firm during a given period equals the maximum amount of consumption opportunities that can be withdrawn from the firm during that period without diminishing the consumption opportunities that can be obtained from the firm in future periods. Accounting income is an upward biased estimate of the true economic income because a firm's net income contains retained earnings that are not actually available for consumption.

QA24-9   The cash flow available to equity shareholders is determined by taking the cash flow from operations, and subtracting (adding) any cash outflows (inflows) from investing activities and any cash outflows (inflows) from financing activities. These leverage-free cash flows measure the consumption opportunities that are available to a firm's owners and contain deductions for whatever investments the firm's management feels are needed to maintain the firm's future earning power.

QA24-10   Foster, Olsen and Shevlin (FOS) analyzed the behavior of the returns on a firm's stock around the time of the announcement of a corporation's quarterly earnings to the public. To do so, they calculated the standardized unexpected earnings (SUEs) for 2,053 firms over 32 quarters of earnings. They found that when corporations announced unexpected good earnings, the stock prices tended to have increased prior to the announcement date, during the period that began 60 days prior to the announcement. Likewise, when a firm announced earnings that were poorer than expected, its stock price tended to decrease prior to the announcement date. On the day just prior to the announcement and the day of the actual announcement, they found that larger earnings surprises in either direction resulted, on average, in larger price reactions in the same direction. These results do not contradict the efficient markets hypothesis since they indicate that the stock market correctly anticipates earnings changes before they are announced and responds accordingly. New information is reacted to both quickly and rationally. However, FOS also discovered that the abnormal returns on stocks associated with earnings announcements continued for two months after the earnings announcement. This does violate the efficient markets hypothesis since it indicates than an investor could earn abnormal returns by trading on these announcements.

Problems

PA24-1   Shareholders in Firm X received the more unpleasant surprise. This can be seen by comparing the standardized unexpected earnings for the two firms:

$$SUE_X = \frac{\$2.00 - \$2.30}{\$0.70} = -0.429$$

$$SUE_Y = \frac{\$3.00 - \$3.50}{\$1.66} = -0.30$$

PA24-2   If Calumet uses FIFO, its cost of goods sold is $12,900 and its ending inventory balance is $3,600. If LIFO is used, its cost of goods sold is $13,500 and its ending inventory balance is $3,000.

Purchases:
January: 500 x $10 =	$ 5,000
May: 500 x $11 =	$ 5,500
September: 500 x $12 =	$ 6,000
Total purchases =	$16,500

	Cost of goods sold	Ending inventory balance
FIFO	500 @ $10 = $ 5,000	
	500 @ $11 = $ 5,500	
	200 @ $12 = $ 2,400	
Total	$12,900	$16,500 - $12,900 = $3,600

	Cost of goods sold	Ending inventory balance
LIFO	500 @ $12 = $ 6,000	
	500 @ $11 = $ 5,500	
	200 @ $10 = $ 2,000	
Total	$13,500	$16,500 - $13,500 = $3,000

PA24-3   Using straight-line depreciation, Inmar will expense $10,000/5 = $2,000 a year. The depreciation factors for the sum-of-the-digits method and the depreciation allowances for each year using this method are provided below:

Year	Depreciation factor		Depreciation allowance
1	$\dfrac{5}{\frac{5(6)}{2}} = 0.333333$		$3,333.33
2	$\dfrac{4}{\frac{5(6)}{2}} = 0.266667$		$2,666.67
3	$\dfrac{3}{\frac{5(6)}{2}} = 0.200000$		$2,000.00
4	$\dfrac{2}{\frac{5(6)}{2}} = 0.133333$		$1,333.33
5	$\dfrac{1}{\frac{5(6)}{2}} = 0.066667$		$ 666.67

PA24-4   The cash flow from operations for the Canton Corporation for 20x2 is calculated below:

Cash inflow from operations

Sales revenues	$10,000	
less increase in A/R	$50	
Cash collections on sales	$ 9,950	
Total cash inflows from operations		+$9,950

Cash outflow from operations

Cost of goods sold	-$ 6,000
General selling and administrative	-$ 1,500
plus depreciation	+$ 500
Taxes paid	-$ 840
	-$ 7,840

Other adjustments to cash flow:

minus increase in inventory	- $ 700	
plus increase in A/P	+$ 100	
plus increase in accrued expenses	+$ 200	
minus interest expense	- $ 400	
	- $ 800	
Total cash outflows		-$8,640
Total cash flows from operations		$1,310

PA24-5   The cash flow from investing activities for the Canton Corporation consists of an additional investment in plant, property and equipment as is revealed by looking at the change in the gross plant, property, and equipment account on the firm's balance sheets. This is a cash outflow from investing activities of $1,000.

PA24-6   The cash flow from financing activities for the Canton Corporation consists of an increase in long-term debt, as indicated by the change in this account on the balance sheets, and the common stock dividends paid of $450.

Increase in long-term debt	+$500	
Common stock dividends	- $450	
Net cash flow from financing activities	+$ 50	

PA24-7   The cash flow from operations for the Infonext Corporation for 20x2 is calculated below:

Cash inflow from operations		
Sales revenues	$22,000	
plus decrease in A/R	$150	
Cash collections on sales	$22,150	
Total cash inflows from operations		+$22,150
Cash outflow from operations		
Cost of goods sold	- $14,300	
Other operating expenses	- $ 2,700	
plus depreciation expense	+$ 800	
minus taxes paid	- $ 1,520	
	- $17,720	
Other adjustments to cash flow:		
minus increase in inventory	- $ 550	
plus increase in A/P	+$ 120	
minus decrease in accrued expenses	- $ 100	
minus interest expense	- $1,200	
	- $1,730	
Total cash outflows		-$19,450
Total cash flows from operations		$ 2,700

PA24-8   The cash flow from investing activities for the Infonext Corporation consists of an additional investment in plant, property and equipment as is revealed by looking at the change in the gross plant, property, and equipment account on the firm's balance sheets. This is a cash outflow from investing activities of $1,100.

PA24-9   The cash flow from financing activities for the Infonext Corporation consists of a decrease in long-term debt of $300, as indicated by the change in this account on the balance sheets, and the common stock dividends paid of $1,000.

Decrease in long-term debt	-$ 300
Common stock dividends	-$1,000
Net cash flow from financing activities	-$1,300

PA24-10   The free cash flow available to equity holders for the Infonext Corporation is the sum of the cash flow from operations, the cash flow from investing activities, and the cash flow from financing activities:

Cash flow from operations	+$2,700
Cash flow from investing activities	- $1,100
Cash flow from financing activities	- $1,300
Total free cash flow	+$ 300

If there are 500,000 shares outstanding, the free cash flow per share is $300,000/500,000 = $0.60. If this is assumed to be a perpetuity, then the present value of the cash flow stream is found by using the following formula:

$$PV = \frac{\text{free cash flow per share}}{\text{required return on equity}} = \frac{\$0.60}{0.15} = \$4.00$$

CFA Exam Solutions*

The following are the guideline answers provided by the AIMR for the CFA Exam questions:

1. B
    Solution:
    Numerator:
    Net income - Preferred dividend
    = $6,500,000 - $500,000
    = $6,000,000

    Denominator:
    100,000 warrants (proceeds $5,000,000) + (-83,333) shares acquired at $60 with $5,000,000 proceeds + 1,000,000 outstanding
    = 1,016,667

    $6,000,000/1,016,667
    = $5.90

2. A

3. D

CHAPTER 25: STOCK VALUATION ISSUES

SOLUTIONS

Questions

QA25-1   A number of investors believe that a cash dividend yield on the S&P 500 Index that is greater than 5% is an indication that the U.S. stock market is underpriced. They, therefore, interpret a 5% cash dividend yield as a buy signal. A 3% cash dividend yield is considered to be a sell signal since they believe that the S&P 500 Index's cash dividend yield can fall only as low as 3% if many common stocks are overpriced.

         Some investors also believe that if stocks in the S&P 500 Index are selling at less than eight times earnings, the U.S. stock market is underpriced and interpret this as a buy signal. These same people believe that when the 500 stocks in the S&P 500 Index have a price-earnings ratio of more than 19, the market is overpriced, and, therefore, it is a good time to sell.

         A disadvantage of using these simple trading rules is that they may give erroneous, and sometimes contradictory signals. In 1938, the price-earnings ratio on the S&P 500 Index was greater than 19, indicating a sell signal, while at the same time the cash dividend yield on the Index indicated a buy signal. Too, in 1992, the cash dividend yield indicated a sell signal that continued for several years while the markets continued to rise. It's possible that the increase in stock repurchases and demographic factors have undermined the future usefulness of the cash dividend yield as a market timing guideline.

QA25-2   Bakshi and Chen hypothesized that when baby boomers reach approximately 50 years of age, they will allocate a greater percentage of their income in the stock market to finance their future retirement needs. Therefore, they concluded that a bull market would begin in about 1996, when the oldest baby boomers entered their fifties, and end before 2026, when the youngest baby boomers reach 65 and retire. Bakshi and Chen also concluded that the flow of savings will reverse in the decade from 2010 to 2020 as the baby boomers begin to retire. After retirement, these baby boomers should begin consuming their savings until the time of their death, so the two researchers conclude that the long bull market will be followed by a long bear market as pension funds, mutual funds, and other financial intermediaries experience continuous annual cash outflows from approximately 2015 to 2040.

QA25-3   There are numerous differences between the new Dot.com companies and the more traditional bricks-and-mortar firms. Traditional firms are able to forecast sales based on sales of past products, but the Dot.com companies are constantly producing new products, and this, combined with new technological innovations, lead to expectations of higher growth rates for these companies. Traditional firms try to increase profits through cost-cutting measures since raising prices is not feasible, while the huge demand for the products of Dot.com companies allow them to raise prices significantly without losing sales. Traditional firms are also typically highly leveraged, resulting in high levels of interest expense, but many Dot.com companies are only equity financed and pay no dividends. Traditional companies also keep employees by giving large pay raises, another fixed cost to them. Employees of Dot.com companies are rewarded with stock options. Traditional companies must often struggle to maintain their share of the market while Dot.com companies work to dominate their markets since there exists a winner-takes-all nature in the Internet business. The first firm to enter a new niche on the world wide web can reap large rewards while late-comers often struggle to try to get a share of that market since web surfers are known to return to the same site rather than spend the time to seek out additional sites.

QA25-4   False. While the power rule model seems to explain *relative* values of Internet firms well, it does not allow us to determine whether the market prices of all such firms are too high or too low. For example, an analyst can use it to determine whether one firm is mispriced relative to another firm, but he cannot determine whether or not the first firm itself is mispriced.

QA25-5   Empirical studies have indicated that stock market returns were average during periods of moderate inflation. During periods of high inflation, real returns were far below average, and in periods of extraordinarily high inflation, real returns were actually negative. This same inverse relationship between stock market returns and inflation has also been observed in non-U.S. markets. So, in the short-run stock prices all over the world move inversely with inflation. In the very long run, however, the data indicates that stock prices adjust to inflation such that long-run average real total returns are unaffected by inflation.

QA25-6   In stage three, the mature growth stage, the industry's product is widely accepted, and it is very competitively priced. Sales revenues are rising, but at a slow rate. The players in the industry consist of a number of stable, profitable, solvent firms. The profits at this stage are gradually beginning to decline, and the firms in the industry tend to be increasing their cash dividend payments.

QA25-7   Many workers save for retirement through tax-sheltered annuity plans offered by their employers, such as the 401K and the 403B plans. Much of the money invested through these plans is directed into one of the many equity mutual funds available in the United States. As more and more people feel a greater need to contribute to their retirement as that stage of their life looms closer, more money gets funneled into these funds. Thus, these equity funds have enjoyed high growth rates during the 1990s. Bakshi and Chen's study of the demographics concluded that baby boomers will start to draw on these savings in the year 2010. If their forecast is correct, the equity funds should continue to experience high growth rates at least until that point in time. (This, in turn, supports the forecast for a bull market during this period, based on the theory of supply and demand. As more and more funds flow into these equity mutual funds and the managers of the funds have to invest most of the funds in equities, in accordance with the funds' objectives, the demand for equities will increase. If the supply of equities does not keep up with this demand, and it is likely that it won't, prices of equities will be driven up.)

QA25-8   In most countries, the stockholders of a bankrupt company are entitled to the assets that the corporation has left after all the firm's debts are paid. If total liabilities exceed the value of the firm's total assets, the creditors keep all the assets as partial payment of their claims and the stockholders are left with nothing. Therefore, the firm's creditors can be thought of as owning the company while, at the same time, selling a call option on the firm's assets to the firm's owners (common stockholders). The exercise price of the option is the face value of the firm's total debt. If the stockholders choose to exercise the option, they call in the firm's total assets and use these assets to pay off the firm's liabilities, keeping any of the remaining assets. They will do so in the case that the value of the assets exceeds the liabilities of the firm. If the firm's assets are less than the liabilities of the firm, the shareholders will allow their option to expire worthless, forfeiting all claims on the bankrupt firm.

QA25-9   One should not automatically assume that an industry or product will move progressively from stage one to stage four of the product life cycle model. This could lead to serious forecasting errors. Some industries, for example, may be in the declining growth stage and move backward into the mature growth stage. Consider the motorcycle manufacturing industry. It had been considered to be in a declining growth stage at a time when motorcycles were associated with ne'er-do-well gangs. Honda, however, came out with a new slogan: "You meet the nicest people on a Honda." This creativity in advertising increased the demand for the product, and the industry was given a new life.

QA25-10   There is a tendency for firms with high ROEs to have high price/book value ratios and firms with low ROEs to have low price/book value ratios. Therefore, if a firm has a high PBV ratio and a low ROE, it is reasonable to suspect that it is overpriced. Likewise, if a firm has a low PBV, but a high ROE, it may be underpriced. A PBV/ROE ratio can be calculated to control for differences in firms' ROEs. The attractiveness of a firm should vary directly with the size of its PBV/ROE ratio. However, one must remember that expected earnings have a larger impact on stock prices than historical accounting measures that are used in the calculation of the book value of a firm and its ROE ratio. Zero and negative ROEs, which are often observed with Internet firms, can also complicate the computations. Nevertheless, the PBV/ROE ratio can be used as a helpful screening tool.

Problems

PA-25-1   There are four steps involved in calculating a practical price/earnings ratio:

Step 1: Determine the market capitalization of the firm. Market capitalization = price x shares outstanding = $76.125(340.8 million) = $25,943.4 million.
Step 2: Multiply the most recent quarter's sales by 4 to determine an annualized sales number. For Amazon, this is $674,042,000 x 4 = $2,704,168,000.
Step 3: Divide the market capitalization by the annualized sales to get a price/sales ratio. $25,943.4/2,704.168 = 9.59.
Step 4: Divide the price/sales ratio by the largest plausible net profit margin to calculate a practical price/earnings ratio for the firm. 9.59/0.005 = 1,918 times.

PA25-2(a)   There are four steps involved in calculating a practical price/earnings ratio:

Step 1: Determine the market capitalization of the firm. Market capitalization = price x shares outstanding = $432.6875(263.2 million shares) = $113,883.35 million.
Step 2: Multiply the most recent quarter's sales by 4 to determine an annualized sales number. For Yahoo, this is $201.083 million x 4 = $804.332 million.
Step 3: Divide the market capitalization by the annualized sales to get a price/sales ratio. $113,883.35/$804.332 = 141.59.
Step 4: Divide the price/sales ratio by the largest plausible net profit margin to calculate a practical price/earnings ratio for the firm. 141.59/0.104 = 1361.44 times

(b)   Based on its practical price/earnings ratio, the fair market value for Yahoo can be determined by multiplying this ratio by your estimate of the normal EPS for the firm. Price = 1361.44 x $0.21 = $285.90. At its December 31, 1999 price of $432.6875, Yahoo appeared to be significantly overpriced and would not have been a good investment.

PA25-3   Yahoo's price/earnings-to-growth rate multiple is 1361.44/55.04% = 24.735. Since the most desirable internet stocks trade at 2.4 to 2.6 times their underlying growth rates, this suggests that Yahoo is significantly overpriced.

PA25-4 (a)   There are four steps involved in calculating a practical price/earnings ratio:

Step 1: Determine the market capitalization of the firm. Market capitalization = price x shares outstanding = $125.1875(129.3 million) = $16,186.74375 million.
Step 2: Multiply the most recent quarter's sales by 4 to determine an annualized sales number. For eBay, this is $73,919,000 x 4 = $295,676,000.
Step 3: Divide the market capitalization by the annualized sales to get a price/sales ratio. $16,186.74375/295.676 = 54.74
Step 4: Divide the price/sales ratio by the largest plausible net profit margin to calculate a practical price/earnings ratio for the firm. 54.74/0.048 = 1,140.42 times.

(b)   Using eBay's 1999 figure as a normal EPS for the firm, the fair market price for the firm is $0.10(1140.42) = $114.04. At its December 31, 1999 price of $125.1875, it was overpriced.

(c)   Finance is not an exact science. Assumptions must be made. In the above example, some of our assumptions were that annualized sales would simply be the most recent quarterly sales times four. We also assumed that the current net profit margin for eBay is the largest plausible one and that its 1999 EPS is at a normal level. As discussed in this chapter, Dot.com firms are hopeful that new products and innovations will result in higher growth levels. This means that investors may expect annual sales to be even larger than what our assumptions would indicate. Furthermore, since there is a winners-take-all attitude with internet companies, the largest plausible net profit margin may be assumed to be much greater than its 1999 figure. Likewise, stock prices are driven by expected earnings, not current earnings. Given the nature of the internet industry, it is unlikely that investors expect the current EPS to continue at its same level in the future.

PA25-5   The price/earnings-to-growth rate for desirable internet companies ranges from 2.4 to 2.6 times. Using eBay's practical price/earnings ratio, we get the following result:
1140.42/g = 2.6; g = 1140.42/2.6 = 438.62%.

PA25-6   Amazon's ranking was given as four, and the regression model determined a value for b of 1.01, so its market capitalization relative to number 1-ranked AOL, would be [market capitalization of AOL = $125.4 billion/$(4)^{1.01}$ = $30.92 billion, so at its given market capitalization of $24.282 billion, it is underpriced relative to AOL.
        eBay's ranking was "6," making its market capitalization under the power rule $125.4 billion/$(6)^{1.01}$ = $20.53 billion. At its given market capitalization of $19.845 billion, it is slightly underpriced relative to AOL. Yahoo's ranking was "2." Employing the power rule, we get a market capitalization of $125.4 billion/$(2)^{1.01}$ = $62.27 billion. At its given market capitalization of $81.132 billion, it is overpriced relative to AOL.

PA25-7 (a)   The exercise price of the call option owned by the stockholders of Castle Pines is equal to the face value of the debt, $50 million

(b)   The intrinsic value per share =

$$P = \frac{MAX[0,(A-D)]}{N} = \frac{MAX[0,(100-50)]}{5} = \frac{50}{5} = \$10.$$

(c)   The total dollar value of the mortgage bond issue = MIN[D, A] = MIN[\$50 million, \$100 million] = \$50 million.

PA25-8 (a)   The intrinsic value per share = $\dfrac{MAX[0,(40-50)]}{5} = \dfrac{0}{5} = \$0.$

The total dollar value of the bond issue = MIN[\$50 million, \$40 million] = \$40 million.

(b)   No. Although the intrinsic value per share is 0, there is time value to the call option as well (two years). This will cause the price per share to be some positive number. It is not a flaw in the model, which calculates only the intrinsic value per share.

PA25-9 (a)   Hasbro's price/book value ratio is \$18.625/9.59 = 1.94 times.

(b)   The first step to be undertaken is to determine a required rate of return for Hasbro. Using the equation of the SML, the required rate of return is determined to be 14.5%: k = 5.1% + 0.96(9.8%) = 14.5%. The constant growth model is then used in its following format:

$$P_0 = \frac{(\text{payout ratio})[1+(ROE \times RR)](ROE)(BV_0)}{k-[ROE \times RR]}$$

$$= \frac{(0.185)[1+(0.1417x0.815)](0.1417)(9.59)}{0.145-[0.1417x0.815]}$$

$$= \frac{0.2804}{0.0295} = \$9.51.$$

(c)   There are a couple of assumptions made when using this model: (1) The firm's payout (and therefore, its retention) ratio remains the same. (2) The ROE will remain the same and all equity investment will come from the firm's retained earnings. (That is, the growth rate is determined as ROE x RR, and the firm's profit margin, use of debt, and asset turnover will remain the same.) Furthermore, in using the SML equation, we assumed the market risk premium to be 9.8%. The beta value is also an estimate, based on the historical returns of Hasbro relative to the market.

Stock prices are based on investor expectations of the future, not on current conditions. It is possible that investors do not believe that Hasbro will continue to grow at a rate of ROE x RR. Perhaps, they believe its profit margins might be squeezed, for example, resulting in a lower ROE, all else equal. This would result in a lower number in the numerator, and a greater spread between the required rate of return and the growth rate, yielding a larger denominator, and lowering the calculated price. Too, recent ventures undertaken by Hasbro may have increased its systematic risk (beta) and may not yet be incorporated in the estimated beta, which is based largely on historical results.

PA25-10 (a)   The implied growth rate is calculated, using the following form of the constant growth dividend discount model:

$$P_0 = \frac{(\text{payout ratio})(1+g)(\text{ROE})(\text{BV}_0)}{k - g}. \text{ Therefore,}$$

$$\$18.625 = \frac{(0.185)(1+g)(0.1417)(9.59)}{0.145 - g};$$

$$\$18.625(0.145 - g) = 0.2514(1+g)$$

$$2.7006 - 18.625g = 0.2514 + 0.2514g$$

$$18.8764g = 2.4492$$

$$g \approx 13\%$$

(b)   The growth rate used in Problem 25-9(b) was given by ROE x RR = (0.1417)(0.815) = 11.5%. This is lower than the 13% growth rate calculated in PA25-10(a) and explains why the price calculated in PA25-9(b) is lower than the current market price of $18.625 that was used to determine the implied growth rate in PA25-10(a).

CFA Exam Solutions*

The following are the guideline answers provided by the AIMR for the CFA Exam questions:

1.   **D**

2.   **D**

3.   **A.   Conclusion Support**

The following factors from Table 1 support Janet Ludlow's conclusion that the electric toothbrush industry is in the maturity (i.e., late) phase of its industry life cycle:

Return on equity. ROE figures for the industry have been generally increasing in the past six years, but the increases are occurring at a decreasing rate. Therefore, the industry may be in the maturity phase of the industry life cycle.

Average P/E. The price-to-earnings ratio for an industry may be interpreted as a measure of the prospective growth rates in earnings and dividends that are anticipated by the market. P/Es tend to be quite volatile; therefore, the P/E for an industry should be compared with P/Es for the market as a whole. As the data in Table 1 indicate, the P/Es for the electric toothbrush industry have been decreasing in the past six years whereas the P/E for the market has nearly doubled. Investors apparently are becoming less optimistic about the growth prospects for the industry and may be characterizing it as mature.

Dividend payout ratio. Mature industries are characterized by high dividend payout ratios. Generally, companies pay higher dividends to shareholders when the companies have fewer opportunities for growth in the market. Dividend payout ratios have been generally increasing in the electric toothbrush industry in the past six years. This characteristic signals an industry in the maturity phase.

Average dividend yield. The dividend yield is an important measure because it, and capital gains make up a stock investor's return. There tends to be an inverse relationship between the level of the dividend yield and the anticipated rate of capital gain (growth). The dividend yield for the electric toothbrush industry has been increasing, whereas the market's dividend yield has been declining. Even though the yield for the electric toothbrush industry is still below that of the market, the gap has narrowed substantially. The implication is that investors perceive less growth potential for the industry than in the past and thus are requiring a higher percentage of their return from yield. The evidence is that the electric toothbrush industry is moving toward the maturity phase of the industry life cycle.

B.   Conclusion Refutation

The following factors from Exhibit 1 refute Ludlow's conclusion:

Growth rate. An industry growth rate of 10 - 15% is too high for a mature industry.
Non-U.S. markets. Some U.S. electric toothbrush companies may be entering fast-growing non-U.S. markets, which remain largely unexploited.

Mail order sales. Some manufacturers have created a new niche in the industry by selling electric toothbrushes directly to customers through mail order. Sales for this industry segment are growing at 40% a year.

Niche markets. Some electric toothbrush manufacturers continue to develop new, unexploited niche markets in the United States based on company reputation, quality, and service.

New entrants. New manufacturers continue to enter the market.

CHAPTER 26: TECHNICAL ANALYSIS

SOLUTIONS

Questions

QA26-1   Technical analysts focus only on historical price and volume information. Factors such as risk, earnings growth rate, and financial ratios are ignored. Volume information is examined in conjunction with price levels to determine support and resistance levels.

QA26-2   Dow theorists define three types of movements in a market index or security price they are analyzing. **Primary trends** are commonly called bear or bull markets. Delineating primary trends is the goal of Dow theory. **Secondary movements** are market collapses or surges upward that last only a few months. Secondary movements are sometimes called **corrections**. **Tertiary moves** refer to the small daily fluctuations. The Dow theory asserts that daily fluctuations are meaningless random wiggles. However, chartists plot daily prices in order to trace the latest developments in the primary trend.

QA26-3   An abortive recovery that followed a series of ascending tops would be a signal to sell. Technicians would say that the price had passed its peak and a primary downtrend was beginning. In other words, they would assert that the stock's price had lost its upward momentum and, therefore, it is time to sell the stock.

QA26-4   Some rate-of-change technicians look at the slope of the moving average price line to determine the direction of price change they expect. Other rate-of-change technicians follow the ratio of the actual price to the moving average price each day. Changes in this ratio above and below unity are interpreted as buy and sell signals.

        Moving averages can be calculated over any number of trading days. A 300-day moving average encompasses 300 trading days, or more than an entire calendar year, and is long enough to smooth over what the Dow theorists call the secondary movements (or corrections) and the tertiary movements (or random daily wiggles). These theorists believe that the 300-day moving average should reveal only the primary (bull or bear market) trend. The 300-day average is so long and so highly smoothed that it will be slow to reveal turning point, however. In contrast, a 10-day moving average is so short that both the primary and the secondary movements are still clearly visible in the graph of the moving average.

QA26-5   The advance-decline line is a measure of market breadth. It is depicted in Figure 26-6 of this chapter. This technical tool probably gave the clearest signal and the longest lead time before the October 1987 crash of any of the technical tools reviewed in Chapter 26.

QA26-6 (a)   The confidence index (CI) is an indicator of investor optimism. The value of the CI varies inversely with the level of bond investors' risk-aversion.

    (b)   The confidence index has an upper value limit of positive one because the average yield of the bonds in the numerator must always be less than the average yield of the bonds in the denominator.

$$BCI = \frac{\text{average yield of } \textit{Barron's } 10 \text{ highest - grade bonds at time t}}{\text{average yield of Dow Jones 40 bonds at time period t}}$$

The average yield of the bonds in the numerator will be less than the average yield of the bonds in the denominator by the amount of the risk premium (or yield spread).

(c) Bond investors are presumed to be more professional, better educated, and wiser investors than common stock investors because more bond investors are institutional investors. Therefore, this indicator of investor optimism is deemed to be more relevant than, say a survey of investors who are amateurs.

QA26-7   A head and shoulder top (HST) is a series of reversals that is supposed to signal that a security's price, a commodity's price, or a market price index has reached a top and will decline in the future. The **left shoulder** denotes a period of heavy buying that pushes the price up to a new peak before a lull in trading allows the price to begin sliding down. The **head** represents a spurt of buying activity in which the price is bid up to a new high followed by another lull in trading that causes the price to fall back below the top of the left shoulder. The **right shoulder** reflects a moderate rally, which lifts the price somewhat, but fails to push prices as high as the top of the head before an additional decline begins. Finally, the **confirmation**, or **breakout**, occurs when the price falls below a straight line, referred to as the neckline, that is tangent to the bottoms (or tops) of the left and right shoulders. When the price drops below the neckline, it is called a breakout, which is supposed to be a sell signal that precedes further price declines.

QA26-8   Technicians sometimes look for a *speculative blowoff* to mark the end of a bull market. A speculative blowoff is a period when a high volume of buying pushes prices up to a peak. A speculative blowoff is supposed to exhaust the enthusiasm of bullish speculators and make way for a bear market to begin. A *selling climax* refers to one occasion when falling prices and high volume are considered bullish. When technicians feel the end of a bear market is near, they watch for a high volume of selling as the last of the bearish investors liquidate their holdings. Such a selling climax is supposed to eliminate the last of the bears, who drive prices down by selling, clearing the way for the market to turn up. Both the speculative blowoff and the selling climax involve high volumes of trading activity that is supposed to mark the end of a price trend.

QA26-9   Most of the tools that the technical analysts use can be applied to analyze individual securities or commodities or to analyze various market indexes, as well.

QA26-10   False. A technician may have a favorite tool that they use. Most technicians, however, realize that technical indicators sometimes issue erroneous buy and sell signals. Therefore, most technicians follow several technical indicators and watch for them to verify or confirm each other's signals.

Problems

PA26-1   The larger-than-average price change coupled with a large volume of shares traded on day 2 suggests that the market probably received new information about Hemmel that changed many investors' assessment of the stock's value on that day. As a result of this information, many investors wanted to buy or sell the stock, causing the price to change significantly. In contrast, the large volume of shares traded on day 9 is probably just a big liquidity trade that was not associated with any information that changed value estimates for Hemmel's stock. The larger than average price move on day 10 is also probably just another meaningless price move; it appears to be unimportant because so few shares were traded on day 10. Since the market was thin (i.e., trading was sparse) on day 10, a few small trades probably moved the price by a larger than average amount simply because the market lacked liquidity-generating trading activity.

PA26-2 (a)   The 5-day moving averages are calculated below:

Day 5: ($29.25 + $31.125 + $32.50 + $33.125 + $33.75)/5 = $159.75/5 = $31.95
Day 6: ($31.125 + $32.50 + $33.125 + $33.75 + $32.875)/5 = $163.375/5
 = $32.675
Day 7: ($32.50 + $33.125 + $33.75 + $32.875 + $32.125)/5 = $164.375/5
 = $32.875
Day 8: ($33.125 + $33.75 + $32.875 + $32.125 + $31.50)/5 = $163.375/5
    = $32.675
Day 9: ($33.75 + $32.875 + $32.125 + $31.50 + $31.75)/5 = $162.00/5 = $32.40
Day 10: ($32.875 + $32.125 + $31.50 + $31.75 + $33.125)/5 = $161.375/5
 = $32.275
Day 11: ($32.125 + $31.50 + $31.75 + $33.125 + $34.50)/5 = $163/5 = $32.60
Day 12: ($31.50 + $31.75 + $33.125 + $34.50 + $34.00)/5 = $164.875/5
 = $32.975
Day 13: ($31.75 + $33.125 + $34.50 + $34.00 + $33.75)/5 = $167.125/5
 = $33.425
Day 14: ($33.125 + $34.50 + $34.00 + $33.75 + $32.625)/5 = $168/5 = $33.60

(b)   The prices range from $29.25 to $34.50, a range of $5.25.
(c)   The moving averages range from $31.95 to $33.60, a range of only $1.65.

PA26-3   The spectacular stock market crash of October 1987 is clearly visible in the **S&P 500** data below:

	Jan.	Feb.	Mar.	Apr.	May	Jun.	Jul.	Aug.	Sep.	Oct.	Nov.	Dec.
Yields-to-maturity												
T-bond	6.97	7.12	7.05	7.80	8.52	8.29	8.24	8.47	9.16	9.30	8.65	8.72
AA	8.86	8.82	8.78	9.31	9.81	9.70	9.64	9.83	10.48	10.62	9.97	10.08
A	9.07	8.94	8.91	9.39	9.91	9.89	9.90	10.16	10.77	10.98	10.51	10.59
BBB	9.47	9.50	9.42	9.55	10.44	10.38	10.42	10.61	11.25	11.55	10.99	11.06
Standard & Poor's 500 Composite Stocks Index												
S&P 500	265	281	293	289	289	301	310	329	319	280	245	241
AA/BBB (CI)	0.935	0.928	0.932	0.975	0.939	0.934	0.925	0.926	0.932	0.919	0.907	0.911

(a)   The fact that all the market interest rates in the table of data were rising throughout the first nine months of 1987 is evidence that the Federal Reserve was tightening monetary policy in the months before the October 1987 crash. This credit tightening doubtless contributed to the October 1987 crash.
(b)   A confidence index (CI) has been constructed using the AA/BBB index shown above.
(c)   The confidence index provided some clear indications of the October 1987 stock market crash when it fell from 0.932 in September to 0.919 in October.
(d)   Unfortunately, the AA/BBB confidence index gave indications of the October 1987 crash that were coincident with the crash and that lagged the event by about one month. Leading indicators are more useful than coincident or lagging indicators. Coincident and lagging indicators are usually only useful to confirm what is already obvious.
(e)   All technical analysis tools give erroneous or lagging indications sometimes; this decreases their value.

PA26-4 (a)   The confidence index (CI) for each year was calculated using the following formula:

$$BCI = \frac{\text{average yield of } Barron's \text{ 10 highest - grade bonds at time t}}{\text{average yield of Dow Jones 40 bonds at time period t}}$$

	Year 1	Year 2	Year 3	Year 4	Year 5
BCI	0.800	0.772	0.773	0.750	0.728

(b)   Chartists would interpret this as an indication of a downturn in the economy since the yield spread is widening. This leads to an expected drop in stock prices.

PA26-5 (a)   The 3-day moving averages are calculated using the following formula:

$$m3dap_t = \frac{P_t + P_{t-1} + P_{t-2}}{3}$$

Date	Close price	3-day moving average
June 1	10596.26	
June 2	10577.89	
June 3	10663.69	10612.61
June 4	10799.84	10680.47
June 7	10909.38	10790.97
June 8	10765.64	10824.95
June 9	10690.29	10788.44
June 10	10621.27	10692.40
June 11	10490.51	10600.69

(b)   On June 8th, the daily price plunges below the moving average. A chartist may be concerned that this signals the beginning of a bear market although he would have more confidence in drawing this conclusion if, perhaps, a longer-period moving average, such as a 150-day moving average, were used. The chartist would probably want to examine much more data than is provided in this problem (for simplicity) before drawing a firm conclusion.

PA26-6   The bar chart for Texaco appears below.

Figure PA26-6: Bar Chart

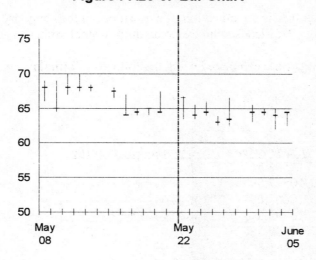

PA26-7   (a) and (b) The moving averages for Texaco's close prices are provided below:

Date (1999)	Close	5-day moving average	10-day moving average
June 4	64.25	**64.1500**	**64.25875**
June 3	62.3125	**65.8750**	**64.27125**
June 2	64.5	**64.4625**	**64.44000**
June 1	64.1875	**64.1750**	**64.39625**
May 28	65.5	**64.0625**	**64.58375**
May 27	62.875	**64.1875**	**64.70250**
May 26	65.25	**64.4875**	**65.32750**
May 25	63.0625	**64.2375**	**65.70250**
May 24	63.625	**64.4375**	**66.25875**
May 21	66.125	**64.9250**	**66.58375**
May 20	64.375		
May 19	64		
May 18	64.0625		
May 17	66.0625		
May 14	67.6875		
May 13	69.125		
May 12	69		
May 11	68.625		
May 10	65.875		

(c)   Note that the 10-day moving averages are higher for Texaco than are the 5-day moving averages. This is because it includes the earlier prices, which were higher, in the calculation. Too, note that the 10-day moving average provides evidence of a smooth decline (with the exception of the average on June 2nd). The 5-day moving average has many more "ups and downs."

PA26-8   A line chart of the Nasdaq close prices appears below:

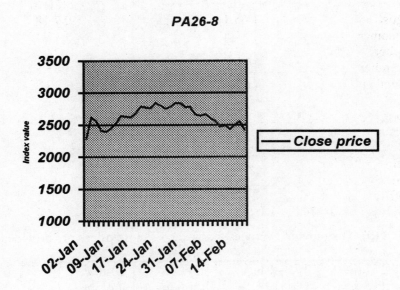

PA26-9   On May 18, 1999, there was a significant increase in the volume of shares traded, accompanied by a price increase for Coca Cola. However, given that this price increase was eliminated within the next few days, it is probably just the result of liquidity trading in the stock rather than the result of any significant new information about the firm.

PA26-10 (a)   The relative strength ratios are provided below:

	Close Price	
Month (1998)	**Coca Cola**	**S&P 500 Index**
June	85.5	1133.84
July	80.5	1120.67
August	65.125	957.28
September	57.625	1017.10
October	67.5625	1098.67
November	70.0625	1163.63
December	67	1229.23

Month	**Relative strength**
June	0.0754
July	0.0718
August	0.0680
September	0.0567
October	0.0615
November	0.0602
December	0.0545

(b)   Coca Cola's relative strength ratios indicates a declining trend in the last half of 1998.

CFA Exam Solutions*

The following are the guideline answers provided by the AIMR for the CFA Exam questions:

1.   D

2.   D

3.   A

4.   **Technical analysis** in the form of charting involves the search for recurrent and predictable patterns in stock prices to enhance returns. The EMH implies that this type of technical analysis is without value. If past prices contain no useful information for predicting future prices, there is no point in following any technical trading rule for timing the purchases and sales of securities. According to weak-form efficiency, no investor can earn excess returns by developing trading rules based on historical price and return information. A simple policy of buying and holding will be at least as good as any technical procedure. Tests generally show that technical trading rules do not produce superior returns after making adjustments for transactions costs and taxes.

CHAPTER 27: FUTURES

SOLUTIONS

Questions

QA27-1   The position of a trader who sells futures without owning an inventory is called a "short futures" position. Selling futures without owning an inventory is almost identical to selling securities short. Declining prices are profitable and rising prices cause losses for the trader. The differences between selling short futures and selling securities short are minor: (1) If the common stock paid any cash dividends, the short seller would have to pay for them out of his own pocket. (2) Commission rates on futures are only a fraction of the commissions on common stock. (3) Income from futures and securities are usually taxed differently. If the trader takes two different positions in the same good simultaneously, the resulting situations are similar. If either the physical commodity or securities were held in two off setting positions, a long position and a short sale, the combination would comprise a hedged position.

QA27-2   The functions performed by the clearing house within a commodity futures exchange are as follows: (1) The clearing house guarantees that every futures contract will be fulfilled. In return for a small insurance fee that it charges on every contract, the parties to every contract are indemnified against losses. The guarantee from the clearing house makes it *unnecessary* to check the credit references of the buyer and seller every time a contract is signed. Futures contracts would not be liquid without the guarantee of some credible institution like the clearing house. The clearing house's guarantee makes the futures contract liquid because the clearing house accumulates the "insurance fees" it collects off of every futures contract and, in addition, requires all exchange members to make substantial contributions to the clearing house's guarantee fund. The guarantee funds at the various commodity exchanges in the U.S. are liquid, multi-million dollar pools of capital that are continuously maintained to insure that plenty of funds will be available to execute transactions in which any buyers and/or sellers default. (2) The clearing house keeps track of the current owner of a contract, thus allowing futures agreements to be sold and resold any number of times. If the contract has not been reversed out of existence, when it matures the original seller will make delivery to the clearing house, and the clearing house will then make delivery to the last buyer of the contract. The intermediate traders who owned a contract temporarily need never be bothered with the delivery process and need never know each other's names.

QA27-3   An inverted market is a commodity market where spot (or the near-term futures) prices are higher than the futures prices on contracts on the same commodity that have more distant maturities. More concisely, an inversion occurs when spot prices are greater than futures prices. Futures might sell at a discount to spot, for example, when the present supply of a commodity is limited, keeping cash and spot prices high, while, at the same time, the growing crop is expected to yield a large harvest so that the expected future supplies will be plentiful and, therefore, available at lower prices after the forthcoming harvest.

QA27-4   This sophistical comment is false. Spot and futures prices are determined simultaneously by supply and demand conditions at the present and in the future. It is naïve to say one price mechanically determines the other price. Of course it is true that in normal markets, carrying costs for storable commodities equals the premium of futures over spot prices. However, this does not mean one period's price determines another period's price simply by adding or subtracting a carrying cost. For non-storable commodities like fresh eggs and live cattle, carrying costs are irrelevant.

Note: In explaining the simultaneity of spot and futures prices, the author sometimes employs the following physical analogy: The commodity can be viewed as flowing into a series of different intertemporal "tubs"--one for each crop harvest. Inflows from the different harvests are consumed currently or else flow into the "future tubs" via futures contracts. The flows to future contracts are *unidirectional* into the future. As a result of this one-way flow, excesses can occur in the "future tubs" (that is, in future time periods) without replenishing the near-term tubs while current shortages exist. In contrast, any current excesses can flow forward in such a manner as to equate the level between tubs and thus allocate consumption smoothly over time. Carrying costs are like "toll costs" between the tubs. This shows how cash, spot, and future prices are all determined simultaneously by current harvests and current consumption. However, due to the unidirectional flow (into the future), future excesses that are anticipated cannot affect the previous (or near-term) periods. Inverted markets can be viewed as being the result of this one-way flow of commodities through time. For graduate classes, the same concepts and some valuable comparative statistics are imparted by reading and discussing the following classic article by J. L. Stein: "The Simultaneous Determination of Spot and Futures Prices," American Economic Review, December 1961, pp. 1012-1025.

QA27-5   False, with a reservation. Consider three categories of speculative activity. First, speculation is stabilizing if performed in a profit-maximizing fashion. By buying low and selling high, speculators maximize their profits, provide demand when supply is great, and thereby prevent prices from plunging lower. Furthermore, the profit-seeking speculators offer inventories for sale when the supply is scarce and thereby prevent prices from rising excessively. The actions of profit-maximizing speculators thus tend to minimize market upswings and downturns; price fluctuations are smoothed by greedy speculation. Second, unprofitable speculation (that is, when a trader buys high and sells low) may be destabilizing. But, unprofitable speculation tends to result in bankruptcy for its practitioners. Therefore, speculators who lose money by buying high and selling low will not destabilize the market for long because they will become bankrupt and seek tasks in other fields where they are able to compete more effectively. Third, buying just after market troughs and selling just after market peaks may have some destabilizing elements. This possibility is overshadowed by the benefits of speculation, which allow for the allocation of consumption over time, the hedging of risk, the creation of constantly changing futures prices that reflect valuable information about the future, the efficient adjustment of prices to new information, the efficient geographic and intertemporal allocation of resources, provisions of liquidity for businessmen dealing in commodities, and provision of uniform prices between geographically separate markets (that is, enforcing the law of one price.)

QA27-6   Commodities that experience the discontinuities caused by periodic harvests are more likely to be traded in futures markets than commodities that are non-perishable and/or are produced continuously. These commodities tend to have stable supply and demand functions, and their prices do not fluctuate with the forecasts of the size of the next harvest. It is not profitable to speculate on such commodities in enough volume to justify the existence (that is, pay the operating costs for) a commodity exchange. However, the manufacturers of these commodities speculate on shifts in the supply and demand of the commodities every time they increase their productive capacity or produce for their inventory. If the market price of any commodity ever experiences substantial fluctuations, that commodity might become profitable to trade on futures exchanges.

QA27-7   Successfully traded commodity futures contracts are those that enjoy sufficient trading volume to make active markets for the contract and generate sufficient trading fees to pay the commodity exchange's cost of keeping the market operating. In general, the following list of statements describes the characteristics of actively traded commodities:

(1)   The commodity should be *gradable* into homogeneous quality categories. This means that one lot of any commodity (such as a boxcar load of sugar) should be interchangeable with any other lot of that commodity.

(2)   *Raw materials* (such as wheat) are traded successfully more frequently than finished goods (such as flour). Money is also a raw material. Money is a raw material on which futures are traded, but futures are not traded on profits because profits can be viewed as a finished good.

(3)   The commodity's cash market price should be determinable by a *clear price discovery process*; there should be no arbitrariness about the price. For example, the price should be determined by supply and demand facts rather than by the whim of an individual or non-market process.

(4)   *Storability* is important; perishable commodities (such as lettuce or fresh flowers) cannot be stored or shipped easily. Since commodity hedgers endeavor to buy at a low price and sell at a high price, they want commodities they can hold in storage cheaply while they await price rises.

(5)   The commodity must *exist in volume*. Rare objects, such as art objects, cannot generate the volume of trading needed to sustain an active market.

(6)   Large amounts of *risk capital* must be committed to carrying the risky inventories needed to make liquid markets. That is, hedgers must be willing to invest millions of dollars in inventories that will fluctuate in value. Then, when the parties investing in inventories of physicals enter the futures market to hedge, they, in turn, create more need for risk capital to finance the speculators' positions. The speculators are needed to bear the risk that the hedgers desire to hedge away.

(7)   The futures contract should be *written clearly and conveniently* for both the buyer and seller. Successful contracts are not written in such dense, legal language that only lawyers can read them.

(8)   The commodity should be *cheaply transportable*. The marketability of a commodity is maximized if it can be shipped inexpensively to buyers.

(9)   The commodity should be *readily describable*. There can be no ambiguity about what is going to be delivered.

(10)   The commodity must experience *price volatility*. The more that the price of a commodity fluctuates, the more risk-averters will want to hedge their inventories and, in turn, the more speculative trading will occur to create these hedges.

(11)   A liquid cash market where the physical commodity is traded should be active before trading in commodity futures contracts is begun. The *prior existence of a viable cash market* means that the price discovery process for the commodity already exists and is discernible.

(12)   The public and the risk-averse manufacturers who will want to hedge their inventories need *education* about the commodity and its futures contract. No one will invest in something they don't understand.

Most of these statements apply to most actively traded commodities. However, every one of the statements above does not apply to every successfully traded commodity. The above list merely suggests what is usually required to trade a contract successfully. For a top-rate academic study on this subject, see Lester Telser and Harlow Higginbotham, "Organized Futures Markets: Costs and Benefits," Journal of Political Economy, October 1977, pages 969-1000. Also see Henry Bakken, Futures Trading In Livestock-- Origins and Concepts, Mimir Publications, Inc., Madison, Wisconsin, 1970.

QA27-8 (a) For a storable physical commodity (like most agricultural commodities), the basis equals the total carrying cost (of storage, insurance, interest expense, property tax, ad infinitum). For example, the carrying cost of 4 cents per bushel per month for the grains is an example of the carrying cost and the basis in a normal market. For non-storable physical commodities (like live cattle and fresh eggs), the carrying cost is more difficult to discern. For example, the distance live cattle must be shipped for delivery and the mode of transportation affects the rate at which their weight declines; as a result, the carrying cost has an effect on the basis that is harder to predict. For non-storable commodities and storable commodities at harvest time, the relative supply and demand determine spot and futures prices, and thus, the basis.

(b) Market interest rates are the main determinant of the basis for those financial futures that are called interest rate futures because market rates determine the carrying cost and the present value for these financial commodities. By algebraically solving for the implicit holding period returns for holding a given interest rate future at different times, one can discern a pattern of returns that resembles a yield curve. Arbitrage will insure that the U.S. Treasury bond yield curve will have an impact on the basis in interest rate futures. In contrast, for stock market index futures, the bull market or bear market expectations determine the basis.

QA27-9 One or more of the following five basis risks usually prevents most hedges from being a perfect hedge:
(1) Location risk. The commodity may not be delivered where it is needed, and, thus, additional shipping costs are incurred.
(2) Delivery date risk. The futures contract's expiration date may not correspond with the date the goods are needed.
(3) Quality risk. The wrong grade may be delivered under the terms of the futures contract; the buyer cannot control precisely the grade that is delivered.
(4) Quantity risk. The futures contract's measure of a unit may not correspond exactly to the quantity being hedged.
(5) Basis Price Difference. The difference between the spot and futures price (that is, the basis) usually changes with the passage of time. These basis changes can cause profits or losses for the hedger.

QA27-10 You could establish a spread position in which you are long in Treasury bond futures and short in the same quantity of Treasury note futures. This way, if the level of interest rates changes, you are protected from gain or loss by the offsetting long and short positions. Furthermore, if the yield curve flattens at any level of market interest rates you will earn a *net profit* from the two positions. You will gain from the long position in Treasury bonds if the long-term rates fall. In addition, you will profit from being short in Treasury note futures if the short-term rates rise. Unfortunately, if your forecast is all wrong and the yield curve changes so that it slopes more steeply upward, you can lose on both the long and the short positions.

QA27-11 The statement is false. Modern telecommunications devices allow geographically disparate markets to compete as different traders in one electronically centralized market. Furthermore, the advantage of having almost identical contracts is that arbitrageurs can use both of them to earn profits by ensuring that the same good does not sell at different prices in different market (that is, by enforcing the law of one price). Stated differently, the two similar contracts will probably generate more total volume of shares traded than if there were only one T-bill futures contract traded.

QA27-12   The investor could deal with the problem in several different ways. First, he could simply sell the Treasury bond--hopefully, before its price declines. Or, he could hedge the endangered long position by taking an equal short position to offset possible losses. Lastly, he could sell T-bill futures short in an amount equal to the long position to hedge the long T-bond.

QA27-13   There are several important differences. First, the owner of a futures contract is *obliged* to accept delivery if the contract is held to maturity, even if taking delivery is financially harmful. In contrast, the owner of the call option need not take delivery unless he finds that it is advantageous to do so. A second difference is in the price adjustments. The price of the futures contract adjusts in order to equate supply and demand. However, with a call option, the exercise price remains fixed, and the option's premium fluctuates. A third difference is that the call buyer enjoys limited liability; no more than the option's premium can be lost. The owner of a futures contract, however, can, through a series of mark-to-market transactions, lose more than was initially invested in the contract.

Being long in a call option and a long futures position are similar in three ways. First, they may both be liquidated before they mature. Second, the owner of both positions profits from price increases in the underlying asset. Third, both financial instruments give their owners more financial leverage than a simple position directly in the security.

Problems

PA27-1   The one-period rate of return for a margined commodity account using T-bills to cover the margin requirement is defined as follows:

$$r = \frac{1}{P_t}(P_{t+1} - P_t) + RFR\left[\frac{P_1 + P_2}{2}\right]$$
$$= (\text{Percent price change}) + (\text{Interest from T - bill})$$

The symbol P_t denotes the market price of the futures contract at time period t; RFR denotes the riskless rate of interest earned on the T-bill given to the broker to hold to meet the margin requirement, and P_1 and P_2 are the beginning and ending values of the margined T-bill, respectively. Returns on margined futures contracts were defined as shown above by Zvi Bodie and Victor Rosansky, "Risk and Return In Commodity Futures," Financial Analysts Journal, pages 38-39, May-June, 1980. Other people have suggested different "correct" answers to this question. Dusak defines the return as in Equation 27-4 in this chapter. (Katherine Dusak, "Futures Trading and Investor Returns: An Investigation of Commodity Market Risk Premiums," Journal of Political Economy, December 1973, pp. 1387-1406.) Fischer Black, in contrast, argues that it is not possible to define the rate of return for a highly leveraged futures contract in "The Pricing of Commodity Contracts," Journal of Financial Economics, January, 1976. Professor Lester Telser argues that margins affect the rates of return, but does not explicitly show how he thinks they should be measured. (L. Telser, Journal of Futures Markets, Volume 11, Number 2, 1981, "Margins and Futures Contracts.")

PA27-2 (a) Jim's fear is that the price will fall before the crop can be harvested and sold. Therefore, Mr. Jones should establish a selling hedge by selling short 8 soybean futures contracts for a total sales price of (5,000 bushels per contract x $6 per bushel x 8 contracts =) $240,000. As a result, he will be long physical soybeans and short an equal quantity of soybean futures.

(b) If the price of soybeans falls to $5, Jim's cash crop has a value of $5 x 40,000 = $200,000. However, assuming that the futures price also falls to $5, he can reverse his futures position by purchasing 8 contracts to lock in a gain of $40,000 on the 8 futures contracts. This $40,000 gain on the futures position will offset the $40,000 loss from the price decline on the value of the harvested soybeans. Thus, an equivalent of the $6 per bushel price has been locked in.

PA27-3 (a) In order to hedge half of his harvest, Mr. Franklin should sell 3 cotton futures contracts at $0.80 per pound, since each contract equals 50,000 pounds. Half of his cotton production equals: 150,000 pounds = 3 contracts x 50,000 pound cotton units.

(b) At 80 cents per pound the total market value of Ed's cash crop is $0.80 x 300,000 = $240,000. At 60 cents per pound the total market value of the crop is only $0.60 x 300,000 = $180,000. If the futures price falls to $0.60 per pound, the total gain on his 3 short cotton futures contracts would be $0.20 x 3 x 50,000 = $30,000. In this situation, he would have been better off if he had hedged his entire crop by using 6 futures contracts instead of hedging only half of the crop because he will lose $0.20 cents a pound on his entire 300,000 pound cotton physicals crop. Ed's hedge will only offset half of this total loss.

PA27-4 (a) Signing the sales contract in July, 20XX made Mr. Sample's Syrup Company short physical syrup. Stated differently, the firm is short processed sugar. If the vice-president's fears of a sugar price rise are valid, the firm should purchase (assume a long position in) six (672,000/112,000 = 6) sugar futures contracts at $0.23 to lock in whatever profit was anticipated on the syrup sale when the contract was signed in July.

(b) If the sugar price goes to $0.35 and no hedge was in place to protect the firm, it would lose $0.12 per pound for a total loss of $80,640. ($0.12 per pound x 672,000 pounds = $80,640.)

PA27-5 (a) Each wheat contract has a total market value of $3 x 5,000 bushels per contract = $15,000. Assuming an initial margin of 10%, the cash outlay is $1,500 per contract. You can purchase 6 contracts for (6 x $1,500 =) $9,000 plus (6 x $40 =) $240 in commission costs. You will have $760 left. But, you will have a bullish long position in wheat futures.

(b) You earn 50 cents per bushel gain, or $0.50 x 6 x 5,000 = $15,000 total gain. From this you must subtract $240 in commissions. Therefore, your net gain is $14,760. Your holding period rate of return is (total net price gain)/(total investment) = ($14,760/$9,000) = 1.64 or 164% over the three months.

(c) If the price of wheat falls to $2.25, you lose 75 cents a bushel for a total loss of $0.75 x 6 x 5,000 = $22,500 plus $240 in commission costs.

PA27-6 Your investment is $15,000 plus $350 in commissions. You gain from the price decline is $50 per contract for a total gain of $50 x 10 contracts x 100 ounces per contract = $50,000 minus the $350 commissions for a net gain of $47,650.

PA27-7 (a) To fully hedge your position, you should sell short ($7,500,000/(150 x $250) =) 200 S&P 500 futures contracts.

(b) The total gross gain on the short futures contract is (150 - 120 =) 30 points on the S&P

500 Index for a total dollar gain of $30 x 200 contracts x $250 = $1,500,000. This $1.5 million gain from being short S&P 500 futures exactly offsets your $1.5 million loss from your long position in the stock market and thus reduces your overall market losses to zero if commission costs are ignored.

PA27-8 (a) If Joe sells short 10 S&P 500 futures contracts, his gain is (130 - 100 =) 30 points per contract on the S&P 500 for a total gain of $30 per contract x 10 contracts x $250 = $75,000. Joe's equity would be his 10% initial margin payment of 10 contracts x 130 per contract x $250 x 0.10 = $32,500 total initial investment. Joe's rate of return on the $32,500 investment would be $75,000/$32,500 = 230.8% for the 6-month period.

(b) If Joe sells short 10 S&P 500 contracts and his forecast is wrong, he loses (130 - 150 =) 20 points per contract on the S&P 500 for a total loss of $20 per contract x 10 contracts x $250 = -$50,000.

PA27-9 (a) Mr. Taylor has contracted to deliver finished condos that he estimates make him short 1.5 million board feet of physical lumber. Mr. Taylor should purchase 10 lumber futures contracts (1,500,000/150,000 = 10) that call for delivery in more than 8 months to hedge his firm's exposure to a loss from its lumber sale. When portions of the needed physical lumber are purchased while the condos are under construction, Taylor can simultaneously reverse out of an equivalent amount of lumber futures contracts in order to keep his hedge in balance.

(b) If the price of lumber rose $12 per 1,000 board foot, Taylor would suffer total commodity losses (i.e., reduced construction profits) of $12 x 1,500 = $18,000 on its lumber position if he did not enter a hedge position.

PA27-10 Bill will profit from a narrowing of the basis between the two futures contracts. He will gain $500 (5,000 x $0.10) on his long position in July corn since the price has increased. He will, however, lose $400 (5,000 x $0.08) on his short position in December corn. His net gain is $500 - $400 = $100.

CFA Exam Solutions*

The following are the guideline answers provided by the AIMR for the CFA Exam questions:

1. A

2. D

3. C
    Solution:
    $2,025 - X = $1500
    X = $525.

    $525/5,000 ounces
    = $0.105 or $0.11 per ounce

    $8 + $0.11 = $8.11 per ounce
    A seller loses when the price rises.

4. **A. What Lane Should Do**

To protect his investment from declining interest rates, Mike Lane should purchase, or "go long," $5 million worth of U.S. Treasury five-year-note futures contracts. Lane can actually purchase any of the traded five-year-note futures contracts, depending on what date he actually plans to invest his $5 million.

B. Effect of Higher Interest Rates on Lane's Position

If rates increase by 100 basis points in three months, the price of these futures contracts will decline and Lane will have a loss in his long futures position. The loss will show up in his mark-to-market position over time and will require him to post additional margin money.

C. Return from Lane's Hedged Position vs. Unhedged Return

Two methods can be used to answer Part C.

One answer is that the return from Lane's hedged position will be lower than the return if he had not hedged. Because of the futures contract's loss in Part B, the higher yield Lane can earn when he purchases a now lower priced (higher yield) U.S. Treasury five-year note in the cash market is "offset" by the loss from the futures contract. The loss is actually added to the now lower price of the U.S. Treasury five-year notes, thus decreasing Lane's realized yield.

A second answer is based on expressing the combined futures contract's price and cash market price in terms of "net price." Net price equals the new cash market price plus the original futures price minus the new futures price. Subtracting net price from 100 gives the investor the realized yield and thus the investor's return from the combined futures and cash markets. Because rates have increased, the new lower cash market price (higher yield) is increased by the loss from the futures contract's position, which reduces realized yield.

5. **Arbitrage transactions.** In a cash-and-carry strategy, which is what this transaction is, the arbitrageur borrows funds at a short-term rate, buys the asset, and sells the futures contract. On the expiration date, the arbitrageur delivers the asset against the futures, repays the loan with interest, and earns a low-risk profit.

List of transactions:

Borrow funds.
Buy the asset.
Sell futures.
Deliver the asset against the futures.
Repay the loan with interest.

Calculation of arbitrage profits. The cash-and-carry model, so called because the trader buys the cash good and carries it to the expiration of the futures contract, may be used to explain the pricing relationship between the futures market and the cash (or spot) market. Simplistically, the expected price (or "fair value") of a futures contract is given by the formula:

Futures price = Cash price + Finance charges - Income.

First, determine whether the futures is overpriced or underpriced relative to cash. Calculate the fair value of the futures contract and compare this value to the contract's actual value. If the actual value is greater than the fair value, the futures contract is overvalued, and a cash-and-carry strategy will result in profits; if the actual value is less than the fair value, the futures contract is undervalued and a reverse cash-and-carry strategy will yield profits.

The theoretical futures price is $101 + $2.50 - $4.50 = $99. Because the actual futures (invoice) price is $100, a profit of $1 can be obtained by employing a cash-and-carry strategy.

6.   **A.   Strategy B's Superiority**

Strategy B is a strip hedge that is constructed by selling (shorting) 100 futures contracts maturing in each of the next three quarters. With the strip hedge in place, each quarter of the coming year is hedged against shifts in interest rates for that quarter. The reason Strategy B will be a more effective hedge than Strategy A for Jacob Bower is that Strategy B is likely to work well whether a parallel shift or a nonparallel shift occurs over the one-year term of Bower's liability. That is, regardless of what happens to the term structure, Strategy B structures the futures hedge so that the rates reflected by the Eurodollar futures cash price match the applicable rates for the underlying liability--the 90-day LIBOR-based rate on Bower's liability. The same is not true for Strategy A. Because Jacob Bower's liability carries a floating interest rate that resets quarterly, he needs a strategy that provides a series of three-month hedges. Strategy A will need to be restructured when the three-month September contract expires. In particular, if the yield curve twists upward (futures yields rise more for distant expirations than for near expirations), Strategy A will produce inferior hedge results.

B.   Scenario in Which Strategy A is Superior

Strategy A is a stack hedge strategy that initially involves selling (shorting) 300 September contracts. Strategy A is rarely better than Strategy B as a hedging or risk-reduction strategy. Only from the perspective of favorable cash flows is Strategy A better than Strategy B. Such cash flows occur only in certain interest rate scenarios. For example Strategy A will work as well as Strategy B for Bower's liability if interest rates (instantaneously) change in parallel fashion. Another interest rate scenario where Strategy A outperforms Strategy B is one in which the yield curve rises but with a twist so that futures yields rise more for near expirations than for distant expirations. Upon expiration of the September contract, Bower will have to roll out his hedge by selling 200 December contracts to hedge the remaining interest payments. This action will have the effect that the cash flow from Strategy A will be larger than the cash flow from Strategy B because the appreciation of the 300 short September futures contracts will be larger than the cumulative appreciation in the 300 contracts shorted in Strategy B (i.e., 100 September, 100 December, and 100 March). Consequently, the cash flow from Strategy A will more than offset the increase in the interest payment on the liability, whereas the cash flow from Strategy B will exactly offset the increase in the interest payment on the liability.

CHAPTER 28: OPTIONS

SOLUTIONS

Questions

QA28-1   The main factors determining the premiums on puts and calls are: (i) The optioned asset's price. The higher the price, the greater the call premium and the smaller the put premium required by the writer. (ii) The duration of the option. The longer the duration is, the higher the premium because there is a greater probability that the option will be exercised if it has a long time until expiration. (iii) Volatility (or, riskiness) of the stock. The greater the volatility of the stock returns, the greater is the probability of a price change that will make it profitable to exercise the option. Writers will, therefore, require higher premiums for both puts and calls. (iv) Striking price. The exercise price may be "points away" from the market price of the underlying asset, either above or below. If it is below, the put writer's risk is reduced, and he would accept a lower premium. If the striking price is above the market price, the put premium would be higher. The reverse is true for call options. (v) The risk-free rate of interest. The risk-free rate (for example, the current Treasury bill rate) has a small positive (negative) effect on call (put) premiums since it represents an opportunity cost. (vi) Cash dividend payments. Dividend payments decrease call premiums and increase put premiums; cash dividend payments work through the price dropoff effect they have on the price of the optioned stock.

QA28-2   Using the put-call parity model,

$$\frac{\text{Exercise price (XP)}}{(1+\text{RFR})^d} = \text{Stock price (P)} + \text{Purchase price of put (POP)} - \text{Call option premium (COP)},$$

we can rearrange terms to see that $P = + \dfrac{XP}{(1+\text{RFR})^d} - POP + COP$. Thus, a long position in the stock can be replicated by purchasing a call on the stock, writing an identical put, and investing in a risk-free asset with a par value equal to the exercise price of the options and a maturity date equal to the expiration date on the options.

QA28-3   The N(x) and N(y) terms can be loosely interpreted as risk-adjusted probabilities that the call option will expire in the money. If both N(x) and N(y) are close to zero, the option would not be exercised, and its value is zero. If both terms are close to 1.0, there is a high probability that the option will be exercised and the option premium will equal the stock price minus the present value of the exercise price of the option:

$$COP = P - \frac{XP}{e^{(\text{RFR})(d)}}.$$

QA28-4   There is a fixed relationship between the price of put and call options with the same maturity date that are written on a single underlying security. This relationship, which is called the <u>put-call parity</u>, is shown below:

$$COP - POP = P - [XP/(1 + RFR)^d]$$

where COP = call premium

POP = put premium

P = price of the underlying security

XP = exercise or strike price

RFR = risk-free rate.

d = the fraction of one year remaining until the option matures, e.g., 0.5 represents one-half of a year, or six months.

The relationship is useful since we can determine the value of a put option if we know the corresponding value of a European call option.

QA28-5 (a)   If we let P stand for the market price of the optioned security and SP denote the call's exercise, then Equation (28-1) defines the intrinsic value of a call.

(Intrinsic value of a call = MAX[0, (P - XP)]   Eqn.(28-1)

Equation (28-1) shows that a call's intrinsic value is the greater of either zero or the quantity (P - XP). The intrinsic value of a call is delineated by the kinked intrinsic value lines in Figure 28-8 in the textbook. The intrinsic value of a call is important because it defines the call's value at expiration (when it has no time value left) , and it sets a floor under the call's premium any time prior to the expiration date.

The vertical distance between the intrinsic value line and the dashed curve tracing out the (Black-Scholes) cost of a call option measures that call's premium over intrinsic value, or the call's time value, or the call's time value.

Figure 28-8 shows that the premium over the intrinsic value of a call is greatest when the market price of the optioned asset equals the exercise price of the option, P = XP. The premium over intrinsic value increases with the length of time remaining until the call expires, increases with the riskiness of the optioned security, varies inversely with the absolute value of the difference between the market price of the optioned asset and the exercise price, $|P - XP|$, tends to increase slightly with the level of interest rates, and decreases with the payment of cash dividends by the optioned stock.

(b)   The intrinsic value of a put option was introduced in Chapter 9:

Intrinsic value of a put = MAX[0, (Exercise price - Price of stock)] (Eqn. 9-7)

A put will be worth only its intrinsic value if it is held until it matures (so that it has no time value.) From Equation (9-7), it can be seen that the intrinsic value of a put equals either zero or the excess of the put's exercise price over the price of the optioned security, whichever is greater. When a put has positive intrinsic value, it is said to be in-the-money.

The premium over intrinsic value for a put is its time value and is defined by Eqn. 9-12 in the textbook.

Time value of a put = POP - MAX[0, (XP -P)]

The time value of a put increases directly with the riskiness or price volatility of the optioned asset, increases with the length of time to expiration of the put, varies inversely with the absolute value of the difference between the market price of the optioned asset and the exercise price, $|P - XP|$, and moves inversely with the level of market interest rates. A put's premium over intrinsic value is largest at the point where the market price of the optioned asset is equal to the option's exercise price, $P = XP$.

QA28-6 If the XYZ Corporation faces tough new competition that reduces sales and profits, then operating the XYZ Corporation will become more risky. The increased riskiness will be reflected in a higher standard deviation of returns for XYZ's stock. Increased riskiness in the optioned security increases the values of both the calls and the puts on the security.

QA28-7 Uncertain. The hedges formed using the hedge ratio are perfect only as long as the price of the optioned asset does not change. If its price changes, so does the value of $N(x)$, and the hedge ratio has to be recomputed and the hedged portfolio rebalanced. The hedge ratio will also change with changes in the risk-free rate of interest, the variance of the returns of the underlying asset, and the time to expiration, as can be seen by examining Equation (28-6) of the textbook:

$$ x = \frac{\ln(P_0 / XP) + [RFR + 0.5VAR(r)]d}{\sigma d^{0.5}} $$

QA28-8 Uncertain. The put-call parity model determines only relative values for the put and the call options. In the situation described, you would know only that either the put or the call is mispriced, but not which one.

QA28-9 The put-call parity model is useful in determining the fair value of a call only if the fair market value of an identical put is known. It is a relative pricing model. The Black-Scholes model can be used to obtain the value of the call directly without knowing the value of the put. The put-call parity model also focuses on expiration date outcomes; that is, it assumes that all options are held to expiration and that all cash flows occur only on the expiration date. In contrast, the Black-Scholes model assumes continuous compounding and focuses on outcomes during the next instant of time. The hedge ratio in the put-call parity model is always equal to 1.0, whereas, in the Black-Scholes model, the hedge ratio is less than one and will change with a change in any one of the other variables in the model--namely, the price of the underlying stock, the time to expiration, the risk-free rate, or the variance of returns on the underlying stock.

QA28-10 False. The hedge ratio, h, in the binomial pricing model can be interpreted as the change in the price of the option for each dollar change in the price of the underlying asset: $h = \frac{COP_u - COP_d}{P_u - P_d}$. The hedge ratio will be higher the more in-the-money the call option is because the more in-the-money the call option, the greater the probability that the option will be exercised. In such a case, the option owners' wealth will increase by almost the same as that of the owners of the underlying asset.

Problems

PA28-1 (a)   Using the Black-Scholes call pricing model, we obtain values for x and y:

$$x = \frac{\ln(42/40) + \left[0.10 + 0.5(0.16)^2\right]0.5}{(0.16)(0.5)^{0.5}} = \frac{0.10519}{0.113137} = 0.929758$$

$$y = 0.929758 - (0.16)(0.5)^{0.5} = 0.816621$$

Inserting these values into the Black-Scholes formula indicates that the value of the call is $4.427.

$$COP_0 = P_0N(x) - XP[e^{(-RFR)d}]N(y) = 42(0.8238) - 40[e^{(-0.10)(0.5)}](0.7939) = \$4.39$$

(b)   By using the call premium calculating above and applying the put-call parity model, we determine that the value of the put is worth 44 cents:

$P + POP - COP = XP/(1 + RFR)^d$, so $POP = XP/(1 + RFR)^d + COP - P$. Since the Black-Scholes model assumes continuous compounding, we substitute $e^{(RFR)(d)}$ for $(1 + RFR)^d$, and the value of the put is $POP = 40(e^{(-0.10)(0.5)}) + \$4.39 - 42 = \$0.44$.

PA28-2   Using the put-call parity model, $P + POP - COP = XP/(1 + RFR)^d$. Therefore, if the options are correctly priced relative to one another, $52 + 1 - \$3.50$ (= 49.50) should equal $50/(1.05)^{0.5}$ (= 48.795). Since the values are not equal to one another, the options are not correctly priced relative to one another; however, you are unable to determine which is mispriced in this case.

PA28-3   To determine how much XYZ's stock would have to increase in six months to make a 10% annual rate of return, we first solve for the semiannual rate of return (denoted sar) required: $(1 + sar)^2 - 1 = 0.10$; sar = 4.88%.

Next, we compound the $2,600 investment at this rate: $2,600(1.0488) = $2, 726.88. This is what is needed for the 4.88% gain. The original option premium is $2,600/(10 round lots x 100 shares = 1,000 shares) = $2.60 per share cost (or option premium). The premium per share with a 4.88% semiannual rate of return added is $2,726.88/(10 x 100) = $2.73. The call premium (COP) would, therefore, have to rise 13 cents ($2.73 - $2.60) to return 4.88% in six months. Since there is slightly less than a one-to-one correspondence between COP and the price of the optioned stock, the price of the stock would also have to increase by almost 13 cents a share, or from $50 to $50.13, to generate the desired 4.88% return. Therefore, the increase on the price of the stock must be almost $0.13/$50 = 0.26% in 6 months to create an annualized return on the call position of 10 percent. Since the slope of the Black-Scholes call pricing curve is slightly less than +1.0, the exact answer for the rate of stock price appreciation is slightly less than 0.26 of 1%, but we are not given enough data in the problem to solve the Black-Scholes call formula, so we must be satisfied with an approximate answer to this question. If the question had given us the data to calculate the hedge ratio, N(x), we could determine an exact answer.

PA28-4(a)   It is easiest to apply the Black-Scholes call pricing model to value the firm as a whole and not on a per share basis. The total debt of $110,000 is the call option's exercise price. Omit the last three zeros and denote the striking price as XP = 110. Azore's total assets

(TA) are analogous to the price of the optioned stock in an ordinary call option model; the total assets are denoted P = $90 after three zeros are omitted. The interest rate is RFR = 0.095, and the standard deviation is 0.4. Inserting these values into the Black-Scholes call option pricing model's formula for x yields:

$$x = \frac{\ln(P/XP) + [RFR + 0.5VAR(r)]d}{\sigma d^{0.5}}$$

$$= \frac{\ln(\$90/\$110) + [0.095 + 0.5(0.16)]1.0}{(0.4)(1.0)} = -0.06$$

$$y = x - \sigma\, d^{0.5} = -0.06 - (0.4)(1.0) = -0.46$$

The values of x and y are substituted into the Black-Scholes call pricing formula to obtain a value for the call option of $10.56:

$$COP_0 = P_0N(x) - XP(e^{(-RFR)(d)})N(y) = \$90N(-0.06) - \$110(e^{(-0.095)})N(-0.46)x$$
$$= \$90(0.4761) - \$110(0.9094)(0.3228) = \$10.56$$

We add back the three zeros that were omitted for the sake of expedition, and the value of Azore's net worth turns out to be $10,560. Subtracting the stock's value of $10,560 from the value of the Azore Corporation's total assets (TA) tells us that the Black-Scholes call pricing model values Azore's bonds at $99,440 (= aggregate debt = $110,000 - $10,560).

The graph on the following page, Figure PA28-4, depicts the use of the Black-Scholes call option pricing model in assessing the values of the securities of a firm that is technically bankrupt.

(b) It is insightful to note that Azore's common stock is worth $10,560 even though the firm's total debt of $110,000 exceeds the value of its total assets. This is because the call option pricing model values the "upside potential" that the Azore Corporation possesses as a going concern. Stated differently, all of Azore's risk is not downside risk; part of this variability of return includes the small possibility that Azore experiences great luck and somehow earns a 10,000 percent rate of return. This chance for great wealth causes the stock to have a positive value.

Figure PA28-4

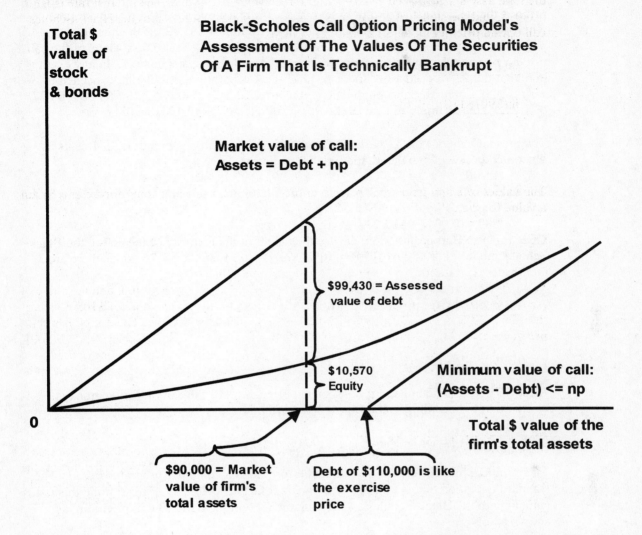

Black-Scholes Call Option Pricing Model's Assessment Of The Values Of The Securities Of A Firm That Is Technically Bankrupt

Total $ value of stock & bonds

Market value of call:
Assets = Debt + np

$99,430 = Assessed value of debt

$10,570 Equity

Minimum value of call:
(Assets - Debt) <= np

0

Total $ value of the firm's total assets

$90,000 = Market value of firm's total assets

Debt of $110,000 is like the exercise price

PA28-5 (a)   The price of Miller Corporation's stock must increase to $85 for Ms. Samples to break even. This conclusion ignores cash dividends, taxes and commission charges. Note that since it is a European call, it can be exercised only on its maturity date. Thus, the P = $85 must occur on the maturity date for her to break even. The resulting gain of $5 a share on the stock that could be earned by exercising the call would just be sufficient to reimburse Ms. Samples for the call premium outlay of COP = $5 when she purchased the call.

(b)   We must first solve for the quarterly rate of return (denoted qr) that is needed to generate an annual return of 20%.

$(1 + qr)^4 - 1 = 0.20$

$(1 + qr)^4 = 1.20$, so $1 + qr = \sqrt[4]{1.20}$, and qr = 4.664%.

Therefore, the call price needed to yield a 4.664% quarterly return (or 20% annual return) on the money invested in call premiums is $5(1.04664) = $5.2332. We are not given enough data to use the Black-Scholes formula to get an exact answer, so approximations must be employed. Since there is slightly less than a one-to-one correspondence between COP and the price of the optioned stock, the price of the stock would also have to increase by almost 23 cents a share above the break-even price to generate the desired 4.664% increase in the funds invested in the calls. Therefore, the price of the stock must rise slightly less than 23 cents above the $85 break-even price when the call was purchased to the higher price of almost $85.23. If the question provided the data to calculate the hedge ratio (e.g., $N(x)$ = about 0.65 = slope of the call pricing curve at P = $85 per share), we could determine an exact answer. In any event, note that the $2.23 cents price increase in Miller Corporation's stock that is needed to earn the 20% annual return on the money invested in calls is only $2.23/$83.00 = 0.027, or 2.7%. This example illustrates the financial leverage available to call buyers.

PA28-6   The present value of the $1 cash dividend to be received in one month is 99.1 cents as illustrated below. Note that d, the time to expiration, is 0.083 = 1/12.

$$\$1.00e^{(-RFR)(d)} = \$1.00e^{(-0.10)(0.083)} = 0.991 = 99.1 \text{ cents}$$

Due to the cash dividend stock price dropoff, we subtract this amount from the current $83 strike price.

$$\$83 - (0.991) = \$82.01 = P$$

Since this is a European option, we use the values at the maturity of the call in the Black-Scholes model: P = $82.01, RFR = 10%, Var(r) = 0.16, and d = 0.25 (since there are 3 months to expiration).

$$x = \frac{\ln(\$82.01/\$80) + [0.10 + 0.5(0.16)]0.25}{(0.16)^{0.5}(0.25)^{0.5}} = \frac{0.06981}{0.2} = 0.34905$$

$$y = 0.34905 - [(0.16)^{0.5}(0.25)^{0.5}] = 0.14905$$

After a $1 cash dividend and the associated price dropoff, the call on Miller stock is worth $6.968, according to the Black-Scholes model:

$$COP = \$82.01(0.6368) - \$80e^{(-0.10)(0.25)}(0.5596) = \$8.56$$

PA28-7   This problem must be solved by trial and error unless a computer program is used. The standard deviation that is implied by the market facts is 0.243857. Substituting this risk statistic into the Black-Scholes call pricing model will yield the $3 call premium, as shown below:

$$x = \frac{\ln(\$50/\$50) + [0.09 + 0.5(0.243857)^2](0.25)}{(0.243857)(0.25)^5} = \frac{0.029933}{0.121928} = 0.245498$$

$$y = 0.245498 - (0.243857)(0.5) = 0.12357$$

$$COP = \$50(0.597) - \$50e^{(-0.09)(0.25)}(0.54922) = \$3.00$$

PA28-8 (a)   We can determine the fair market value of the call option on BBB stock by employing the Black-Scholes model:

$$x = \frac{\ln(\$65/\$60) + [0.10 + 0.5(0.18)^2](0.25)}{(0.18)(0.25)^{0.5}} = \frac{0.10905}{0.09} = 1.21166$$

$$y = 1.21166 - (0.18)(0.25)^{0.5} = 1.12166$$

COP = $65[N(1.21166)] - $60e^{(-0.10)(0.25)}[N(1.12166)] = $65(0.888) - $60(0.975)(0.867) = $57.72 - $50.7195 = $7.00.

Since $7.00 > $6.20, the option is undervalued.

(b)   If you believe in your analysis, you should purchase the undervalued calls on BBB stock. Note: The hedge ratio is $N(x) = N(1.211) = 0.888$, so to create a risk-free hedge, you should sell 0.888 share of stock short for every call and invest the proceeds of the short sale at the risk-free rate.

PA28-9 (a)   The value of the premium for a call on ZBZ stock is calculated with the Black-Scholes formula below:

$$x = \frac{\ln(\$40/\$35) + \left[0.08 + 0.5(0.4)^2\right](0.3333)}{(0.4)(0.3333)^{0.5}} = \frac{0.186859}{0.230928} = 0.809165$$

$y = 0.809165 - (0.4)(0.3333)^{0.5} = 0.578236$

COP = $40(0.790719) - $35e^{(-0.08)(0.3333)}(0.718398) = $7.146

(b)   The put premium for ZBZ stock is calculated with the put-call parity model as follows:

POP = COP - P + XP/(1 + RFR)^d. We will substitute $e^{(-RFR)(d)}$ for $(1 + RFR)^d$ since the Black-Scholes model assumes continuous compounding.

POP = $7.146 - $40 + $35e^{(-0.08)(0.3333)} = $1.225

PA28-10   The hedge ratio is $N(x) = 0.9$ = the slope of the positively sloped call pricing curve. Therefore, if the optioned stock's price declines by $1.00, a call on that stock should decline by $N(x)$(stock price change) = (0.9)($1.00) = $0.90. The standard deviation and the interest rate are sophistical. The sophistry was included in this problem to remind the students that much of the information they hear in real life is irrelevant and they must, therefore, sort out the relevant facts, and that the call pricing model is fairly simple once you understand it.

CFA Exam Solutions*

The following are the guideline answers provided by the AIMR for the CFA Exam questions:

1.   B

2.   Three prominent pricing inconsistencies are apparent in Table 20 for the Furniture City call options:

    1.   The June call option at a strike price of $110 is undervalued. A call option that is in the money should be worth at least as much as its intrinsic value. The intrinsic value of a call option is the maximum of either zero or the difference between the security price and the exercise price (S - E). The June $110 option, therefore, should be worth at least $119.50 - $110.00, or $9.50. The current price of $8 7/8 implies that the option is undervalued.

2. The August call option at a strike price of $120 is undervalued. Call options having the same strike price but with longer maturities are more valuable than those with shorter maturities because the stock has more time in which to rise above the strike price; that is, the time value increases with maturity. The August $120 option of $3 is below the July $120 option of $3 3/4; therefore, the August $120 option is undervalued. Alternatively, the July $120 option could be said to be overvalued.

3. The September call option at a strike price of $130 is overvalued. Call options having the same maturity but with higher strike prices that are more out of the money are worth less because a larger and less likely move in the stock price will be needed for the option to pay off. The September $130 option is priced higher than the September $120 option; therefore, the September $130 option is overvalued. Alternatively, the September $120 option could be said to be undervalued.

3. A. **Critique of Belief**

Joel Franklin's belief is incorrect. There are two fundamental kinds of options: American style and European style. An American option permits the owner to exercise the option at any time before or at expiration. The owner of a European option may exercise it only at expiration. If an option is at expiration, it will have the same value whether it is American or European.

The owner of an American option can treat the option as a European option simply by postponing the decision to exercise until expiration/. Therefore, the American option cannot be worth less than the European option. However, the American option can be worth more. The American option will be worth more if circumstances make exercise of the option before its expiration desirable. So, it may have a higher premium.

B. **European-Style Option's Value**

The formula to calculate a call option using put-call parity is $c = S + p - Xe^{-rt}$

where c = the price of a European call option at time t
S = the price of the underlying stock at time t
p = the price of a European put at time t
X = the exercise price for the option
t = time to expiration = one year

Therefore, from the information give,

Call option = $4.408 = $43 + 4.00 - 45e^{-.055}$

C. **Effect of Variables**

	Effect on Call Option's Value
i. An increase in short-term interest rate	Positive
ii. An increase in stock price volatility	Positive
iii. A decrease in time to option expiration	Negative

CHAPTER 29: ALTERNATIVE INVESTMENTS

SOLUTIONS

Questions

QA29-1   An REIT is a real estate investment trust. REITs are commercial investment portfolios that are patterned after closed-end investment companies. The portfolios of equity REITs have over 75% of their funds invested in equity positions in real estate, while mortgage REITs have over 75% of their funds invested in mortgages. Equity REITs manage the properties in which they invest, and their shareholders receive rental income as well as income from capital appreciation if the property is sold for a gain. Mortgage REITs lend money to builders and make loan collections. Their shareholders receive interest income and capital appreciation income from improvement in the prices of loans.

QA29-2   Uncertain. While the standard deviations for the returns on direct residential, farm, and business real estate are all lower than those for the S&P 500 Index, the small cap stocks index, and the commodity futures index, these statistics are suspect. This is because residential, farm, and business real estate transactions occur infrequently, and the data are typically measured less accurately than the data from assets that are traded frequently. Appraised real estate values are used in the calculations because market transaction data cannot be observed frequently. The standard deviations for the returns on REITs, which are based on market values rather than appraised values, do not seem to indicate low risk.

QA29-3   One advantage of investing in real estate is due to the current tax laws that allow mortgage interest expense, property taxes, and some other expenses to be tax deductible, thereby allowing real estate owners to benefit from the tax savings involved. Secondly, real estate investors can borrow more money for their investment than can investors in other securities, which enables them to utilize more financial leverage. The real estate owners may also have some control over decisions regarding the property, and these decisions can increase the market value of the property, whereas investors in the stock of a corporation have little impact on managerial decisions. Real estate investments can provide investors with geographic diversification, and geographically disparate real estate investments tend to be uncorrelated with each other and with non-real estate investments. Too, high positive correlations between all types of real estate prices and inflation document the fact that real estate is a good inflation hedge. Additionally, the typical owner of a single-family residence obtains psychic income from home ownership that inflates the values of these homes above what they are worth based on their investment merits alone.

        On the negative side, real estate investments involve large idiosyncratic risks for most investors. Most parcels of real estate are not easy to divide into smaller pieces, and, therefore, the properties represent a relatively large portion of the investor's total portfolio. Too, the cost of acquiring information on real estate investment opportunities is high since every piece of real estate is unique, and existing flaws with a particular piece of property may not become evident until after the property is purchased. Transactions costs are also high since real estate brokers charge high commissions. Maintenance and management costs are substantial as well, and these are costs that are not incurred by investors in securities. Real estate investors also face the risk of neighborhood deterioration and the risk that the current tax laws will be changed, eliminating the valuable income tax deductions now available (political risk).

QA29-4 Hedge funds are actively managed portfolios that hold positions in publicly traded securities. Unlike U.S. mutual funds, U.S. hedge funds are not regulated by the Investment Company Act of 1940. Most hedge funds are organized as limited partnerships, but some operate as limited liability corporations. Hedge fund managers have more leeway than mutual fund managers. The National Securities Markets Improvement Act of 1996 (NSMIA) allows hedge fund managers to use leverage, sell short, buy put and call options, trade futures contracts and other derivatives, buy shares in other investment companies, take concentrated positions in only a few assets, and take an active role in the governance of corporations in which they invest. On the other hand, in order to remain unregulated, hedge funds may have no more than 500 investors, and the law allows them to accept money only from experienced individual investors that have a minimum of $5 million to invest. Institutional investors must have at least $25 million to invest.

QA29-5 A "sister fund" is an off-shore hedge fund that is set up to invest similarly or identically to its U.S.-based hedge fund. The off-shore fund provides non-U.S. investors the opportunity to avoid taxation and allows the domestic U.S. hedge fund to have more than 500 investors without coming under U.S. government regulation.

QA29-6 Uncertain. A study by Brown, Goetzmann, and Ibbotson reported that over a seven-year sample period the average hedge fund earned a lower average rate of return than the S&P 500 Index. However, the average hedge fund also had a lower standard deviation of returns than the S&P 500 Index, and the average betas for the hedge funds were low. When these researchers measured the risk-adjusted performance of the hedge funds using both the SHARPE and TREYNOR measures, the hedge funds were found to have outperformed the S&P 500 Index. On the other hand, results of a study by Ackermann, McEnally, and Ravenscraft caused that team of researchers to conclude that the hedge funds were unable to beat the market on a consistent basis when total risk-adjusted returns were used. The performance statistics for the hedge fund industry are, however, subject to survivorship bias, which can skew the results of the studies.

QA29-7 Domestic hedge funds must register with the SEC and are subject to the minimal regulations imposed by the National Securities Markets Improvement Act of 1996. Almost all domestic hedge funds are headquartered in the U.S. Off-shore hedge funds are headquartered outside the U.S., are not required to register with the SEC, and are largely unregulated.

QA29-8 False. Although stock prices are negatively correlated with inflation during sample periods of less than one year, they are uncorrelated with inflation over longer periods and have provided a better long-run inflation hedge than either gold or silver.

QA29-9 Gold bullion and physical silver offer investors two advantages: catastrophe insurance and diversification. Gold and silver are both portable stores of value that are readily accepted as mediums of exchange when a catastrophe occurs that causes the purchasing power of money to decline rapidly. They are also global commodities that are resistant to being influenced by current events. Their prices are not highly correlated with either stock or bond prices. This gives gold and silver the capacity to reduce the risk of a diversified portfolio that is heavily invested in financial securities.

QA29-10 Both gold and silver have values beyond their values as money. Both are now used as raw materials in various industrial applications. The demand for either gold or silver is determined by the needs of these industries. Because there are different supply and demand forces for gold and for silver, the price of silver has not remained highly positively correlated with the price of gold.

Problems

PA29-1 Because we are calculating *expected* returns, the arithmetic averages should be used. $E(r_p) = 0.5(13.3\%) + 0.5(15.3\%) = 14.3\%$. The variance of the portfolio is calculated as follows:

$$VAR(r_p) = (0.5)^2(17.3)^2 + (0.5)^2(16.4)^2 + 2(0.5)(0.5)(0.3)(17.3)(16.4) = 184.6205$$

The standard deviation is the square root of the variance and is equal to 13.6%.

PA29-2 Because we are calculating *expected* returns, the arithmetic averages should be used. $E(r_p) = 0.5(15.3\%) + (0.5)(11.1\%) = 13.2\%$. The variance of the portfolio is calculated as follows:

$$VAR(r_p) = (0.5)^2(16.4)^2 + (0.5)^2(34.1)^2 + 2(0.5)(0.5)(-0.4)(16.4)(34.1) = 246.0945$$

The standard deviation is the square root of the variance and is equal to 15.7%.

PA29-3 Because we are calculating *expected* returns, the arithmetic averages should be used. $E(r_p) = 0.25(11.1\%) + 0.25(15.5\%) + 0.5(15.3\%) = 14.3\%$. The variance of the portfolio is calculated as follows:

$$VAR(r_p) = (0.25)^2(34.1)^2 + (0.25)^2(72.5)^2 + (0.5)^2(16.4)^2 + 2(0.25)(0.25)(0.8)(34.1)(72.5)$$
$$+ 2(0.25)(0.5)(-0.1)(72.5)(16.4) + 2(0.25)(0.5)(-0.4)(34.1)(16.4) = 630.0072$$

The standard deviation of the portfolio is the square root of the variance and is equal to 25.1%.

PA29-4 The portfolio that is invested in gold, silver, and the S&P 500 Index has both a higher expected return and more risk than does the portfolio that is invested in only gold and the S&P 500 Index. The higher expected return is the result of the higher expected return on silver. The investment in silver also has a much higher risk (standard deviation = 72.5%) than either gold or the S&P 500 index, and while it is negatively correlated with the S&P 500 Index, silver has a high positive correlation with gold. This limits the amount of risk diversification potential that it offers to this portfolio.

PA29-5 The real returns are calculated by subtracting the average inflation rate from the geometric averages. Geometric averages are used because we are looking for the *compounded* annual real returns. The real returns are shown below:

Equity REIT:	12.0% - 5.2% = 6.8%
Mortgage REIT:	3.1% - 5.2% = -2.1%
S&P 500 Index:	14.1% - 5.2% = 8.9%
Gold:	7.0% - 5.2% = 1.8%
Silver:	5% - 5.2% = -0.2%
T-bill:	8.7% - 5.2% = 3.5%

An investment in the S&P 500 Index offered the highest real return; an investment in mortgage REITs offered the lowest real return.

PA29-6 Gabe and Ginny's mortgage loan would be for 0.8($270,000) = $216,000. Their monthly mortgage payment is calculated as follows:

$$\$216,000 = payment \sum_{t=1}^{360} \frac{1}{(1 + \frac{0.09}{12})^t}$$

$$payment = \frac{\$216,000}{124.2819} = \$1,738$$

PA29-7 The amortization schedule for the first year of Gabe and Ginny's mortgage is shown below:

(1) Month	(2) Beginning mortgage balance	(3) Mortgage payment [from P29-6]	(4) Interest payment [(0.09/12 times Column (2)]	(5) Principal payment [Column (3) - Column (4)]	(6) Ending mortgage balance [Column (1) - Column (5)]
1	$216,000	$1,738	$1,620	$ 118	$215,882
2	$215,882	$1,738	$1,619	$ 119	$225,763
3	$215,763	$1,738	$1,618	$ 120	$215,643
4	$215,643	$1,738	$1,617	$ 121	$215,522
5	$215,522	$1,738	$1,616	$ 122	$215,400
6	$215,400	$1,738	$1,616	$ 122	$215,278
7	$215,278	$1,738	$1,615	$ 123	$215,155
8	$215,155	$1,738	$1,614	$ 124	$215,031
9	$215,031	$1,738	$1,613	$ 125	$214,906
10	$214,906	$1,738	$1,612	$ 126	$214,780
11	$214,780	$1,738	$1,611	$ 127	$214,653
12	$214,653	$1,738	$1,610	$ 128	$214,525
Totals		$20,856.00	$19,381.00	$1,475.00	

PA29-8 Budget for Purchase of a $270,000 Home With 20% Down:

Monthly payments:

Mortgage (from PA29-6)	$1,738
Real estate taxes ($2,600/12)	217
Gas, electricity, water	200
Home insurance	70
Repairs and upkeep	50
Total monthly payments	$2,275

Monthly savings:

Income tax reduction [($1,615* + $217) x 0.28]	$ 513
Price appreciation [0.05 x $270,000 = $13,500; $13,500/12 = $1,125]	1,125
Equity accumulation (from PA29-7, $1,475 will be paid off the first year, and this represents $1,475/12 = $123 per month)	123
Total monthly savings	$1,761

*$1,615 = average monthly interest payment

Excess of monthly payments over savings ($2,275 - $1,761)	$ 514

PA29-9 The only monthly reduction in actual cash outflows as a result of the home purchase is the monthly tax savings of $513, so the monthly cash outflow will be $2,275 - $513 = $1,762.

PA29-10 Zero. In 20X1, the fund lost money, so the manager receives only his fixed fee. In 20X2, the $50 billion loss from the previous year must be made up before any incentive bonus is paid, and at the end of 20X2, the fund's net asset value was only $565 billion.

CFA Exam Solutions*

The following are the guideline answers provided by the AIMR for the CFA Exam questions:

1. A

2. A

3. Several characteristics could account for the difference in the performances of the two indexes, including the following:

- **Appraisal basis vs. transaction basis.** The CREF Index would incorporate predominantly appraisal-based information, whereas the EREIT Index would be transaction based (i.e., based on market prices of REIT shares). The possibility exists that the information in the appraisal-based indexes lags that of a market-based index. The reason for the lag is that appraisals are performed only periodically (e.g., quarterly) on values that essentially change daily. The use of appraisal-based information also produces smoothing bias.

- **Unleveraged vs. leveraged properties.** The CREF Index might include only unleveraged real estate properties. The EREIT Index would typically include equity REITs that hold both leveraged and unleveraged properties. In general, one would expect the performances of leveraged and unleveraged real estate to differ. Other things being equal, leveraged real estate returns should be more volatile than unleveraged returns.

- **Returns before advisory fees vs. returns after advisory fees.** Both indexes would reflect the deduction of property management fees, but the CREF Index would most likely exclude the fees paid to *investment managers*, whereas the EREIT Index would include compensation to investment managers. The exclusion of investment fees from the CREF Index would impart an upward bias to the CREF Index vis-à-vis the EREIT Index.

- **Liquidity premium.** The EREIT Index would reflect a premium in comparison with the CREF Index because of the easier conversion of the REIT stock to cash with little loss in value on a publicly traded exchange.

- **Correlation.** Equity REITs are more closely correlated with common stock performance than CREFs, which are correlated closely with the underlying real estate property performance.

4. The consultant's statement is an expression of the naïve idea that the "uniqueness" of real estate is such that the common sense rules of portfolio analysis and construction do not apply: "just make 'good buys' until the money runs out and all will be well." This unacceptable view disregards the basic principles of diversification, proportionality in asset-class exposures, and risk/return balance. How "good" a specific property is depends on how well it fits with the other holdings in the portfolio and what effect it will have on the portfolio's risk and return objectives. Prospective real estate investments should be examined not only on their own merits but also for their impact on the investor's overall real estate portfolio and on how the entire real estate segment fits into and affects the investor's portfolio as a whole.

    This approach also requires: (1) setting risk and return objectives for the real estate segment of the portfolio that are compatible with those for the portfolio as a whole; (2) devising a portfolio acquisition strategy to achieve the stated goals; and (3) evaluating the extent to which each individual property conforms to the strategy and is likely to contribute to attainment of the objectives of both the real estate segment and the total portfolio.

    The addition of a given property may or may not improve realized portfolio return for any given time period, and it may or may not prove to be an inflation hedge. If an asset class's characteristics change, historical relationships as revealed in "the data" may not hold. For example, some recent research indicates that real estate currently exhibits no correlation with inflation; if no positive correlation exists, real estate's inflation-hedge value will be small or nonexistent. The explanation seems plausible; High vacancy rates may have "decoupled" market rent levels (and real estate values) from inflation in recent years. The consultant should disclose this aspect.

5. Capital market theory holds that efficient markets prevent mispricing of assets and that expected return is proportionate to the level of risk taken. In this instance, real estate is expected to provide the same return as stocks and a higher return than bonds. Yet, it is expected to provide this return at a lower level of risk than both bonds and stocks. If these expectations were realistic, investors

would sell the other asset classes and buy real estate, pushing down its return until it was proportionate to the level of risk.

Appraised values differ from transaction prices, reducing the accuracy of return and volatility measures for real estate. Capital market theory was developed and applied to the stock market, which is a very liquid market with relatively small transaction costs. In contrast to the stock market, real estate markets are very thin and lack liquidity.